# MARKETING
## Phrase Book

### Gail Hamilton

Hamilton House

Hamilton House, 27 Leuty Avenue
Toronto, Ontario, Canada M4E 2R2




**Canadian Cataloguing in Publication Data**

Hamilton, Gail (Margaret Gail)
   Marketing phrase book

2$^{nd}$ ed.
ISBN 0-9680853-4-2


1. Advertising – Terminology.  I. Title.

HF5825.H35 1999       659.1'03       C99-930413-5




Printed in Canada

# CONTENTS

    Thousands of powerful marketing phrases are arranged
alphabetically by key word for easy access. Use them as
building blocks to create successful promotions.

    Mix and match from columns of choices to instantly produce
a dynamite name for your big sales event.

    Need to get your major selling point noticed? Choose the
exclamation that best expresses your message. Put it where it
really stands out. Listen to the cash register ring.

    Suggestions to improve your all-important reply coupon.

    All those vital words and phrases you need to tie your thoughts
together and make your promotions flow convincingly.

    The crucial core vocabulary of marketing, the words that pack
the punch and pull in the dollars. Grouped by meaning to
spark your imagination, they provide the impact you need for
real selling power.

# INTRODUCTION

Your business depends on successful marketing. Whether you are the local plumber or a huge multinational, you must get your message across effectively.

And now the *Marketing Phrase Book* puts the language of the marketplace, the language that sells, right at your fingertips!

The *Marketing Phrase Book* contains a huge, infinitely versatile collection of phrases designed solely for marketing. The kind of phrases selling millions of dollars worth of products and services every day. No matter what your business, this unique, easy-to-use resource will put sizzle in your advertising, boost your results and practically do your promoting for you.

How does it work?

Easy! Just look up your key words and you'll find a lavish array of ways to use them. Find what you want to say but can't put your finger on. Discover the "trigger" words that set customers reaching for their pocketbooks.

The phrases provide a springboard for your imagination, helping you come up with exciting new ways to get your message across. And, above all, they are dynamic construction blocks to build high-powered advertising and promotions tailored exactly to your needs.


## Small Business Owners

If you produce your own advertising, the *Marketing Phrase Book* is a must. It's the easy way to increase your sales and free up precious time to spend on your business. Get more attention faster, reach more people, and never struggle for words again.

## New Entrepreneurs

You've got a great idea. You've taken that scary, thrilling leap out on your own. Now you have to make it work. The *Marketing Phrase Book* lets you quickly learn the language that attracts customers and racks up sales. Add instant professional polish to your promotions and pizzaz to your everyday selling techniques without hiring expensive outside expertise. Most important of all, get a head start on success when you need it most.

## Salespeople and Executives

Does your livelihood depend on your ability to promote your company's product or service? The *Marketing Phrase Book* helps you turn out terrific letters, persuasive proposals and reports, compelling speeches and sales talks, and dynamite presentations. Give yourself that crucial competitive edge and let others wonder what your secret is.

## Marketing Professionals

Whether you're part of an advertising agency, a public relations firm or the company marketing department, the *Marketing Phrase Book* remains an endlessly valuable resource. When you're expected to repeat your last triumph with something equally brilliant, only different, you and your staff can have all the red-hot promotional language at hand for instant reference. Make the *Marketing Phrase Book* a solid foundation for your own creativity. Revitalize and update your work. Spark new ideas. Save valuable time and come out on top when you're under pressure to perform.

# SELLING IS SIMPLE

Using a few common sense rules, <u>anyone</u> can sell.

## Promote the Benefits Rather than the Features

A feature is a characteristic of your product. Wheels are a feature of a car. A benefit answers the customer's basic question, "What can this feature do for me?" Wheels carry the customer speedily and safely to wherever he or she wants to go. Customers buy benefits, not features.

## Tip!

List the features of your product or service. Opposite each feature, describe the benefit to your customers. Ask how it will make their lives easier, better, safer, more fun. Rank the benefits in order of importance. These are your sales points. The most important benefit is your strongest sales point.

## Identify Your Target Audience

Think from their point of view. Are they pet owners, retired people, golfers, new mothers, basketball fans? Do they want to save money or time, enjoy themselves, improve skills, be comfortable, try something new, feel secure? Which of your benefits will help fulfil these desires? Give these benefits your greatest emphasis.

## Boost Customer Confidence

Be ready to reassure strongly on price, delivery, reliability, guarantee, performance, service and quality.

## Tip!

A simple way to find out why people buy is to *talk* to your customers and find out what is most important to them.

## Decide Your Goal and Stick to It

Do you want to generate inquiries, boost sales, increase store visits, introduce a new service, keep in touch? Trying to do too many things obscures your message.

## Use the Tried-and-true Sequence Known as A-I-D-A : Attention, Interest, Desire, Action

### Attention

You have only a few seconds to grab attention. Put your strongest selling point, your biggest benefit first.

### Interest

Show the need your customer has for your product. If you are selling gloves, for instance, talk about the importance of protecting your hands well on cold winter days.

### Desire

Show how the your product or service can solve the problem. This creates the desire to buy to fill the need. "Our fine, hand-knitted gloves keep your hands warm so you are always comfortable no matter what the weather."

### Action

Ask for immediate action. Tell your customers exactly what you want them to do, whether it is to buy your product, visit a store, mail the coupon, call for details, ask for a free sample or demonstration. Provide enough information to get your customers to take the next step.

### Tip!

Make action as easy as possible. Include your company name, address and phone number on every piece of promotion. Provide store hours, locations, clear directions or a map. Make sure catalogs have easy order forms. List dealers. Indicate which credit cards you accept.

## Action Incentives Work

Price discounts, special price reductions, new lower prices, bargain prices, limited quantities, easy payment plans, handy discount coupons, bonus gifts for acting before a deadline – all persuade your customer to act now so as not to miss out on your terrific offer.

Don't overlook the power of contests, giveaways, celebration events, etc. to stir up interest.

Use the word "free" as much as possible.

## Tip!

A good guarantee helps overcome fears that a product might not perform as expected.

## Powerful Sales Tools

**Testimonials and Endorsements**. People trust statements which come from a disinterested third party. Use quotes from satisfied customers.

**Comparisons**. Compare your product to that of your competition, showing how yours is superior.

**Reliability**. Mention the number of years your company has been in business, number of outlets, employees, etc.

**Specific facts**. Numbers, statistics and exact information add strong credibility.

**Repetition**. The more places the customer can see your promotion, the more familiar you become and the readier the customer is to buy.

## Relax and Let Your Mind Run Free

Jot down everything you can think of as it comes to you without worrying about order or editing. Browse the *Marketing Phrase Book* for suggestions. When you are done, choose the best ideas for your promotion. Your headline will probably jump out at you from the material.

## Address One Person at a Time

Pretend you are enthusiastically persuading a close friend to buy your product. Remember that "you" is the word lets customers relate personally.

## Keep it Simple

Rework until your message can be understood immediately. Read what you've written aloud to make sure it flows clearly and smoothly.

## Layout

Your message must be seen at a glance. Avoid clutter. Make sure your promotion is easy to read and well-balanced with text and graphics strongly focused on your main idea.

Have the eye drawn to a starting point from which all else flows naturally.

Color attracts.

Use white space effectively and generously.

Break up large text blocks with headlines, white space or visuals.

Too many different typefaces are difficult to read.

# HOW TO USE THE PHRASES

**Step One**

Decide on your purpose. For instance, you wish to promote the sale of roses from your florist shop.

**Step Two**

The phrases are arranged alphabetically by key word. When you see the word **"product"** or **"service"**, that is your cue to insert the specific product or service you are promoting.

> Look up **"FINE"** and choose a phrase, such as **" when only the finest will do"**.

> Look up **"AFFORDABLE"** and choose a phrase such as **"far more affordable than you think"**.

> Look up **"GUARANTEE"** and choose a phrase such as, **"great low prices guaranteed"**.

> Look up **"SELECT"** and choose as phrase such as **"will help you select exactly the product you need"**.

> Look up **"CARE"** and choose a phrase such as **"show that special someone how much you care"**.

**Step Three**

Combine the phrases into a vigorous marketing appeal that brings the customers and the money rolling in:

> **"When only the finest will do**, send red roses. An armful of lush, fragrant blooms is **far more affordable than you think**. Throughout June, **great low prices are guaranteed.** Our friendly staff **will help you select exactly the roses you need** to **show that someone special how much you care**. Order by phone today or come in and see for yourself at any of our convenient locations."

## SAMPLE ENTRY

### COST
- Now you can beat the high cost of
- The low low cost will surprise you
- What's the start-up cost to you
- Does anyone need to know it costs nearly nothing to produce
- Less costly than ever
- Provided at no additional cost
- You would expect it to cost more but it doesn't
- All these terrific extras included at no extra cost
- At no cost or obligation to you
- By far the most cost effective way to
- Reduced cost while improving strength and safety
- At absolutely no extra cost no matter when you buy
- Lower costs mean more of your money can work for you
- Helping you keep your costs in line
- So you can keep the lid on costs
- Twice the value at no extra cost
- We know you have to keep your costs down
- Helps lower overall costs by

**Cost:** price, value, worth, market value, amount, figure, valuation, quotation, demand, asking price, appraisement, appraisal, dollar value, expenditure, expense, charge, rate
*See also:* **CHARGE, DOLLAR, EXPENSE, MONEY, PRICE, SAVINGS, VALUE**

"COST" is the key word present in every phrase. Where appropriate, a number of alternatives to "cost" are suggested below the bulleted list of phrases.

**"See also: CHARGE, DOLLAR, EXPENSE, MONEY, PRICE, SAVINGS, VALUE"** indicates that under these entries you will find more phrases related to the meaning you are searching for.

# MARKETING
# PHRASES

**ABILITY**
- Because of our ability to provide a high level of service
- With proven ability to deliver the best value for your money
- We're famous for our ability to solve problems
- Acclaimed for its ability to perform
- Increasing your ability to enjoy

**Ability:** aptitude, artistry, bent, craft, competence, capacity, command, facility, flair, forte, genius, instinct, knack power, prowess, proficiency, wit, skill

*See also:* **CAPACITY, COMMAND, CRAFT, GENIUS, POWER, SKILL**

**ABOUT**
- That's what we're all about
- It's all about you
- When you're wondering what to do about
- There's absolutely no doubt about it

*See also:* **CONCERN**

**ABOVE**
- A cut above the rest
- Standing out above all competitors
- Imagine being above it all

*See also:* **BEST, EXCEPTIONAL, FINE**

**ACCENT**
- A great accent equals a lasting impression
- Putting the accent on
- The accent is on quality
- Use it to accent any decor, any flight of fancy
- Assorted colourful accent items
- Accent on savings

**ACCESS**
- You'll have preferential access to
- And you enjoy easy access anywhere in
- Can be accessed by phone, fax or
- With quick and personal access to
- Providing ready access day or night
- Now you can have unlimited access to all these services plus
- For immediate access
- Convenient access, 24 hours a day
- With instant access to so many benefits

- Request access today
- Gain direct access to
- Make sure you have the access and support you need to
- Access is the issue
- Gives you immediate access to essential information
- Giving you even faster access to

**Access:** approachability, admission, admittance, entry, entree
*See also:* **ADMISSION, ROAD, PATH, WAY**

## ACCESSIBLE

- Easily accessible at any time
- Are you looking for something a little more accessible
- Making this service accessible to you
- When you're up against the clock, accessibility is everything

**Accessible:** approachable, familiar, friendly, informal, genial, open, manageable
*See also:* **AVAILABLE, READY**

## ACCESSORY

- And, of course, it's accessory to
- The accessory that makes all the rest of it work
- Accessorize with style
- Comes with a wide variety of sleek accessories

## ACCOMMODATION

- In the best accommodation available
- Always happy to make accommodation for
- To appreciate the luxurious accommodations

*See also:* **AGREEMENT**

## ACCOMPLISH

- Doing what has never been accomplished before
- Showing just how much we were able to accomplish with
- Well-known for accomplishing things others can't

**Achieve:** acquire, attain, complete, realize, attain, succeed, gain, triumph, earn, fulfil, bring about, obtain, perform, secure, reach, finish
*See also:* **ACHIEVE, SUCCEED**

## ACCOMPLISHMENT

- We believe the greater accomplishment lies in
- An accomplishment we're justly proud of
- Our biggest accomplishment yet is helping you to

*See also:* **ACHIEVEMENT, SUCCESS**

## ACCORD
- An idea that will promote family accord
- Striving to be in accord with your wishes
- In accord with the most advanced ideas of the time

*See also:* **AGREE, MATCH**

## ACCOUNTABLE
- Always accountable to you
- You want a company that's accountable
- Accountability is at the core

## ACCURATE
- More accurate, more valid than ever
- It would be more than accurate to say we are the finest
- We aim for the utmost accuracy

*See also:* **RIGHT**

## ACHIEVE
- Rarely does someone achieve such a combination of advantages
- A combination of advantages never achieved before
- Here's how you can achieve

*See also:* **ACCOMPLISH, ACT, CREATE, BUILD, DO, PERFORM**

## ACHIEVEMENT
- Our greatest achievement just may be gaining your confidence
- Our most amazing achievement yet
- Not only do we get to boast proudly of our achievements
- Recognized for our achievements and ability to

*See also:* **ACCOMPLISHMENT, BREAKTHROUGH**

## ACT
- All so you can act more efficiently
- But you must act quickly
- Time to stop talking and start acting

*See also:* **ACCOMPLISH, ACHIEVE, DO, MOVE, PERFORM**

## ACTION
- Come in and watch the action
- Designed for those who want a little more action
- See all of the action all of the time
- Triple action works swiftly to
- Getting you breathtakingly close to the action
- Built to see action

- Helping you develop an action plan
- It's easy to find where the action is
- Catch all the action with

**Action:** act, deed, transaction, adventure, effort, endeavour, enterprise, dispatch, handiwork

*See also:* **ACTIVITY, ADVENTURE, EXCITEMENT, FUN**

## ACTIVITY

- Our sole activity is serving your needs
- As we step up our activities at this time of year
- Just about the most fun activity you'll ever find
- All our activities have been directed toward pleasing you

*See also:* **ACTION, ADVENTURE, EXCITEMENT, FUN**

## ADAPT

- Adapt to meet a fresh attack
- To quickly adapt to meet changing conditions
- Helping you adapt to a changing, exciting, modern world
- Can be easily adapted to your particular needs

*See also:* **CHANGE, FIT, FLEXIBLE, VERSATILE**

## ADD

- Nothing added, nothing removed
- Please add us to your list
- Making the right things add up
- Just add our product and capture success
- It all adds up to satisfaction
- Add-on value

## ADDITION

- This lively addition is designed for your pleasure
- A great new addition to
- Come and see the most recent additions to our line
- A terrific last-minute addition to
- With this latest addition, it's easier than ever to

## ADJUST

- Adjusts to several different sizes
- You'll be amazed at how quickly you can adjust to comfort
- Adjusted exactly to your requirements

**Adjust:** Adapt, fit, regulate, fine-tune, focus, bring into line, settle, resolve, compromise

*See also:* **ACCOMMODATION, ADAPT, COMPROMISE, FIT**

## ADMIRE
- If you've always admired other people's
- Now it's time for others to admire you
- You no longer have to admire from afar
- We know you'll admire our
- Now you can do more than just admire it

## ADMISSION
- Free with admission
- For one low low price of admission
- There is absolutely no admission charge
- Merely the price of admission gets you all this and more

*See also:* **ACCESS**

## ADVANCE
- One advance after another keeps us in the forefront of
- Stay on top of the latest advances
- Advances in techniques give you
- Combines the most recent advances with
- The most advanced product you could use

**Advance:** progress, headway, improvement, creation, invention, finding, breakthrough

*See also:* **BREAKTHROUGH, PROGRESS**

## ADVANTAGE
- Take advantage of this once-in-a-lifetime opportunity
- Take of advantage of the rewards and benefits of
- If you're looking for a definite advantage, come to us
- It's to your immediate advantage to
- Take advantage of savings up to
- The advantage is very clear
- You're already at an advantage because
- Consider the many advantages of
- Wide range of significant business and personal advantages
- It's advantages like these that have made us the leader
- Has the added advantage of
- Lets you enjoy all these advantages
- Get all the advantages without the pain
- Here are some of the hidden advantages of

*See also:* **BENEFIT**

## ADVENTURE
- The adventure takes flight

- Join the adventure
- There's an adventure for everyone
- Uncommon adventures
- Planning an adventure is an adventure in itself
- The adventure is all yours
- We've got just the adventure you're looking for
- Offering you a new adventure in

*See also:* **CHALLENGE, RISK, VENTURE**

### ADVERTISE
- This sale will not be advertised
- Advertise where buyers and sellers meet
- Red-hot advertising campaign
- Proof that it pays to advertise
- Exactly as advertised
- Get the most when you advertise
- Watch for our advertised sales
- Come in for our sizzling advertised specials

**Advertise:** publicize, bill, announce, broadcast, make known, publish, declare, promulgate, proclaim, herald, trumpet, ballyhoo, advance, promote, push, call attention to, boast, vaunt, post, display, circulate, distribute, propagate, spread, scatter, disseminate, disperse

*See also:* **ANNOUNCE, PROMOTE, PROMOTION, SELL, SALE**

### ADVICE
- The best advice for
- You'll continue to get expert advice
- Get advice either in person or by phone
- We offer advice that meets your needs today
- If it's time for some advice, you can turn to us
- Great prices and friendly advice
- Count on us to provide focused advice
- Where to find essential and free advice
- The most helpful buying advice is at your fingertips
- When you're searching for advice you can trust
- Information and advice you just won't find anywhere else
- Free technical advice when you need it, day or night

*See also:* **COUNSEL, EXPERT, GUIDANCE, HELP, INFORMATION, PLAN, PROFESSIONAL, WISDOM**

### AFFORD
- Prices you can afford
- And you'll still be able to afford

- Easy to afford
- Okay, so you can't afford the most expensive

*See also:* **MANAGE**

## AFFORDABLE

- More affordable than ever
- For the surprising affordable price of
- Easy and affordable
- Far more affordable than you think
- Now made more affordable
- Very affordable for every pocketbook
- Firmly in the affordable price class
- Let us help you find the must suitable and affordable
- Not to mention, of course, more affordable
- Affordability is a given

## AGAIN

- You'd definitely do it again
- We keep you coming back again and again
- We've done it again

## AGE

- It's a coming of age for a whole generation
- Is it time you came of age
- Regardless of age or income
- A whole new age has arrived
- Appeals to any age, from youngest to oldest
- Now that you've reached the age of wisdom
- Youth is not a matter of age
- Reverse the aging process

**Age:** seniority, maturity, epoch, era, season, mature, ripen, mellow

## AGREE

- When you see it, you'll just have to agree
- We're sure you'll agree they're extra special
- Apparently, the rest of the country agrees
- I think you'll agree right away that

**Agree:** concur, harmonize, allow, approve, accept, consent, acknowledge, conform, match

*See also:* **ACCORD, MATCH**

## AGREEMENT

- A clear and concise agreement for your benefit

- A far better agreement than others offer
- To quickly and easily come to the best agreement

*See also:* ACCOMMODATION, ALLIANCE

## AHEAD
- How to get ahead and save at the same time
- Gives you more of what you need to get ahead
- Get ahead and stay ahead with
- Always full steam ahead
- We're always looking ahead
- Here's a look at what you'll see in the weeks ahead
- And that's because we look ahead of the trends
- Light years ahead of the competition
- We began thinking ahead a long time ago

*See also:* FUTURE

## AIM
- Aim higher, choose the best
- We aim to please
- We know what you're aiming for
- Helping with all your aims

*See also:* GOAL

## ALIVE
- Comes alive with the excitement of
- Come alive to the promise
- When it 's so wonderful to be alive
- We'll have you feeling more alive than ever

## ALL
- That's all there is to it
- It's all here waiting for you
- Yes, you can have it all
- But that's not all

## ALLIANCE
- Just about the smartest alliance you could make
- Alliances with the very best all across the country
- With strategic alliances in

*See also:* ACCOMMODATION, AGREEMENT

## ALONE
- You are not alone in thinking this way

- Why keep going it alone when you can call in the professionals
- Can virtually stand alone
- Success is rarely achieved alone

## ALREADY

- If you don't have one already
- Already on its way to you
- You might already qualify for

*See also:* **NOW**

## ALTERNATIVE

- Presenting the affordable alternative
- Shouldn't you consider the alternative that's already been chosen by thousands of others
- A credible alternative to the usual leaders in the field
- The handy and secure alternative to
- Now there's an easy alternative
- The simple alternative is now easily available
- There simply is no alternative to
- The only alternative
- At last, a reasonable alternative to
- Now, the perfect alternative
- Looking for an alternative
- Basic alternatives to

*See also:* **CHANGE, CHOICE, RAIN CHECK**

## ALWAYS

- Always there when you need it
- Always on the job
- You know we're always there for you

## AMAZE

- It astounds and amazes you
- Continues to amaze us all
- Just how amazing is this

*See also:* **SURPRISE**

## AMENITY

- Providing you with all the amenities of a much larger
- The amenities most people really want
- The best amenities for you, our best customer

*See also:* **COMFORT, PLEASURE**

## ANALYSE
- Takes the time to analyse your needs
- After analysing and comparing hundreds of
- Made for people who love to analyse

## ANALYSIS
- Free in-depth analysis is the first step
- Call today for your free analysis and price quotation
- In the final analysis, you'll find we're the best

*See also:* **GUIDANCE, HELP, INFORMATION**

## ANGLE
- Angling in on the best
- We've got all the angles covered for you
- Consider all the angles on
- What's your angle
- See from a brand new angle

*See also:* **PLAN, TAKE**

## ANNOUNCE
- We are pleased to announce that
- The first to announce a reduction in
- Our company is delighted to announce that we are now offering
- Announcing big changes at

*See also:* **ADVERTISE**

## ANNOUNCEMENT
- Here is an important announcement
- The announcement everyone's been waiting for
- Get ready for a stupendous announcement from

## ANSWER
- You already know the answer
- Giving you a clear, unmistakable answer
- Because we're here to answer your questions
- Here's the answer to all your problems
- Nobody knows the answer like we do
- We answer only to you
- The fastest way to get the answer you're looking for
- Answering the big questions
- The answer is already in your hands
- When you need answers that work, look to us
- We have all the answers

- We're making it a lot easier to get straight answers
- The place to go for answers to
- We've got more answers than you have questions
- If you've got questions, we've got answers

**Answer:** acknowledgement, confirmation, reply, response, return, solution, explanation, justification, reason, key, clue, satisfy

*See also:* **APPROACH, ANALYSIS, INFORMATION, KEY, REASON, RESPONSE, SOLUTION**

## ANTICIPATE
- It's time to anticipate that delicious feeling of
- Anticipate a high degree of satisfaction
- The more you anticipate it, the better it gets

*See also:* **AHEAD, FUTURE**

## ANXIOUS
- We are anxious to be of service to you
- Anxiously awaiting the newest breakthrough in
- No need to be anxious any more about your

## ANYBODY
- Anybody can do it
- It isn't just anybody that can
- More than anybody else, we strive to serve you

*See also:* **PEOPLE**

## ANYTHING
- Anything goes
- Go anywhere, do anything
- You won't find anything better in the whole region
- Anything can happen with

## ANYWHERE
- Ready anywhere, anytime
- Anywhere there is a need
- Put it anywhere, watch it perform

## APART
- Another thing that sets us apart from other
- Together or apart, we're always ready to help
- Apart from the savings, there are many other reasons to

*See also:* **UNIQUE**

## APPEAL
- There's no denying the subtle appeal of
- Rich history and lasting appeal
- The perennial appeal of
- Surrender to the overwhelming appeal of
- Nothing could be more appealing than this

**Appeal:** attraction, attractiveness, interest, allure, charm, fascination, entice, invite, tempt

*See also:* **ATTRACTIVE, ATTRACTION, TEMPT**

## APPEARANCE
- Dramatically minimizes the appearance of
- Can greatly improve the appearance of your
- Would you like a classic appearance
- Appearances can be deceiving

*See also:* **ASPECT, LOOK**

## APPLICATION
- After only one application, you'll see a big difference
- Your application will be accepted immediately
- Gives you a huge choice of applications

*See also:* **USE**

## APPLY
- Easy to apply
- Once you apply it, you'll never again go back to
- Apply for yours today by calling

*See also:* **USE**

## APPOINTMENT
- Call today for your appointment or walk in anytime
- You appointment is waiting
- By appointment only
- One appointment you can't afford to miss

## APPRECIATE
- It's about appreciating the little things in life
- You'll appreciate the value
- A way to show just how much we appreciate your business

*See also:* **THANKS**

## APPRECIATION
- Showing a keen appreciation for

- This is the kind of appreciation you get when you come to us for
- Constant appreciation in value is only one benefit of

**Appreciation:** recognition, comprehension, gratitude, thanks, thankfulness, thanksgiving, acknowledgement, tribute, praise, applause
*See also:* **THANKS, TRIBUTE**

## APPROACH

- A completely different approach to
- A safe, effective approach to
- We offer a dynamic new approach to
- To learn more about our disciplined approach to
- A very rational approach to
- Ultimately, our risk-averse approach pays off for you
- Finding the approach that works for you

*See also:* **ANSWER, DIRECTION**

## AREA

- Serving your area for thirty years
- You won't find a better in the whole area
- This is one area where we can't be beaten
- An entire area devoted to your satisfaction

## ARRANGE

- Makes it so simple to arrange
- We can arrange it while you wait
- You'll be surprised at how quickly we can arrange to

*See also:* **ORDER**

## ARRANGEMENT

- For the sake of comfortable arrangements
- We make all the arrangements for you
- What better arrangement than this
- Ask for the kind of arrangement you want

*See also:* **ORDER**

## ARRAY

- Come and see our lavish array of
- Offering an interesting array of
- Add to this our astonishing array of choices in

*See also:* **CHOICE, DISPLAY**

## ARRIVAL

- Announcing the arrival of

- The minute our new arrivals get here, you'll know
- An arrival worth waiting for
- Includes the latest arrivals

## ARRIVE

- The newest models have just now arrived
- Now you can be here when they arrive
- For those people who have finally arrived
- Arriving just in time for your

*See also:* **HIT**

## ART

- Skilled in the delicate art of
- State of the art
- We've turned this service into an art
- An impressive work of art created by

*See also:* **CRAFT, SKILL**

## ASK

- Just ask our helpful staff
- What more could you ask
- Now, the only thing you'll need to ask for is
- Funny you should ask
- Ask about our new reward program
- Ask for it by name
- Ask about how you can get
- For complete details, ask or visit
- We asked you how we're doing
- The names smart shoppers ask for
- And be sure to ask about

**Ask:** inquire, query, question, request, petition, plead, apply to , turn to, solicit, clamour for, beg, beseech, supplicate, entreat, implore, cry to, demand, call for, invite, beckon, test, pump, grill, expect, count on, require, order, command, inspire, encourage, induce

*See also:* **COMMAND, DEMAND, QUESTION**

## ASPECT

- Introducing a luxurious aspect to any
- And this is only one aspect of
- From whatever aspect you look at it
- The increasingly exciting aspects of

*See also:* **LOOK**

**ASSIST**
- We have assisted thousands to
- Standing ready to assist you at any moment
- Tell us how we may assist you

*See also:* **HELP**

**ASSISTANCE**
- We're talking hands-on assistance here
- Providing you with personal assistance
- Whatever assistance you need, we're ready to provide

**Assistance:** help, aid, boost, relief, service, benefit, lift, protection, friendship, backing, care, helping hand, sustenance, advocacy, sponsorship, advancement,

*See also:* **COMFORT, HELP**

**ASSOCIATE**
- Just call one of our expert associates
- We have trained associates to help you
- Our associates are the best in the business

*See also:* **EXPERT, PROFESSIONAL, STAFF, SALESPEOPLE**

**ASSORTMENT**
- We offer a full assortment of
- Save on our complete assortment of
- Offering an assortment of delectable products
- You'll find a great assortment at
- A diverse assortment rolled into one
- Have just the assortment you want

*See also:* **VARIETY**

**ASSURANCE**
- Your assurance of quality
- Just one more assurance of
- Providing the rock-solid assurance you need
- Our name is your best assurance of

*See also:* **CERTAINTY, GUARANTEE, WARRANTY**

**ASSURE**
- You'll also be assured of
- Rest assured that the very best
- You can be assured that
- One look will assure you

## ATMOSPHERE
- Embracing a deliciously intimate atmosphere of
- Add lots of atmosphere with
- Above all, the atmosphere is one of refinement and sophistication
- Famous for its friendly atmosphere

**Atmosphere:** Environment, medium, milieu, setting, surroundings, mood, ambiance, sphere, tone, aura, tenor, character, spirit, temper, feeling, vibration, vibes
*See also:* **CLIMATE, SPIRIT**

## ATTACK
- To quickly neutralize the attack
- Guarding you against attacks of
- When you're having an attack of
- Attacking the problem from all directions

*See also:* **WAR**

## ATTENTION
- Someone has finally paid attention to the fact that
- Nothing draws attention like a
- Getting a lot of attention right now
- Enjoy a level of personal attention that
- At last, getting the attention you deserve

*See also:* **CONCERN**

## ATTITUDE
- We've got the right attitude
- It takes more than the right attitude to
- Lose that by-the-book attitude
- Attitude is what really counts
- Along with it comes a whole new attitude
- We give you some attitude

## ATTRACTION
- The list of attractions is as diverse and it is long
- Here's what the big attraction is
- Offering more attractions for less money
- Give in to the attraction
- Feel an irresistible attraction drawing you in

**Attraction:** interest, fascination, charm, magnetism, allure, enticement, temptation, enchantment, bewitchment, witchery, glamour, captivation, seduction
*See also:* **APPEAL, SEDUCTION**

18

## ATTRACTIVE
- Because we're offering extremely attractive terms
- When you want to be at your most attractive
- A very attractive offer is waiting for you
- You can be even more attractive with

## AUTOMATIC
- After that, everything is almost automatic
- Approval is automatic
- Automatically better
- In this uncertain world, nothing is automatic except

## AVAILABLE
- All products featured here are available at
- Products exclusively available at
- Available in a wide range of
- This quality product is available exclusively through your local dealer
- It's all available now at
- Now available at an unbelievable low price including
- Quite simply the most comprehensive set available
- Not available in all markets
- Now available through your local store
- Now available exclusively at
- Available until supplies run out
- The finest available anywhere

**Available:** handy, of service, usable, on hand, accessible, on tap, convenient, reachable, at one's fingertips, on command
*See also:* **ACCESSIBLE, READY**

## AVOID
- Avoid costly errors
- Helping you avoid all that confusion and worry
- Here's away to avoid those dreadful

## AWARD
- With award-winning service, year after year
- Consistently winning industry and consumer awards
- With our reputation, awards come easily
- Nobody has won more awards than

## AWARENESS
- Raising awareness of

- Awareness of our product has been steadily increasing
- By now, awareness is penetrating the farthest corners of

## BABY

- For all your baby needs
- The one thing babies know for sure
- Baby yourself for once
- So simple even a baby could use it

**Baby:** infant, newborn, babe, toddler, tot, tiny top, preschooler, juvenile, adolescent

## BACK

- If you're not satisfied, send it back
- It's back and it's fantastic
- We're back on track
- Great prices are back
- Bound to keep you coming back for more
- You'll always come back to
- You also get the confidence of being backed by

## BACKYARD

- Excellence right in our own backyard
- Look no further than your own backyard
- Turn your backyard into a
- As comfortable as your own back yard

*See also:* **NEIGHBORHOOD**

## BALANCE

- Striking the right balance
- We balance your needs against your
- When you want a truly balanced approach
- Helping you keep your balance in an unpredictable world

## BANK

- Bank on us
- Buy our produce and put all your savings in the bank
- You'll be laughing all the way to the bank

*See also:* **DEPEND, RELY, TRUST**

## BARGAIN

- Walk away with a bargain
- Bargains galore
- The bargain shop

- It's a real bargain
- You won't find a better bargain anywhere
- Bargain, anyone
- The best bargain you'll find for miles

**Bargain:** agreement, understanding, contract, settlement, bond, discount, reduction, good deal, buy, giveaway, steal, barter, trade, swap, traffic, peddle, vend, sell, exchange, dicker
*See also:* **DEAL**

**BARGOON**
- Big big bargoons
- Bargoons for everyone
- Hunt yourself up a real, old-fashioned bargoon

**BASE**
- We're based here because you are
- Building from a strong base
- Our base is wide and deep
- Helping to establish a firm base

*See also:* **FOUNDATION**

**BASICS**
- Back to basics
- Sensible basics for you
- First, we get the basics right
- The best priced basics
- Return to basics for
- Have all gone back to the basics

**BEAT**
- We'll beat any current advertised price
- We'll meet and beat any lower prices
- We haven't missed a beat
- You can't beat our
- We will beat any advertised price by

*See also:* **CONQUER**

**BEAUTIFUL**
- As beautiful as it is useful
- Just happens to be the most beautiful
- Be more beautiful than ever before
- So beautiful the world stops in its tracks

**Beautiful:** comely, attractive, handsome, lovely, becoming, eye-filling, good-looking, shapely, glamorous, sexy, charming, engaging, captivating, enthralling, enchanting, alluring, fascinating, winsome, winning, bewitching, enticing, empting, seductive, ravishing, personable, pleasant, divine, elegant, graceful, artistic, dainty, delicate, exquisite, superb, matchless, gorgeous, first-class, first-rate, dazzling, radiant, resplendent, shining, lustrous

*See also:* **ATTRACTIVE, SEXY**

## BEAUTIFY

- Guaranteed to beautify your
- For those who want to beautify
- You too can do even more to beautify your

**Beautify:** adorn, improve, grace, prettify, smarten, dress up, embellish, elaborate, enhance, heighten, set off, enrich, sweeten, ornament, bedeck, deck, deck out, array, decorate, emblazon, furbish, restore, doll up, dude up, preen

## BEAUTY

- Gives years of lasting beauty
- Treat yourself to unsurpassed beauty
- And the beauty of it is
- Rediscover your own natural beauty
- Provides a more concentrated beauty
- The beauty that lasts a lifetime
- Adds beauty and elegance to
- Add exciting new warmth and beauty to
- Combines natural beauty with the finest in service
- Lasting beauty is yours to keep
- We create beauty year round
- Order this versatile beauty today
- Order today and enjoy colorful, carefree beauty at its best

*See also:* **CHARM**

## BEEF

- Beef it up
- Whatever your beef is about, we can take care of it
- Our new, beefed-up operation puts muscle into
- Now you can do more than listen to them beef

## BEGIN

- To begin with
- So before you begin, visit us
- One very smart way to begin is to

- We help you begin and keep you on track

*See also:* **START**

## BEGINNER

- Perfect for beginners
- Cash in on beginner's luck
- Even if you're just a beginner, you can
- We cater to beginners

**Beginner:** neophyte, novice, tyro, amateur, rookie, newcomer, initiator

## BEGINNING

- It's beginning to dawn on people that
- And this is just the beginning
- More than merely a great beginning
- A scrumptious beginning
- With you from beginning to end

*See also:* **START**

## BEHIND

- Everybody is behind you
- Behind you all the way
- When you're feeling a little behind, we can help
- So that you'll never get behind in

*See also:* **HELP, SUPPORT**

## BELIEF

- It's one of our core beliefs that
- Firmly founded on the belief that
- More than just a belief
- Always in tune with your beliefs
- If you subscribe to these beliefs, we're the folks you want to come to

*See also:* **FEELING, IDEA, OPINION, PHILOSOPHY, PRINCIPLE**

## BELIEVE

- Standing together for the things we believe
- Now you know who to believe
- At our company, we believe
- It's hard believe that something can be so good
- Standing tall for what you believe
- Helping you believe in yourself even more
- Seeing is believing
- You won't believe it until you actually come and see for yourself

- When it comes right down to the things you believe in
- Talk to the people who believe in you
- We have always believed in offering the best

## BELIEVER
- I'm a believer
- We'll turn you into a believer
- Believers flock to the source
- Join thousands of new believers in

## BENCHMARK
- Establishes a new benchmark within
- We've always been the benchmark for
- Benchmark products and benchmark services
- The test of a real benchmark has always been

*See also:* **STANDARD**

## BENEFIT
- Another nice benefit is
- You could benefit from our help
- One more hidden benefit becomes obvious when
- Its benefits are far more profound that any such product on the market to date
- Just one more added benefit available through
- Yet another direct benefit come from
- Something that can benefit everyone
- Outstanding benefits for years to come
- The most benefits for both of you
- Of course you'll enjoy the same benefits as before
- Including benefits usually reserved for
- You too can benefit from
- You'll also get other exceptional benefits
- And money-saving financial benefits
- Benefits that go far beyond
- The benefits are endless
- The benefits add up daily
- More benefits for you and your family with only a little cost
- Just add up the benefits
- Only a few years ago, nobody could have imagined benefits like these
- And many other fabulous benefits
- With it come the benefits you want
- Provides benefits right from the start

**Benefit:** advantage, well-being, betterment, improvement, advancement, promotion, gain, help, aid, service, profit, advance, assist, contribute to
*See also:* **ADVANTAGE, HELP, IMPROVE**

## BEST
- Bringing the best to you
- And best of all
- Best in the industry
- Settle for nothing less than the best
- Be sure you have the best
- The best for your peace of mind
- You deserve the very best
- Next best thing to
- The best thing since
- Bringing the best to you
- Our best ever selection of
- The best deals are at
- The best in town
- We've saved the best for you
- Bringing you the very best available
- Best of all, it costs so little
- Don't let it get the best of you
- Simply the best anywhere
- One of the very best things about it is
- The best of all possible worlds
- The best you've ever seen

**Best:** excellent, unexcelled, unparalleled, unsurpassed, fine, superfine, first-class, first-rate, crack, superior, choice, select, top, tip-top, tops, paramount, capital, outstanding, foremost, preeminent, venerable, highest, peerless, perfect, superlative, consummate, pure, genuine, sterling, gilt-edged, sound, wholesome, golden, advantageous, best-suited, right, correct, fitting, apt, enviable, covetable, supreme
*See also:* **CHOICE, EXCELLENCE, PREMIUM, SUPERIOR**

## BEST-SELLING
- Has been the best-selling product in its class for years
- There's a good reason why this product has become the best-selling phenomenon it is
- This is our best-selling product
- Catapaulted into best-seller position
- A real best-seller day in, day out
- We have more best-sellers in one location than any other

## BETTER

- Products that let you make better use of
- Nobody does it better
- Better than anything else
- It just keeps getting better and better
- And its gets even better
- By making better things, we are making things better
- For better or for worse, you have to stick together
- And that makes us feel a whole lot better too
- This better enables us to help you
- Brighter, bolder, better than ever
- Our best selling product just got better
- We're always one better
- Now we have a better way to
- It doesn't get any better than this
- We get better every year

*See also:* **IMPROVE**

## BIG

- The big one is here
- Our biggest ever
- It's not just big that counts
- Gets even bigger

**Big:** large, huge, enormous, giant, whacking, prodigious, immense, colossal, monstrous, humungous, gigantic, ginormous, tremendous, towering, great, vast, extensive, voluminous, grand, grandiose, majestic, august, massive, gargantuan, significant, weighty

*See also:* **GIANT**

## BITE

- Don't worry, it won't bite
- At last, something with real bite to it
- Don't let problems bite into your profits

## BLAHS

- Beat the beauty blahs
- Blahs begone
- Banish the blahs forever

## BLAST

- Prepare for a blast
- A big blast of value
- Blast-off with

- Come and have a blast

## BLEND

- Creates a unique product by blending the best of each
- Built or easy blending
- A contagious blend of
- A unique blend of
- Won't just blend in
- A conspicuous blend designed to stand out
- Be sure to try our special blend of
- Seasoned with a delicate blend of
- Each blend contains a unique
- An affordable blend of luxury and performance

*See also:* **MIX**

## BLITZ

- Sales blitz
- The blitz is on
- The blitz is about to hit

## BLOCKBUSTER

- Look inside for more blockbuster savings
- A real blockbuster of a sale
- A blockbuster is coming

*See also:* **BIG, GIANT**

## BLOW OUT

- Value blow out
- Don't miss our summer blow out sale
- Blow out prices
- The biggest blow out of all

## BOAST

- Boasts some of the finest
- We don't usually boast about it, but
- Soon you'll be boasting about
- It's no idle boast that

*See also:* **PRIDE**

## BODY

- Proud of a healthy, toned body
- A highly responsive extension of your mind and body
- A wide range of body enjoyment

- Turn your body over to the joys of
*See also:* **SKIN**

## BONUS
- Plus a special bonus offer
- Free blockbuster bonus
- Another added bonus is
- Welcome bonus for all new customers
- You'll receive a welcome extra bonus of
- Get your free bonus today

**Bonus:** reward, award, prize, gift, present, endowment, largess, freebie, dividend, extra, plus, surplus, gain, fringe benefit, prerequisite, perk, compensation, recompense, remuneration, emolument, repayment, premium, bounty, inducement, encouragement, stimulation, bribe, bait, payment
*See also:* **GIFT, PREMIUM**

## BOOK
- Book now to ensure your place
- We go by the book
- Look in the book to find us
- For real assurance, book ahead

## BOOM
- Grab your part of the boom in
- Join a booming industry
- Business is booming
- The biggest boom ever has just hit town
- Boomtimes are here, yipee

**Boom:** progress, prosper, thrive, flourish, luxuriate, burgeon, mushroom, explode, spring up, burst forth, rise, grow, increase, gain, add to
*See also:* **GROW, INCREASE**

## BOOST
- With a little boost from
- We give you the boost you need to
- Boosts performance amazingly
- Often it only takes the smallest boost to help you

*See also:* **HELP**

## BORN
- Maybe you were born with it
- Born to succeed

- Some people are just born to be the best—and you're one of them
- For those of you who weren't born yesterday

## BOSS

- Be your own boss right away
- Now no one can boss you around any more
- With us, you're the boss
- The best boss is yourself
- No more bosses to keep you jumping

## BOTH

- Now you can have the best of both
- For the both of you
- Both of you will want to try it
- Both are winners

## BOTTOM

- Got you covered from top to bottom
- Let's start from the bottom
- A complete overhaul from the bottom up
- Start on the bottom and work your way up

## BOTTOM LINE

- Concentrate on the most important bottom line of all
- Because results are the bottom line
- The truth always shows up in the bottom line
- Translates into a strong bottom line
- Nothing does more for your bottom line than the right people with the right skills to
- The bottom line is your top priority

*See also:* **PROFIT**

## BOUNTY

- Beauty from the bounty of
- Coming to you from the bounty of
- Bounty enough for everyone

*See also:* **BONUS, GIFT, PROFIT**

## BRACING

- The gently bracing quality of
- Bracing as a brisk, bright morning in spring
- Gives a bracing boost just when you need it
- Savour the bracing tang of

# BRAG

- Pardon us for bragging
- Giving you something to brag about
- Our bragging days have just begun
- Our customers are bragging about
- The bragging rights are all yours

*See also:* **BOAST**

# BRAIN

- Brain power is featured
- The brains of the operation is
- First, we use our brains
- Appeals to a lot more than your brain

# BRAND

- The most reliable brand to look for is
- Thousands of different name brand products in stock
- Save on all our brand name products
- Brand names, low low prices
- The kind of national brand quality you can trust
- We carry the top brand names in
- Top quality brand names in
- Your value brand is here
- National brand quality at our great prices
- Bringing your more famous brands
- Brand names for less
- The brands you want
- Best brands available
- Put your trust in a brand doctors have been recommending
- We carry all brand name products
- More famous brands

*See also:* **SORT**

# BREAK

- Take a break from your daily routine and visit us today
- Give yourself that well-deserved break in your day
- Visit us for a great break on your
- You worked hard for this break
- Give yourself a break
- Take a break with something you can relate to
- Break out now
- Make the break
- Break away to freedom

30

- This time, you get the breaks

## BREAKAWAY

- Treat yourself to a breakaway today
- Breakaway prices let you break out of your
- For your biggest breakaway ever

## BREAKTHROUGH

- A technological breakthrough
- Dramatic new breakthrough
- We make the breakthroughs first
- This could be your big breakthrough
- Showing you our breakthroughs in design and performance

*See also:* **ACHIEVEMENT, ADVANCE, INFORMATION, LEAP, RESEARCH**

## BREATH

- We'll take your breath away
- Giving you a chance to catch your breath
- You'll catch your breath at your first sight of

## BREATHE

- Breathe a little easier with
- Gives you room to breathe
- Just breathe deeply and relax

## BREEZE

- Light as a summer breeze
- Let's you breeze right through
- With our help, it'll be a breeze
- Breezing through that used to take hours

*See also:* **EASY**

## BRING

- We are pleased to bring you
- Bringing you only the best
- Nobody brings you better
- Bringing you for the very first time

*See also:* **CARRY**

## BROCHURE

- Present this brochure at a participating location
- Also includes a detailed brochure

- Call today for our information-packed brochure
- Be sure to pick up a brochure
- Details in the accompanying brochure

*See also:* **ADVERTISE, INFORMATION**

## BROKE

- Go from broke to
- Go for broke
- You'll never end up broke if you follow these principles
- If it ain't broke, don't fix it

## BROWSE

- Drop by to browse through
- Come in and browse
- You're always welcome just to browse
- You'd be surprised what you'll find just by browsing
- Browse through and find valuable information

*See also:* **LOOK, SEE**

## BUCK

- Buck buster
- Get bucks back on
- Saves you big bucks on
- Soon you'll be the person with the bucks
- Looks like a million bucks

*See also:* **CASH, DOLLAR, MONEY, SAVE, SAVINGS**

## BUDGET

- When you're on a tight budget
- Also available to suit your budget
- For all tastes and all budgets
- A huge selection of styles for every home and budget
- Something to please every budget
- Tailored to fit your budget

**Budget:** estimate, financial statement, costs, operating expenses, overhead, plan, blueprint, program, allowance, share, allotment, percentage, quota, cost out

*See also:* **PLAN, PROGRAM**

## BUILD

- Will build what others call the best
- Building toughness and dependability into
- Building a lifetime of knowledge, values and confidence

- Build on what you've begun
- Together, we're building something no one could construct alone
- Nobody builds them as well as we do

*See also:* **CREATE, DEVELOP, MAKE**

## BUILT

- Built for trouble-free operation
- So thoughtfully built that
- Not everyone is built alike
- Built tougher and stronger

## BULK

- We carry bulk products
- Bulk up your bank account
- Bulk savings every day
- Ask about our bulk prices

*See also:* **QUANTITY**

## BUSINESS

- Because we value your business
- A business growing through excellent communications
- Now you can be in business for yourself
- Want to perk up your business
- No matter what business you're in, you need
- In business you've got to control costs
- Ready to do business with you
- Help you manage the business you've always dreamed of
- Working to gain a deep understanding of your business
- On the right track for business
- A business measured in minutes
- You don't get anywhere in this business by standing still
- Best for business, best for you
- No business was lost to
- See what you can do for your business
- Best for your growing business
- Lets you concentrate on doing business
- Investing time in your business pays off
- Can handle serious business
- Helps you do business faster and more professionally
- Understanding the unique and specialized needs of your business
- This fabulous business opportunity
- Let's do business together
- You'll like the way we do business

- We're open for business seven days a week
- Not only do we offer you business a winning edge
- Working harder for your business
- Direct application in your day-to-day business
- Committed to helping your business take off
- Get to know businesses like yours
- Where business is bound for
- Give your business a big advantage
- Responds to the needs of business today
- Designed to help your business grow
- Primed and ready to take your business to a higher level than ever before
- For vital savings on everyday business needs
- The big solution for small business

**Business:** occupation, profession, trade, line, vocation, avocation, career, following, calling, pursuit, craft, metier, employment, job, work, living, livelihood, means of support, bread and butter, industry, enterprise, barter, exchange, commerce, interchange, dealings, truck, intercourse, traffic, transaction, affairs, ventures, negotiation, bargaining, issue, merchandising, selling, promoting, company, corporation, firm, house, establishment, shop, store, partnership, team, concern, affair, question

## BUTTON
- All at the touch of a button
- Cute as a button
- Push-button convenience
- We pushed all the right buttons

## BUY
- Special buy, priced to sell
- Buy with confidence
- We'll spend the time to help you get the best buy
- When it comes to buying and selling, nobody comes close to
- It's a real buy
- You don't have to buy into
- Super buy on
- Your best buy every day
- Best buy anywhere
- You won't get a better buy than this
- Buy now, pay later
- We buy and sell
- See and buy
- Best buy price

- Unbeatable buy
- Find out just how much you buy for only
- Don't buy from anyone else until you talk to us
- You can be confident about buying from
- The best time to buy is now
- Nothing else to buy
- There's no obligation to buy anything else
- Before you go rushing out to buy
- That's why you've got to buy a
- How do you buy success
- Your absolute best buy on
- Huge buying power working for you
- Know your needs before you buy
- The more you buy, the more you save
- The best place to buy your

**Buy:** purchase, pick up, pay for, get one's hands on, invest in, come by, acquire, put money into, obtain, get, procure, secure, hire, engage, take on, snap up
*See also:* **INVEST, PURCHASE**

## BUYER
- Offered for the privileged buyer who will take advantage
- Today's buyer must be educated
- For the buyer who knows what she wants
- Attracts potential buyers within hours
- Our buyers are the shrewdest

*See also:* **CUSTOMER**

## BUYS
- Great buys on selected merchandise
- More great buys inside
- We've rounded up the best buys from all across our stores
- Buy more, save more
- The best buys are sitting on our shelves waiting for you
- Hottest buys ever
- Check out these hot buys
- You won't want to miss any of these super buys

*See also:* **BARGAIN**

## CALCULATE
- Precisely calculated for you by our computers
- After you do the calculations, you'll see why we're the best
- Calculated to please you

- You might call us the calculating sort
- We've done all the calculations for you

*See also:* **ADD**

## CALL

- Heed the call to action now
- You'll never have to make another call
- Call right away
- For a good, old-fashioned service call
- If you're interested, please call us at
- That's why you might seriously consider giving us a call
- Calling all buyers
- Call us today for prompt, professional service
- Call on us, day or night, to
- Please call ahead
- One call lets you do all this
- Call us today for immediate attention
- We're waiting for your call
- One call is all it takes
- It'll take only a minute to call and book your appointment
- Call for your nearest dealer
- The moment we get your call, we're on our way
- Please call on us for all your needs
- Call to find out about
- The best hours to call are
- On call, twenty-four hours a day
- With one phone call, all this could be yours
- Call us in advance to beat the rush
- It all starts with one phone call
- Give us a call at
- It's your call all the way
- You've called upon us to
- You are invited to call
- Or make a quick call to
- Has just issued a wake-up call to
- Answer the call
- The smartest call you'll ever make
- Just call our toll-free number today
- So you'll never miss another important call again
- Call, write or fax us for more information today
- Just call, toll-free, for our information package
- Call now for free information and estimates
- So give us a call right now

- Always at your beck and call
*See also:* **TELEPHONE, TOUCH**

## CALLER
- Experts to answer out callers' needs
- If you're a first-time caller we will give you an extra bonus
- Each caller is treated with the utmost respect and courtesy

## CAPABILITY
- Increasing your capability
- Integrates all of these full-featured capabilities
- Our design capabilities are seemingly endless
- Combines the rugged capabilities of
*See also:* **ABILITY, SKILL**

## CAPACITY
- Now we have the capacity to
- With a bigger than ever capacity to
- We've increased out capacity to serve you better
- No one else has this kind of capacity
*See also:* **ABILITY, CRAFT, SKILL**

## CAPTURE
- That captures it all
- Capture the feeling
- Nothing else captures the joy of
- Capture this special moment forever
- We capture smiles

## CARD
- And now use your new credit card and receive
- Apply for our credit card today
- The only card that counts
- When you use your card you benefit

## CARE
- It's important to know how to care for
- How you take care of yourself says a lot about you
- We care about what you have to say
- You want to be able to take care of yourself
- Easy-care convenience
- Care, convenience and confidentiality
- Show him or her how much you care

- We show how deeply we care
- We care about all your needs
- Visit our care centre for detailed service
- We care about the way our product works for you
- Show that special someone how much you care
- When you really care, you want nothing but the best
- Caring for you, day and night
- Still made with good, old-fashioned care

**Care:** attention, vigilance, caution, watchfulness, concern, regard, mindfulness, consciousness, prudence, awareness, circumspection, care for, watch out for, look after, be concerned for, be solicitous, attend to, deal with, take up, take action on, cherish, protection, safeguard
*See also:* **CONCERN**

## CAREER

- Now it's time for your career to take off
- We've made a career of it
- A career of caring for our customers
- We know how much your career matters to you

## CAREFUL

- Please be careful out there
- Very careful with your precious treasures
- For a careful buyer like you
- Careful service is our hallmark

## CARESS

- The sweet caress of
- Gentle as a caress
- Save all your caresses for

## CARNIVAL

- Carnival of savings
- Turns life into a merry carnival
- Join the carnival
- The carnival of value starts today

*See also:* **CELEBRATION**

## CARRY

- We also carry a great selection of
- We carry everything you're looking for
- We carry an excellent choice of
- Cash and carry every day

• Carrying out studies to show you
*See also:* **DO**

## CASH
• You pocket cash as soon as you buy
• Get cash back with the purchase of any
• Lots of cash savers
• Heard about cash back
• Cash in today
• Putting more cash in your pocket immediately
• You can even get cash back
• Selling for cash
• Cash on the barrel head
• Turn you products into cash
• More flexibility in managing cash flow
• Cash in literally overnight
• Start collecting cash right away
*See also:* **BUCKS, DOLLAR, MONEY**

## CATALOG/CATALOGUE
• Reply now for our new full color catalogue
• Call for a complete product catalogue
• Catalogue of savings
• Many items also available in our catalogue

## CATCH
• A very long way to go to catch up to us
• Catch the latest news and views
• Catch the brass ring today
• The excitement is catching
• Catch a falling star
• Everyone is catching on fast
*See also:* **CAPTURE**

## CATER
• Catering to the growing need for
• We cater to your every need
• Nobody caters better to
• Sit back and be catered to
*See also:* **PAMPER, SERVE**

## CELEBRATE
• We're celebrating

- It's your time to celebrate
- Celebrate triumphs and set new goals
- Celebrate in a memorable way
- We're celebrating
- What better way to celebrate
- Come help us celebrate
- Celebrating with some of our hottest prices ever

*See also:* **CHRISTMAS, EASTER, HOLIDAY**

## CELEBRATION
- Bring the celebration home with
- Join the celebration today
- It's our anniversary celebration
- And the celebration just goes on and on

*See also:* **CARNIVAL, FESTIVE, HOLIDAYS**

## CELEBRITY
- Meet our most popular celebrity
- You become an instant celebrity
- The celebrity of our company is well founded
- Enjoying well-earned celebrity

*See also:* **STAR**

## CENTURY
- Has been used for centuries throughout the world
- Now we're growing into the next century
- The next century will be our century
- The only product designed for the twenty-first century

*See also:* **TIME**

## CERTAINTY
- That's the certainty
- You can say it with absolute certainty
- The certainty will always remain
- Your satisfaction is a certainty

*See also:* **GUARANTEE, WARRANTY**

## CERTIFICATE
- Purchase any time and receive a gift certificate
- Have you considered a gift certificate
- A gift certificate laden with delectable possibilities
- Everyone loves to receive the surprise of a gift certificate

## CHALLENGE
- The sort of challenge our people have always delivered on
- Challenges the status quo
- Rising to the challenge
- Meeting today's challenges
- A team of experts to help you overcome the toughest challenges
- Thriving on new creative challenges
- Responding to these challenges is no easy thing
- Finding fresh challenges in looking at
- Solving tomorrow's challenges
- Exceptional challenges require exceptional people

**Challenge:** invitation, dare, call, summons, venture, hazard, risk, puzzle, knot, barrier, defy, stimulate, excite, inspire, spur on, invigorate, jog, fan
*See also:* **PROBLEM, RISK, VENTURE**

## CHAMPION
- A champion in the global battle for supremacy
- Turn yourself into a champion
- Stand with the champions
- The real champions are often unexpected
- Champions at your service

**Champion:** protector, defender, guardian, friend, winner, victor, leader, champ, hero, knight, supporter, advocate, backer, fighter, guard
*See also:* **PROTECT**

## CHANCE
- Finally giving everyone a chance to
- Automatically gives you the chance to
- We leave nothing to chance
- Nothing should be left to chance when you life is involved
- Don't take chances with your most precious possessions
- Know they shouldn't take chances with
- Take a chance with us

*See also:* **OPPORTUNITY**

## CHANGE
- Which you can change as often as you like
- Can change all that in a hurry
- Things have certainly changed
- Very soon you'll notice a real change
- Devoted to bringing change to
- We listened and we changed
- Are you looking for a change of scene

41

- Have changed a lot over the years
- It's time for a change
- A truly substantive change
- Constitutes a major change
- Major changes at all levels benefits you
- The biggest change you'll have to deal with is
- This change of mindset has just begun
- We have changed for the better
- You have the freedom, the power to change
- It's costs a little change to stay in step with
- We're changing to respond better to emerging needs
- You'll notice some real changes in how we work
- We've made some exciting new changes

**Change:** transform, moderate, temper, alter, correct, modify, convert, mutate, transfigure, retool, remodel, switch, replace, exchange, translate, reconstruct, reorder, recast, reorganize, innovation, novelty, revolution, transition, evolution, barter, trade, swap
*See also:* **ADAPT, COMPROMISE, DIFFERENCE, FLEXIBLE, VERSATILE**

## CHARACTER
- You can sense the character
- Now that's a product with character
- Founded on strength of character
- You can tell just by the character of
- Changing character to suit you

## CHARGE
- Leading the charge to
- Charges payable at time of purchase
- All at no extra charge
- No extra charge for the smiles
- No hidden charges
- Taking charge of your life
- There are no service charges for this service

**Charge:** ask, expect, ask a price, levy, assess, appraise, tax, exact, bill, debit, defer payment, buy on the layaway/installment plan, take on credit and account
*See also:* **COST, PRICE**

## CHARISMA
- Amazing talent and irresistible charisma
- You, too, can have this kind of charisma

- Feel the charisma
*See also:* **CHARM**

## CHARM
- Experience the unique charm of
- Accomplished with charm and skill
- Acquire the charm of
- This charm can fill your home and your life
*See also:* **BEAUTY**

## CHECK
- Dive in and check out these great values
- Check out our terrific selection
- Check out the following
- Check us out today at
- Every time you check out
- And check out the more than

## CHERISH
- Cherish the simple dreams of
- Something to cherish
- Make them feel cherished
- We cherish your patronage

## CHIC
- It's pure chic
- Arrive with breath-taking chic
- Chic that cannot be imitated
- You too can achieve this kind of chic
*See also:* **ELEGANT, STYLE**

## CHILD
- Pamper your inner child
- Even a child could do it
- Makes it child's play to
*See also:* **KIDS, YOUTH**

## CHILDHOOD
- Cherish the special time of childhood
- Relive your childhood with
- The joy of childhood can be repeated here
- What is more precious than a happy childhood

## CHOICE

- It's your choice
- Make the right choice
- Equipping you to make a better choice
- A far easier choice
- By choice, not default
- Your choice is perfectly clear
- For so many, the choice includes
- The authentic choice
- Plus your choice of
- More choice than anywhere else in town
- The best choice for you
- Making your choice really count
- Shouldn't you have a choice
- Customer's choice
- The smart choice for the ultimate
- Your first choice for
- Your choice for only
- Gives you a multitude of choices
- The perfect choice for do-it-yourselfers
- There is no better choice than
- The intelligent choice in
- It's the clear choice
- The finest choice for discriminating shoppers
- First and only choice
- There's only one choice
- The one with the most choice
- Here are some healthy choices
- Now you can make informed choices about everything we have to offer
- A world of choices at your fingertips
- Some choices are more important than others
- There are lots and lots of choices for
- Providing more choices than any other
- When it's real choice you want, come to us

**Choice:** selection, alternative, option, decision, commitment, possibility, answer, solution, way, substitute, discrimination, vote, equivalent, preference, pleasure, taste, wish, desire, inclination, elect, select, elite, pick, best part, prize, best, rarest, prime, treasure, gem, cream of the crop, paragon, nonesuch, nonpareil, one in a million, champion, prodigy
*See also:* **ARRAY, BEST, CHOOSE, DECIDE, OPTION, PICK, RAIN CHECK, SELECT**

## CHOOSE

- We can help you choose the right product or service for you
- Here's how to choose
- You'll never have to choose between
- Smart people choose us first
- Helping you choose the product that is right for you
- Why choose when you can have it all
- To help you choose wisely and well
- Why not choose the best
- Choose from an incredible selection of
- You get to choose
- Never hard to choose
- Easier than ever to choose the product that's right for you
- To help you choose the right product
- Smart people choose
- Right away you see how easy it is to choose

**Choose:** select, pick, draw, sort, fancy, favor, desire, balance, weigh, discriminate, judge, decide, opt, see fit, embrace, elect
*See also:* **CHOICE, DECIDE, PICK, SELECT**

## CHOP

- Chop your bill in half
- When you really need to chop your costs
- Chop time, chop effort, increase your return
- Chopper specials
- The price chopper

*See also:* **CUT**

## CHRISTMAS

- Get what you want for Christmas
- A Christmas-time double bonus
- Come to us for all your Christmas gifts
- Let the Christmas season light up your heart
- The finest Christmas gift anyone could receive
- This Christmas, don't miss out
- Want to jingle somebody's bells this Christmas
- Give someone a memorable Christmas
- For someone special on your Christmas list
- As much as part of Christmas as decorating the tree
- Christmas is an important time for your family
- Christmas is the season of giving
- Make Christmas magic for someone on your list
- Make a Christmas wish come true

- For a very merry Christmas
- Make Christmas merry
- A Christmas treat that's jingle-licious
- A very welcome Christmas gift
- Celebrating isn't just for Christmas and the New Year
- With Christmas just around the corner

**Christmas:** Yule, Yuletide, Noel, holiday season, Christmastime, Christmastide

*See also:* **CELEBRATE, HOLIDAY**

## CHUNK

- You don't have to pay it all in one chunk
- Keep a big chunk of cash for yourself
- When you've invested a chunk of time in

## CIRCUMSTANCES

- Extraordinary measures for extraordinary circumstances
- Under the circumstances, the very best choice
- Fitted to your circumstances
- No matter what your circumstances

*See also:* **REASON**

## CIVILIZATION

- You're never far from civilization
- One of the big advances of civilization
- Make civilization a little kinder

## CLAIM

- Good luck finding another product that can claim that
- All our claims are true
- After you've checked out the claims of the competition, come back

## CLASS

- Add class and distinction
- In a class of its own
- The largest in its class
- A whole new class of
- Go to the head of the class
- The very best in its class
- Puts you into a class of your own
- Executive class luxury

*See also:* **GROUP**

## CLASSIC
- Always a classic
- New classics, traditional quality
- Clean and classic
- From classic to dramatic
- One of the classics that's been around forever
- A classic in our time

*See also:* **STANDARD, TIMELESS**

## CLEAN
- Clean value
- Clean up on savings
- Clean, quick and easy
- For gentle cleansing action

## CLEAR
- Everything must be cleared for new products
- One thing becomes crystal clear
- We want to be perfectly clear about
- It's the clear choice

## CLEARANCE
- Inventory clearance, everything must go
- Warehouse clearance at warehouse prices
- The clearance of the year
- A special clearance of
- Monster clearance means monster savings
- Factory outlet clearance
- The final clearance is your last chance to save big
- Semi-annual floor clearance
- Factory direct clearance sale

*See also:* **SALE**

## CLICK
- Really clicks for
- This will click with you
- When something clicks inside your head

## CLIENT
- Our program works for each client
- Every one of our clients has unique needs
- Our clients are people just like you
- So that we can better serve our ever-increasing client base

- Serving an increasingly diverse clientele
- Our clients built our business
- Here's what our clients say
- Your clients will never know the difference
- Our clients love us
- Our clients know they can count on
- Our complete dedication to our clients' success
- Seizing opportunities on behalf of our clients

*See also:* **CUSTOMER**

## CLIMATE

- In a climate fraught with constant change
- Creating the right climate for
- A climate of friendliness and cooperation
- In today's tough climate, you need

*See also:* **ATMOSPHERE**

## CLOCK

- Round-the-clock service
- Enjoy round-the-clock access to
- When you have to beat the clock
- You don't have to be afraid of the clock
- Turn the clock into a friend, not an enemy

*See also:* **TIME**

## CLOSE

- Close at hand for today and the future
- Closer than you think
- Get close to the best
- So close you can almost smell it
- We're conveniently close by
- View it up close
- Up close and personal
- Nothing else comes close to
- We're close to where you live

## CLUB

- Value club
- Like having your own private club
- Join the club - it's free
- Become an instant member of the club
- Get all the benefits of belonging to the club

## COINCIDENCE
- It's no coincidence that there's something great about
- More than just a coincidence
- A lucky coincidence helps you to

## COLD
- This season, come in from the cold
- Beat the cold rush
- Save cold cash on hot values

## COLLABORATE
- We collaborate with you to
- When you're looking for the best people to collaborate
- An outstanding collaborative effort

*See also:* **TEAM**

## COLLABORATION
- The result of inspired collaboration
- Replaced with a newfound collaboration
- This collaboration is a real first
- A historic collaboration has taken place

*See also:* **TEAMWORK**

## COLLECT
- Start collecting right away
- If you hurry, you can collect every one
- Collect your savings now

**Collect:** accumulate, heap up, pile, stack up, compile, amass, cumulate, squirrel away, hoard, stow away, gather, pull in, harvest, reap, garner, store up, stock up, lay by, lay up, lay in, stash away, reserve, set aside, save, stash

*See also:* **SAVE**

## COLLECTION
- Keep your collection up-to-date with
- Don't forget about these useful collections
- Presenting our premium collection
- Offering the only collection of its kind ever
- An extraordinary collection of
- A must-have addition to your collection
- Some of the hottest pieces in the collection
- Introducing our designer collection
- Part of the newest collection available

- We've put together a careful collection of

## COLLECTOR

- The best put together into a collector's edition
- The smartest collectors get here first
- Designed for collectors of fine items everywhere

## COLOR

- Put some color into your life
- Drenched in rich, luscious color
- In the colors you want
- Colors that wake you up fast
- Nothing looks newer than layers of color
- A shimmer of color, a swish of grace
- Color that lasts and lasts
- For subtle color, a lighter shade of pale
- Are you becoming color-wary
- Fashion colors for spring
- Available in assorted designer colors
- Add a splash of color to your
- In subtle color blends
- In all these new colors
- All-new colors, patterns and styles
- Lets your colors come out bright, not dull

## COMBINATION

- A potent combination of
- Make a combination to fit your needs
- An unbeatable combination of
- Sample exotic combinations of
- One impressive combination does it all
- The most extraordinary combination of
- The winning combination
- Choose any combination of
- What an outstanding combination of
- A knockout combination of first class
- You get an outstanding combination of
- Combination of exceptional personal service and
- Hundreds of design choice combinations

*See also:* **BLEND, MIX**

## COMBINE

- What do you get when you combine

- You can combine as many as you please
- Now you have a chance to combine
- Combined especially for you

*See also:* **BLEND, MIX**

## COME
- Come and get it for less
- We hope you'll come in soon
- Come and select that special gift
- Come in today and see our new spring line
- Come in and view our selection

*See also:* **VISIT**

## COMEBACK
- We're on the comeback trail
- Making a comeback no one can ignore
- Staging a spectacular comeback

*See also:* **RETURN**

## COMFORT
- Takes you to the next level of comfort
- Your quest for comfort is finally satisfied
- Slip on casual comfort
- Comfort like you've never felt before
- Surround yourself with comfort
- We can all use little comfort to get us through the final days of winter
- The quintessential comfort
- Comfort and pleasure you desire need not be at odds with prices
- Get into real comfort now
- Enter the comfort zone
- Comfort has never been so reasonably priced
- Counting on comfort, again and again
- With all the amenities and comforts of

*See also:* **AMENITY, EASE, PLEASURE, SOFT**

## COMFORTABLE
- You'll feel comfortable and in control
- So comfortable you won't want to leave
- In the supremely comfortable
- Faster and more comfortable
- Whatever you're comfortable with
- We know you're comfortable with that

## COMMAND

- Puts you in total command of
- Your wish is our command
- In command of more services at once than any other
- For you, it's a command performance

*See also:* **CONTROL**

## COMMENT

- When you make a comment, we listen hard
- Your comments keep us in touch with your tastes and expectations
- So please feed us with your comments, they're important

*See also:* **SUGGESTION**

## COMMIT

- Committed to helping you maintain
- Committed to quality, value, selection and service
- Professional, knowledgeable, committed to you

**Commit:** entrust, commend, confide, vest in, charge with, assign, authorize, pledge, promise, swear, covenant, vow, bind, engage, undertake, attest, certify, guarantee, vouch, answer for, oblige

*See also:* **PLEDGE**

## COMMITMENT

- A combination of creativity, commitment and caring
- We'll show a commitment you can really depend on
- Is our commitment to deliver the best service available with the results you expect
- Attest to the versatility and commitment of
- Considering a quarter of a century of commitment to
- For people who hate commitments
- A perfect compliment to any occasion
- Our commitment to you includes

## COMMODITY

- The single most precious commodity is
- What's the hottest commodity today
- The most sought-after commodity in
- Offering you a very valuable commodity

## COMMON

- Has a lot in common with the real thing
- We all have one thing in common
- Sharing common values

• We seem to have a common thought in mind

## COMMUNICATE
• Communicate faster
• A new way to communicate
• You need more ways to communicate
• Working to communicate with you

**Communicate:** inform, tell speak, advise, notify, mention, point out, bring to attention, let know, enlighten, clue in, announce, publish, convey, get across, say, voice, utter, reveal, divulge, make known, uncover, lay open, impart, pass along, interface, chat, talk, get in touch, contact, call, telephone

*See also:* **TALK, TELL, SAY**

## COMMUNICATION
• Opening more lines of communication to you
• Honest and open communication
• Growing through good communication
• Communication is everything

## COMMUNITY
• Connects you to the fastest growing community in the world
• Flocking to a safe new community
• Join a community of people and resources
• Owned and operated by a member of your own community
• Caring about our community
• A terrific part of your community
• Putting us well ahead of the average community
• Speaking about its integration into the world community
• Proud to have served the community for the past number of years

## COMPANY
• You're in good company
• A good, solid company that will really help you to
• The company that's been trusted for years
• Company's coming

*See also:* **BUSINESS**

## COMPARE
• Compare our low prices
• We invite you to compare
• Dare to compare
• Compare our price and quality

- Compare at
- Only when you compare will you understand
- Just compare
- You'll love how easy it is to compare
- Compare us with any other

## COMPARISON
- That's why we invite comparison
- We're all for comparisons
- Standing up under the most exacting comparison

## COMPATIBILITY
- You'll get optimum performance and compatibility
- Engineered for compatibility with
- Compatibility with your needs is the first thing we take into account

## COMPATIBLE
- So compatible with
- Handsome and compatible
- You'll find it a very compatible fit

## COMPETE
- Our experience and skill can help you compete more effectively
- To compete and succeed today, you need the right tools
- Competing better than ever
- Helping you compete at your best

**Compete:** contend, strive, struggle, fight, wrestle, jockey, spar, participate, contest, challenge, play against
*See also:* **BATTLE, FIGHT**

## COMPETITION
- Everyone loves us except the competition
- It doesn't matter what the competition's got
- Everyone loves us except the competition
- Giving you an edge on the competition
- We offer something the competition doesn't
- Blow the competition away with
- Got what it takes to stay ahead of the competition
- Working harder to help you stay ahead of the competition

## COMPETITIVE
- It's all about staying competitive
- Gaining a competitive advantage means setting yourself apart

- Also proud of our high-quality, competitively priced products and services
- Eminently competitive
- Able to bring you consistently competitive pricing
- Staying competitive to keep your business

## COMPETITOR

- We'll match any competitor's price
- We won't be undersold by local competitors
- Has proven a worthy competitor for the world's leading
- Two things our competitors don't want you to see
- Why customers buy from us eight times as often as they buy from our nearest competitor
- Our competitors don't think so
- We go way beyond our competitors in terms of performance
- After careful comparison with our competitors

## COMPLETE

- Now you can do a complete study of
- No other product offers more complete
- Complete service round the clock

## COMPLETION

- Serving you from concept to completion
- Guiding you to completion
- The completion of a brilliant idea

*See also:* **END, FINISH**

## COMPLEX

- It's unique complex of
- Helping you with the most complex problems
- Sometimes choosing can be very complex
- Taking the complexity out of

## COMPLIMENT

- The ideal compliment to
- You'll soon be getting a lot more compliments
- It's a natural compliment to
- When you're looking for something to compliment
- Here are some of the compliments we've been getting
- The best compliment is your business
- Enjoy it compliments of

## COMPREHENSIVE
- Making it as comprehensive as possible
- Look to us for the most comprehensive coverage
- Comprehensive service is our secret

## COMPROMISE
- Why compromise when you can easily get the best
- A comfortable compromise between
- Built without compromise
- Absolutely no compromise on quality or service
- Without compromising one iota
- The one thing you won't find is a compromise

## CONCENTRATE
- Allowing you to concentrate on what's important to you
- Offering concentrated value
- So you're free to concentrate on the important stuff

*See also:* **FOCUS**

## CONCEPT
- Based on a proven concept
- The guiding principles of the concept
- Introducing a new and exciting concept
- That is the most breathtaking concept to arrive in recent years
- One of the best-known concepts in

*See also:* **IDEA, INFORMATION, PLAN**

## CONCERN
- What are your biggest concerns today
- Your concerns are valid
- It's only natural to be concerned about your
- We can help with all your concerns
- Turning complicated concerns into simple solutions

*See also:* **CHALLENGE, CARE, PROBLEM**

## CONDITION
- All in top condition
- Creating the conditions you need to thrive
- Withstands the toughest conditions imaginable
- Subject to certain conditions

## CONFIDENCE
- Moving with confidence

- Adding a new dimension of confidence to the process
- Quickly, efficiently and with confidence
- You can have confidence in us
- Giving you confidence to

*See also:* **PRIDE, TRUST**


## CONFIDENTIAL

- Can actually provide you with confidential service
- All transactions are confidential
- With complete confidentiality just for you

*See also:* **SECRET**


## CONNECT

- Inviting you to connect with
- We'll do our best to connect you with
- It keeps you connected with family and friends
- Connecting people to people
- Get connected

*See also:* **JOIN**


## CONNECTION

- All the connections you need are right here
- People are starting to make the connection
- Make the most of your connections
- Giving you the connections to
- We've got the connections you need


## CONQUER

- Have already conquered the world of
- Feel like a conquering hero
- Ready to conquer those stubborn problems that

*See also:* **BEAT, VICTORY, WIN**


## CONSIDER

- If you've always been reluctant, consider this
- You are invited to consider purchasing
- If you're considering a change, come to us
- Before you buy, please consider these facts

*See also:* **THINK**


## CONSTRAINT

- Instead of having to work within the constraints of
- Finally free of the constraints of

- Break loose from old constraints

## CONSULTANT
- Skilled consultants will help you with
- Try our friendly and knowledgeable consultants
- Maybe you should try the consultants the consultants consult.

*See also:* **EXPERT, PROFESSIONAL, STAFF**

## CONSULTATION
- Call for consultation or visit our showroom
- For consultation or booking, please call
- Offering ongoing consultation with your
- Call today for a no-cost, no-obligation consultation
- Free in-home consultation
- Unlimited free consultation

## CONSUMER
- An integral part of today's consumer mix
- The most important consideration is you, the consumer
- Consumers' choice
- From the consumer point of view
- You're a very informed consumer

*See also:* **CUSTOMER**

## CONTACT
- For more information, simply contact
- Giving you the contacts you need to
- Contact our friendly staff today

*See also:* **CALL**

## CONTROL
- When it's something you need to control
- Now you can take control over all your
- The easy way to stay in control
- For the first time, we're able to control
- Control is something you're interested in
- Now you can take control of
- Always under your control
- Take control of your life now
- Be in control all the time
- Wouldn't it be nice to feel more in control

*See also:* **COMMAND, POWER**

## CONVENIENCE
- The ultimate in convenience
- Minor investment, major convenience
- The convenience of compact size
- Every possible convenience
- For your convenience
- The dawn of a whole new era of convenience
- The best in quality, price, service and convenience
- Open for your shopping convenience

**Convenience:** utility, leisure, ease, free, freedom, spare time, advantage, accommodation, service, amenity
*See also:* **AMENITY, COMFORT, EASE**

## CONVENIENT
- Find out how quick and convenient
- Designed to be fast, easy and convenient
- Not to mention all the convenient services thoughtful extras
- Always working to make it more convenient for you
- It's much less expensive and more convenient than

## CONVENTIONAL
- Your reliance on the conventional is about to change forever
- Nothing is conventional here
- You're not a conventional person, so why use a conventional
- Escape the conventional

## CONVINCE
- Very convincing data will change your mind
- You'll never again have to convince anyone of anything
- Let us convince you about

**Convince:** persuade, reassure, affirm, bring round, win over, sell, satisfy, assure, prove to

## COOK
- Find out what's cooking
- We're cooking up a storm
- Too tired to cook
- Cooking up something hot with you

## COOL
- Stay cool all the time
- Keep your cool
- The ultimate in cool

- We'll help you keep your cool all summer long
- For cool people like you

## COOPERATION
- Now in cooperation with many of the nation's most prestigious
- A masterpiece of cooperation
- Your cooperation is essential

## COORDINATE
- All the better to coordinate
- A coordinated effort which not only links
- We do all the coordinating
- Everything coordinates beautifully after you've been to our experts

## COPY
- Something anybody can copy
- You can copy this success
- You don't want to be just another copy of
- We don't copy anybody
- Always an original, never a copy

*See also:* **DUPLICATE**

## CORNERSTONE
- Trust, integrity and truth are the cornerstones of
- Your satisfaction is the cornerstone of our business
- Built upon a solid cornerstone of

*See also:* **BASE, BASICS, FOUNDATION**

## CORPORATE
- Springs from our unique corporate spirit
- Another example of our corporate imagination
- Take advantage of our corporate strengths
- Fine corporate skills that have taken decades to hone

*See also:* **BUSINESS**

## COST
- Beat the high cost of
- The low cost will surprise you
- What's the start-up cost to you
- Does anyone need to know it cost nearly nothing to produce
- Less costly than ever
- Provided at no additional cost
- You would expect it to cost more but it doesn't

- Included at no extra cost
- At no cost or obligation
- Cost effective solutions
- Reduced cost while improving strength and safety
- At no extra cost to you
- Twice the value at no added cost
- Lower costs mean more of your money can work for you
- Helping you keep your costs in line
- So you can keep the lid on costs
- We know you have to keep your costs down
- Helps lower overall costs by

**Cost:** price, value, worth, market value, amount, figure, valuation, quotation, demand, asking price, appraisement, appraisal, dollar value, expenditure, expense, charge, rate, hire
*See also:* **CHARGE, DOLLAR, MONEY, PRICE, SAVINGS, VALUE**

## COUNSEL
- Ready to counsel you about
- When you're looking for trustworthy counsel
- Counselling you about your most urgent requirements

*See also:* **ADVICE**

## COUNT
- Naturally, we can count you among our special friends
- Count on us for more
- Where it counts the most
- You can count on us for everyday low prices
- You can always count on us for
- An organization you can count on
- You don't count the cost when

## COUPON
- Receive a coupon redeemable at
- Valuable coupon inside
- Just complete and mail the coupon
- Money-deposit coupons enclosed
- Save money with substantial coupons inside
- In partnership with retailers, we're bringing you these excellent coupons
- Look for the free coupons on offer
- Save more when you use our in-store coupons

## COVER

- Covers twice the area
- Making sure you're covered
- We've got every angle covered
- Making sure we've got you covered

## COVERAGE

- Just the right amount of coverage
- Offers a wide range of coverage
- For a little extra coverage
- Unrivalled coverage for

## CRAFT

- Quality-crafted to last
- Crafted with skill and love
- Wait till you see how well-crafted our product is

*See also:* **ART, SKILL**

## CREATE

- Allows you to create a whole new
- You can create a better life for yourself and your family
- Created with you in mind
- We set out to create an all-new
- Now you can easily create a dramatic
- Creates new value
- That's why we've created the new
- Can be created in seconds
- When it comes to creating the best

*See also:* **ACCOMPLISH, ACHIEVE, ACT, BUILD, DO, MAKE, PERFORM**

## CREATIVITY

- The height of creativity
- Fostering creativity among our staff
- Combine your creativity with our expertise

## CREDIBILITY

- Gives you instant credibility
- Our credibility is enormous
- Just look at our credibility and make your decision
- Nobody has more credibility when it comes to

*See also:* **BELIEF, GUARANTEE**

## CREDIT

- Give yourself the credit you deserve with
- There's plenty of credit to go around
- Your credit is always good at
- Proud to take credit for

## CREW

- Not to mention a topnotch crew of
- Become a part of the whole merry crew
- Our crew can be on the job within hours
- Highly trained crews descend upon

*See also:* **STAFF, TEAM**

## CROWD

- Above the crowd
- You're not a part of the crowd
- Standing apart from the crowd
- Join the crowd flocking to
- There's a reason why crowds are coming to

## CRY

- Enough to make a grown man cry
- A need crying out to be filled
- No longer a voice crying in the wilderness
- Cries of delight greet the sight of

## CUISINE

- Exquisite international cuisine
- Cuisine to die for
- For a totally different and exciting cuisine
- Be sure to try our unusual and scrumptious cuisine

*See also:* **COOK, TASTE**

## CURVE

- The most challenging curve
- It's called the learning curve
- When life throws you a curve, we can help
- Sleek curves gleaming in the sun

## CUSHION

- Further cushioned by
- Providing you with a cushion of safety
- Cushions the shock of

- Cushioning you from any rude fluctuations in

*See also:* **PROTECT**

## CUSTOM

- Quality custom crafted
- Manufacturers of custom products since
- Custom-made just for you
- It's our custom to please
- A world-famous name in custom products
- We value your custom enormously

## CUSTOMER

- From the very beginning of a customer relationship
- To better serve our customer needs
- Steadily improving customer service
- You can count on us for dedicated customer care
- We enjoy a very high customer return rate
- We're giving customers what they want—quality and value
- The satisfied customer specialists
- Building customer satisfaction
- Because ultimately, this business is about customer service
- Customer service is our top priority
- Offering exclusive products to a wide range of customers
- We go right where the customer lives and works
- Offer limited to new customers
- For nearly half a century, we've world closely with our customers
- Thank you to all our loyal customers
- Customers are demanding more and faster service every day
- Keeps customers coming back year after year
- Certainly be a hidden treasure for our customers
- We satisfy the most demanding customers
- Finding new customers is easy
- Our customers come first
- The endless process of finding new customers
- Taking care of our regular customers first
- You'll find new customers faster and easier than ever before
- Our customers always come first
- Most of our business is satisfied repeat customers
- Satisfying an unlimited number of customers
- Giving customers a good impression is critical to

**Customer:** patron, client, clientele, buyer, shopper, purchaser, vendee, marketer

*See also:* **BUYER, CLIENT**

## CUSTOMER SERVICE

- Customer service information
- Our concern with quality can be seen in our customer service
- Customer service is our middle name
- The fastest, finest customer service in the business
- Let's talk customer service
- When you shop, you're also looking for customer service

## CUT

- A cut above the rest
- Not just cutting it any more
- Make the cut
- No one cuts it like us
- We cut our prices to the bone
- Come to us for cut-rate service and products
- Cost-cutting is the name of the game

## DAMAGE

- Dramatically reduces risk of damage
- Very fast damage control
- Call us before the damage is done
- Protects against loss or damage
- Sometimes it's impossible to prevent damage to
- Guard against hidden damage from

## DAREDEVIL

- Maintaining your daredevil image
- Even daredevils would be pleased
- The place where daredevils shop
- You don't have to be a daredevil to enjoy

*See also:* **HERO**

## DARK

- You'll never be left in the dark again
- If you're in the dark about what to do
- Come on out of the dark

## DATA

- Just massaging your data won't always work
- Actually getting your data into some kind of shape
- Providing the data you need to decide
- Get more data here than anyone else give on

*See also:* **INFORMATION**

## DATABASE
- Inside every underfed corporate database
- Once you're part of our database, you benefit from
- A gigantic database at your service
- Choose from our huge database of
- Take advantage of the biggest database in the business

*See also:* **INFORMATION**

## DATE
- We'll arrange for a convenient time and date to
- Put an asterisk beside this date
- Mark a new date on your calendar
- We've got a date with you
- The biggest date of the year is rapidly approaching
- The most important date for renewing

*See also:* **TIME**

## DAWN
- Dawn of new value
- The dawn of a new era is upon us
- The enormous value of this product is just beginning to dawn on the world
- A new day is dawning for you

*See also:* **BEGINNING, MORNING, START**

## DAY
- We look forward to the day when
- Just knowing you're getting the most out of each day
- Make it the best part of your day
- Start your day the best way with
- Make us a regular part of your day
- After just one day you'll see the change
- This could be your lucky day
- A bright new day is dawning for you
- Not since the grand old days of

*See also:* **TIME**

## DAZZLE
- Dazzle them thoroughly
- Look past the dazzle and see the solid quality
- You'll be dazzled by
- With dazzling speed and efficiency

# DEAL

- A great deal now
- You can deal direct when you call us
- Everything you need to know to make a great deal
- We have your best deal right here
- Let's make a deal
- A lovely deal every day
- Wake up to a terrific deal
- Check out this fabulous deal
- Double double deal
- Here's the straight deal
- When problems seem more than you can deal with
- Come in and make your most advantageous deal
- The right deal, the right protection for you
- It's a done deal
- Hurry in for the deal of the century
- When you have a great deal riding upon
- A deal worth talking about
- Come in for humungous deals on
- Be sure to check out every one of these deals
- More sweet deals from
- Back page deals, front page value
- Just a few of this week's unbeatable deals
- You'll find better deals here
- Best deals in town
- We will beat any competitive deals
- Family deals for family value
- The finest deals are made when
- Exclusive deals on selected merchandise
- The greatest deals ever
- Unbelievable deals in
- Amazing deals on all the best
- Hot deals on hot products

*See also:* **BARGAIN, BARGOON, COST, PRICE, VALUE**

# DEALER

- We've sold more products than any other dealer
- Strong dealer support is a priority
- Call today to order or for the name of the dealer nearest you
- We're a fast, reliable, full-service dealer
- Call your dealer right away and schedule an appointment
- See your dealer for a wide variety of
- Only at your product dealer

67

- See your local dealer now
- More dealers recommend us than any other
- The only dealer offering this unique
- Dealers wanted

*See also:* **SALESPEOPLE**

## DEALERSHIP

- Stop by the dealership anytime
- Better service from our dealership
- Drop into our dealership and see for yourself
- A dealership that always stands behind its customers

## DECIDE

- You decide
- We decided right off the bat
- When you have to decide in a hurry
- Helping you decide which is the best for you
- Look at our low low prices before you decide
- But you have to decide today

*See also:* **CHOOSE**

## DECISION

- The business decision of a lifetime
- We leave the decision to you
- The most important decision you may ever face
- Decisions, decisions, decisions
- The best decision is the one that's right for you
- We're here to help you make a very significant decision
- A whole new approach to decision-making
- This could be the smartest decision you ever made
- Make your own decision about the need for
- Making your buying decisions the right ones
- Sound decisions to ensure a strong future

*See also:* **CHOICE**

## DECOR

- A huge range available to suit your decor
- You can tell from the decor that you're an original
- A decor that expresses the inner you
- Time for a change of decor
- More than just the decor

*See also:* **ATMOSPHERE**

## DECORATE
- Decorating with
- Your most important decorating decision
- It's easy to decorate when you choose our products
- When you decide to decorate, come to us

## DECORATIVE
- The decorative appeal and color of
- For a truly whimsical decorative effect
- The fine decorative piece can be yours for only
- Useful and decorative at the same time

## DECORATOR
- Decorator-inspired
- The most talented decorators are consulted
- Everyone will think you hired a decorator
- Our decorator will coordinate it all specially for you

*See also:* **EXPERT**

## DEDICATE
- We are dedicated to providing you with the best service, knowledge and advice
- Find out just how dedicated we are
- We dedicate this product to you
- The result of awesome dedication on the part of
- Dedicated service people at your beck and call

*See also:* **COMMIT**

## DEFENCE
- Stimulates your body's natural defences
- Your first line of defence
- You best defence is
- We take defence against disease very seriously

*See also:* **PROTECT**

## DELICIOUS
- Simply delicious
- Are you dreaming of something dangerously delicious
- So delicious, it's hard to believe they're
- Deliciously yours

## DELIVER
- We know how to deliver

- Delivering cost-effectively under remarkable pressures
- Delivering more than
- For a nominal fee, we'll deliver right to your door
- Delivered to every home
- We never promise more than we can deliver
- We deliver every day
- We deliver to your home or job site
- We deliver quality
- Delivered straight to you
- Now delivering to your area
- We over-deliver just to make sure
- And that's exactly what our product delivers

## DELIVERY
- Plus free delivery on all major
- Competitive pricing, fast delivery and high-quality work
- For even faster delivery
- Delivery anywhere on the planet
- Free delivery day or night
- Increasing the speed of delivery via increased efficiency
- Ask our staff about our delivery service
- No extra charge for delivery
- Delivery is available whenever you call

## DEMAND
- Back by popular demand
- Held over by popular demand
- Meeting the growing demand for
- Huge market demand
- Best quality because you demand it
- Filling the exacting demands of our customers
- To handle the exploding demand for
- Sky-high demand for
- The extreme demands of

*See also:* **ASK, COMMAND**

## DEMONSTRATION
- Free demonstration on request
- For the best demonstration, come in and see it in operation
- There's no better demonstration of
- Call for a personal demonstration and be convinced

*See also:* **SHOW**

**DEPEND**
- You know you can depend on yourself
- When you have to depend on
- You can always depend on us for
- Finally, a product you can depend on

*See also:* **RELY, TRUST**

**DEPENDABILITY**
- A reputation for rugged dependability
- Top-class dependability in a tough world
- We know the first thing you look for is dependability
- Putting dependability first

**DESERVE**
- You deserve the same careful treatment as
- Your family deserves the best
- Come down and get what you deserve
- Giving you the service and quality you deserve
- You've earned it and you deserve it

*See also:* **EARN**

**DESIGN**
- Representing the very best in design
- A very intelligent design for a very intelligent buyer
- Have spent a great deal of time to design the perfect
- Design a product capable of fulfilling the demand potentials buyers will put on it
- Providing complete design and construction
- Innovative design combined with quality
- Hot design, hot looks, hot value
- A plan designed specifically for you
- Committing ourselves to fine design and workmanship
- Exclusive design from our own workshop
- Eye-catching designs add spice and zip
- Designed to make you happy
- Allowing you to explore alternatives in design

*See also:* **AIM, GOAL, OPINION, PHILOSOPHY, PLAN, PRINCIPLE, SYSTEM**

**DESIGNER**
- Designer quality at off-the-rack prices
- Looks as though a famous designer created it
- Our designers are always on call for

- It took a great designer to create something this elegantly simple
- Our professional designers created this delightful

*See also:* **EXPERT, PROFESSIONAL**

## DESIRE

- Something you may dearly desire
- Gratify your every desire
- See it and desire it
- Built to fulfil your fondest desire

*See also:* **NEED, WANT, WISH**

## DESTINATION

- Your fashion destination
- Has become a popular destination for
- The destination of choice for
- The first destination is your home
- Has always been a favorite destination
- A truly marketable destination for your clientele

*See also:* **PLACE, STORE**

## DETAIL

- Every detail reflects an integrity of design that
- Beautifully detailed
- Every electrifying detail is captured
- Detail captured in true-too-life perfection
- Intricately detailed design and finishing
- We take care of every detail for you
- One more detail you won't have to think about
- In every finely engineered detail
- For more details, call anytime
- See full details at your nearest area
- Just ask for more details when you call
- Here's how to get full details quickly and easily
- With all the delicious details provided by
- Watch for more details
- Among the most delightful details are
- Ask your store for details
- Call for friendly, no-pressure details
- Our details make the difference

## DEVELOP

- We'll continue to develop exciting new products just for you
- Carefully developing a relationship with you

72

- Come and see what develops
- Working hard to develop better and better products and services for you

*See also:* **BUILD**

## DEVELOPMENT

- One of the primary participants in the development of
- Actively involved in the development of
- Everyone involved in this dramatic development
- This development directly impacts upon you
- Benefit immediately from this exciting new development

*See also:* **ADVANCE, EVENT**

## DIFFERENCE

- Compare the difference
- That's the difference between
- A difference you'll remember
- You'll feel the difference the very first time you
- And this makes all the difference
- The difference quality makes
- Just look at the difference
- Experience the difference, feel the thrill
- Making all the difference in your success
- The difference between merely correct and truly inspired
- Delivers a difference you can feel
- Our true point of difference
- See, hear, feel, savour the difference
- The difference is in the details
- You can spot the difference right away

*See also:* **CHANGE**

## DIFFERENT

- What's different about out product is
- Determined to be different
- Now for a truly different
- For those who prefer something a bit different
- Dramatically different
- You're an individualist, you want to be different
- How different can you get

## DIFFICULT

- We know how difficult it can be to
- No longer need be difficult to

- A difficult problem with an easy solution
- When you're wrestling with a really difficult decision

## DIMENSION

- To provide an extra dimension in the continued growth of
- Gives added dimension at an affordable price
- A whole new dimension in
- Elevating the product to a new dimension
- Of awe-inspiring dimensions
- Enter a new dimension today

*See also:* SIZE

## DINE

- Two can dine for the price of one
- Dine out every day
- Imagine dining in such splendor
- For your fine dining pleasure
- Delicious dining at a more affordable price

## DIRECT

- Buy direct from the manufacturer
- Direct from Europe
- Directing every critical stage of the operation
- The savings go directly to you
- Up-front and direct

## DIRECTION

- Under the direction of new owners
- We'll point you in the right direction
- Takes you in a whole new direction
- A direction you perhaps haven't thought of
- Our directions are a lot easier to follow

*See also:* APPROACH

## DISCONTINUE

- We'll never discontinue this vital service
- Great deals on discontinued stock
- Save on a huge selection of discontinued items

## DISCOUNT

- We will give you a discount equal to
- Now discounted to save you moeny
- Special offer discount

- Special discount for this week only
- Get the biggest discount here
- Over and above any discount
- Just call our service to enjoy further savings and discounts

*See also:* **DEAL, PRICE, SAVINGS**

## DISCOVER
- Helps you discover a better way of
- Discover what it's all about
- Discover the world of
- Just waiting for you to discover them
- You'll also discover
- Discover a new way to
- Visitors delight as they discover

*See also:* **FIND**

## DISCOVERY
- The unmatchable thrill of discovery
- The biggest, most exciting discovery yet
- A discovery that could change your life
- Working on new discoveries every day

*See also:* **ADVANCE, DEVELOPMENT**

## DISPLAY
- See our fantastic display
- Displaying all the signs of a real winner
- Our display model explains it all
- Don't miss our exciting display at

*See also:* **ARRAY, CHOICE, SHOW, SHOWROOM**

## DISTINCTIVE
- Refreshingly distinctive
- As distinctive as those who use it
- A very distinctive touch
- Distinctively yours
- A distinctive style no one could miss

## DISTINGUISH
- Only one of the things that distinguish
- Has distinguished itself once again
- Can satisfy even distinguished tastes like yours
- Rapidly distinguishing ourselves from the rest of the pack

## DO

- It's not that we do, it's how we do it
- You can do it at home in your spare time
- The power to do more and do it better
- Here's what we'll do for you
- Look what you can do in just one day
- Here's what we do
- Now you can do virtually all of your
- We're doing something about it
- You've got better things to do than
- All you have to do to join the party is
- Nobody today knows how to do it better than
- Does it all, all at once

*See also:* **ACT, ACTION, ACHIEVE, ACCOMPLISH, PERFORM**

## DO-IT-YOURSELF

- You can do-it-yourself easily with help from
- We're the place for the do-it-yourselfer
- Help for the do-it-yourselfer
- Great for the ambitious do-it-yourselfer

## DOLLAR

- A way to get top dollar for
- Savings by the dollar
- Earn an honest dollar more easily
- Useful methods to maximize your dollar
- Make your dollar go further than ever before
- Dollar days are here again
- Taking better care of your dollar
- Helping you make every dollar count
- Dollar for dollar, feature for feature
- Squeeze more from your dollar
- Special dollar buys
- Benefit from yet another source of easy dollars

*See also:* **BUY, CASH, DEAL, MONEY, SAVINGS**

## DOMESTIC

- Both domestically and internationally
- Improves domestic management
- The best domestic product you can buy
- A big player in your domestic affairs

*See also:* **LOCAL**

**DONE**
- Helping you get things done with
- And we've done just that
- No longer just done in the more expensive circles
- Now you can be finally done with

*See also:* **END, FINISH**

**DOOR**
- You'll never have to knock on another door
- Come knock on our door
- Right at your door
- Delivered to your door day or night
- Opens doors you never dreamed possible
- Now a new door swings open for you

**DOORCRASHER**
- Doorcrasher specials for all you early birds
- You can't beat a doorcrasher like this
- Come early for our doorcrasher deals

**DOORSTEP**
- Is now available right on your doorstep
- The help you need could be standing on your doorstep
- Doorstep to doorstep in record time

*See also:* **HOME**

**DOUBLE**
- Double the value
- Double your fun with
- Double value for half the effort

*See also:* **PAIR**

**DOWN PAYMENT**
- A small down payment will hold these items until you need them
- No down payment until
- And we won't even ask you for a down payment
- The smallest down payment you'll ever find
- The down payment is easily negotiable

**DOWN**
- Goes down good
- Get down and dirty
- As prices go down, value shoots up

- Prices are dropping down, down, down
- No money down

## DOWNTOWN
- Shop downtown at
- Just minutes from downtown
- Now you can bring downtown home with you
- Country values, downtown convenience

## DRAMA
- With all the drama of
- Capture total drama in
- Share the drama by
- You won't find better drama than this
- Caught up in the drama, the sheer thrill of

*See also:* **EXCITEMENT**

## DREAM
- More than you ever dreamed possible
- Build your own dream
- You've been dreaming of this ever since
- You can make your life's dream come true
- If you've ever dreamed of
- Why dream when you can actually do it
- Sets you on your way to building your dream
- A place to dream about
- Dream about what to do with all the money you've just saved
- With a lot of other people who share your dream
- It's what you've always been dreaming of
- Plan your dream now
- Now is the time to create your dream
- Fulfil a different dream
- The possession that others can only dream about
- Dreams can come true
- People like you have been turning dreams into reality for years
- Don't put your dreams on hold
- For people who believe that dreams really do become real

*See also:* **DESIRE, WISH**

## DRESS
- Dress up your home with
- We don't have to dress it up with fancy words
- Dressy in a very comfortable way

- Dressing up an old idea with a whole new twist

## DRIVE
- With enthusiasm and drive you can
- Barely an hour's drive from
- Have the foresight and drive to
- To arrange a test drive, call
- It's worth the drive to our location to

## DROP
- Shop till you drop
- Drop in to see us soon
- Prices are dropping rapidly
- Just watch our prices drop
- You're always welcome to drop in
- Inviting you to drop in and chat
- More and more people are dropping in to take a look at our

*See also:* **VISIT**

## DUE
- Now get your just due
- Get your deliveries exactly when they're due
- Due to skyrocketing interest in
- Everyone gets their dues
- You've paid your dues, now get your reward

**Due:** payable, in arrears, mature, outstanding, receivable, owing, unpaid, rightful, proper, correct

*See also:* **DESERVE, OWE**

## DUMP
- It's time to dump that old attitude
- Send that outdated contraption to the dump
- When you're down in the dumps, here's the cure

## DUPLICATE
- Once again we've duplicated our previous triumph
- Now you can duplicate this success
- Has never before been duplicated

*See also:* **COPY**

## EARLY
- Early bird special
- It's never too early to

- Get here early to make sure you get your
- Early results are astonishing

*See also:* **SOON**

## EARN

- Not only do you earn valuable
- Earn with every purchase you make
- We'll earn your business
- You've earned a rest
- Keep what you've earned by
- Earn big money by

**Earn:** gain, acquire, obtain, secure, get, profit, benefit, avail, procure, gather, garner, glean, reap, make, clear, pocket, pull down, bag, gross, net, take home, make a pretty penny, bring home the bacon, merit, deserve, win, cause, bring about, yield

*See also:* **DESERVE, WORK**

## EARTH

- Nourished by the elements of Earth
- You wonder where on Earth we'd be without it
- Earth-friendly
- Kind to the Earth we live on

*See also:* **ENVIRONMENT**

## EASE

- To gently ease away dirt and grime
- The unstudied ease of classic
- Now you can do it with the greatest of ease
- Ease your way with

*See also:* **COMFORT**

## EASTER

- A happy parade of Easter values
- The Easter bunny has arrived
- Easter Carnival
- Easter on parade
- Easter hunt for value
- Whopper eggs for Easter
- A joyous Easter to all our clients
- The Easter bunny follows the signs to great bargains
- Take a look in our Easter basket
- Hop to it Easter deals
- Easter savings on

- Have a safe and happy Easter
- Special treats for Easter enjoyment
- Make this Easter holiday weekend a memorable event for the whole family
- Egg-cellent Easter deals
- Every Easter bunny loves a deal
- Easter specials for special people
- Surprise some bunny special for Easter
- Look at these Easter discounts
- Easter greetings to everyone
- Hop in for your Easter basket
- A tisket, a tasket, a yummy Easter basket
- Come join us for Easter
- Stroll in for Easter savings
- Some bunny special deserves an Easter treat
- Egg-ceptional Easter savings
- Easter egg-stravaganza
- Hop on in for a Happy Easter

*See also:* **CELEBRATE, FESTIVE, HOLIDAY**

## EASY

- Discover just how easy it is
- Makes it easy for you to become successful
- The quick and easy solution
- It's as easy as one, two, three
- Makes for easy eating
- Taking it easy with
- That's so easy to get into
- Yes, it's easy to
- Makes it delightfully easy for you to
- It's the easy way to
- We make saving money as easy as
- It's that easy
- As easy as turning on your PC
- See how easy it is to
- To find out just how easy it is to
- Simple instructions make it easy
- Everything is so easy it can be done while
- Easier and quicker
- This task has never been easier
- It's never been easier to
- To make things even easier for you

**Easy:** simple, plain, obvious, effortless, hands-down, smooth sailing,

pushover, piece of cake, picnic, breeze, duck soup, child's play, no sweat, comfortable, carefree, casual, lenient, indulgent, natural, flowing, suave, leisurely, unhurried
*See also:* **SIMPLE**

## EAT
- Ready to eat
- Why eat out when you can cook up such delicious
- Make eating an even greater pleasure with

*See also:* **COOK, DINE, TREAT**

## ECONOMIC
- Regardless of economic conditions
- Take advantage of an economic upturn by
- In today's tough economic climate you need extra protection
- When you make economic decisions, consider this

*See also:* **FINANCIAL**

## ECONOMICAL
- Economical value
- A very popular and economical to dress up your
- When you want to make the most economical choice
- Economical and beautiful at the same time

**Economical:** thrifty, economizing, saving, sparing, prudent, careful, conservative, frugal, money-saving, cost-effective, high-yield, low-cost, budget, low-budget, low-income

## ECONOMY
- Meeting the challenge of today's global economy
- Don't let the economy get you down
- No matter what the economy is doing, you can thrive
- We can give you economies of scale

## EDGE
- Relish the cutting edge best
- Even those who live on the edge know
- If you like your items to be on the leading-edge
- Moving ahead at a fever pitch
- Adding an edge or spark to your newest
- We give you the edge you need
- Your edge on the future
- You'll be on the leading edge of

*See also:* **ADVANTAGE**

## EDUCATIONAL
- Will prove highly educational
- Your children need educational toys
- Visiting our store can be a very educational experience

## EFFECT
- Now you can get the desired effect from merely
- For best effect, use it often
- The beneficial effects will delight you

**Effect:** consequence, outcome, result, conclusion, issue, end, upshot, event, sequel, aftermath, fallout, side effect, punch, vigor, strength, potency, impact, influence, meaning, sense
*See also:* **RESULT, USE**

## EFFECTIVE
- Here's what makes it so effective
- Fast and effective solutions to
- An effective plan you can put into action right away
- You want a product that's effective and economical

**Effective:** capable, competent, effectual, efficient, adequate, sufficient, useful, serviceable, practical, real, valid, striking, telling, impressive, pointed, moving, arousing, powerful, potent, forcible, influential
*See also:* **USEFUL**

## EFFICIENCY
- More efficiency is something we don't take lightly
- Tooled for efficiency, not effect
- We know efficiency is your number one concern
- Gives greater efficiency with less
- You benefit directly from the increased efficiency
- Efficiency has increased dramatically in the last few years

## EFFICIENT
- Runs more efficiently
- Simple and efficient – and simply the best
- Always striving for greater efficiency
- The most efficient product you can find on the market
- This efficient system pays off for you right away

**Efficient:** effective, valid, active, productive, high-powered, competent, fit, on the ball, qualified, eligible, proficient, adept, accomplished, polished, practised, experienced, clever, deft, adroit, talented, economical, thrifty, saving

## EFFORT
- We've put a great deal of effort into
- We know how much effort it takes to
- Honoring the effort you've put into
- One of the first organizations to combine our efforts with
- The first to actually put a coordinated effort together
- Combining efforts to enhance
- After a lot of hard work and effort

*See also:* **STRIVE, WORK**

## ELEGANCE
- Elegance is the social tone here
- Timeless elegance
- A look of sleek elegance
- Inspired by the elegance and charm of old world
- The purest form of elegance
- Embodies timeless, streamlined elegance befitting

*See also:* **BEAUTY**

## ELEGANT
- It is extremely elegant
- Breathtakingly elegant, full of superb grace
- A supremely elegant solution to
- The cool, elegant way to
- Wait until they see how elegant you've become

**Elegant:** luxurious, posh, sumptuous, grand, fine, rich, swank, gorgeous, ornamental, ornate, excellent, choice, superior, select, exquisite, tasteful, well-made, urbane, sophisticated, polished, chi-chi, stylish, fashionable, cultured, cultivated, well-bred, debonair, dapper, charmer, polite, charming, courteous, genteel, gracious, correct, discriminating, refined, intelligent, well-proportioned, balanced, harmonious, aesthetic, artistic

*See also:* **BEAUTIFUL, CHIC, STYLE**

## ELEMENT
- The primary element is value
- One of the essential elements in your
- Here are the elements to watch for

*See also:* **BASICS**

## ELIGIBLE
- You may be fully eligible for
- Your whole family is now eligible to join
- Making you eligible for even bigger benefits

- We're contacting all eligible people
- Find out now if you're eligible for extra savings

## ELIMINATE
- Now you can eliminate many of the effects of
- Virtually eliminates the problem of
- Eliminate worry and stress with

## EMBRACE
- You'll love the way it embraces
- Embrace the future with enthusiasm
- Embraces you with pure pleasure

*See also:* **JOIN**

## ENCHANTRESS
- Turn yourself into an enchantress fast
- Fit for an enchantress
- A spell woven by an enchantress

## ENCOURAGE
- We encourage you to watch for
- The results are so encouraging that
- You'll be really encouraged to know that

## END
- And it doesn't end there
- Just no end in sight
- The end of all your troubles is now within your reach

*See also:* **FINAL, FINISH, LAST**

## ENDORSEMENT
- Our personal seal of endorsement
- Satisfied customers have been sending us endorsements
- Just look at these endorsements and see how good

*See also:* **SUPPORT**

## ENERGIZE
- You'll feel energized and full of vigor
- Energize yourself with
- Refreshing and energizing
- Your life will be energized immediately

*See also:* **INSPIRE, REJUVENATE**

## ENERGY
- Gets that extra energy from
- High energy products for high energy people
- Provides you with plenty of energy to cope with stress and feel great
- For everyone who needs more energy
- Embraced by the energy of

**Energy:** vigor, vitality, brio, get up and go, force, power, guts, nerve, potency, drive, push, muscle, ambition, enterprise, spirit, dash, vivacity, verve, flair, fire, zing, glow, fervency, ardor, bounce, sprightliness, buoyancy, cheer, ebullience, sparkle, effervescence, vim, zip, zeal, passion, pep, exuberance, enthusiasm
*See also:* **ENTHUSIASM, PASSION, POWER**

## ENHANCE
- Enhances without overpowering
- The idea is to quickly and easily enhance
- Built to enhance and maintain
- And to further enhance your

*See also:* **ADVERTISE, HELP, IMPROVE, PROMOTE**

## ENHANCEMENT
- Their timely enhancement through
- It's an enhancement you can't do without
- Enjoy even further enhancements
- A number of enhancements quickly improve your

*See also:* **IMPROVEMENT**

## ENJOY
- Making them a pleasure to enjoy
- Dream of enjoying
- Everything you need to enjoy
- Go on, enjoy the goodness of
- Do you enjoy working with
- So you can enjoy it even more
- Do something you really enjoy
- If you enjoy working with

**Enjoy:** take pleasure in, rejoice, revel, riot, groove, luxuriate, bask, savor, appreciate, indulge, love, fancy, benefit from, profit, make the most of, delight in

## ENJOYMENT
- Your enjoyment gets greater every day
- Working hard to create enjoyment for you

86

● Just watch the enjoyment on their faces

**Enjoyment:** delight, gladness, cheer, pleasure, gratification, satisfaction, zest, relish, gusto, exhilaration, transport, ecstasy, mirth, glee, merriment, jollity, gaiety, happiness, elation, bliss, felicity, contentment, ease, comfort, kick, bang, thrill, amusement, entertainment, recreation

*See also:* **HAPPY, NICE**

## ENOUGH

● And if all this first class service isn't enough
● One is often enough
● More than enough for
● Now there's enough for everybody

## ENRICH

● Enrich your life with
● One of the most enriching experiences you can have
● Uniquely enriched with

*See also:* **INCREASE**

## ENROLL

● Enroll now for your free trial
● Call to enroll today
● If you haven't yet enrolled, now is the time
● Now you can enroll in our exclusive

## ENSURE

● We can ensure that you are taken care of immediately
● We have ensured that only the best
● Ensure your pleasure with
● A staff of hundreds all working to ensure the utmost

## ENTER

● Enter now to win one of these great prizes
● You can enter today if you hurry
● Enter a dazzling new realm of
● You're invited to enter the open door of opportunity

## ENTERTAINING

● Entertaining made easy with
● A highly entertaining way to spend an evening
● Take a moment to entertain a totally new idea
● Makes entertaining a snap

**ENTERTAINMENT**
- It's great entertainment
- A treasure trove of marvellous entertainment
- Giving you more for your entertainment dollar
- If it's entertainment you're looking for, you've certaintly come to the right place

*See also:* **ENJOYMENT**

**ENTHUSIASM**
- We hope you share renewed enthusiasm
- Given with pleasure and enthusiasm
- The overwhelming enthusiasm shows in

*See also:* **ENERGIZE, ENJOYMENT**

**ENTHUSIAST**
- For the enthusiast in the family
- Offers enthusiasts a whole range
- For amateurs and enthusiasts alike
- We'll turn you into an enthusiast for

**ENVIRONMENT**
- In a highly professional environment
- Now you can do your part for the environment by
- Require specific knowledge, skills and attitudes in this environment
- Thrive in a safe and challenging environment
- A highly protective environment
- We care about the environment
- Adds up to an environment of excellence
- Thrive in a challenging and ever-evolving environment
- Effectiveness with the environment in mind
- While going easy on the environment

*See also:* **ATMOSPHERE, EARTH, HOME, NATURE, SETTING**

**ENVIRONMENTAL**
- Makes it a sound environmental choice
- Environmentally friendly and best value too
- Up to the highest environmental standards
- Passes all environmental tests with flying colors

*See also:* **CLEAN, NATURAL**

**EQUAL**
- Not every product is created equal
- Equal to the very best

- All things being equal, ours is the finest
- More than equal to the job of

**EQUIP**
- Equipping you splendidly for the job ahead
- Equipped with everything you need to
- Specially equipped with
- Comes fully equipped with

**EQUIPMENT**
- You just need the right equipment
- Better equipment means better results
- We have all the equipment to help you
- Reducing the equipment you have to have

**ERA**
- Promising a brand new era in
- The era of total comfort has arrived
- It's our era now
- Don't be stuck with the baggage of a bygone era

*See also:* **TIME**

**ESSENTIAL**
- Absolutely essential to your success
- Start with the essentials
- Enterprising essentials get you going in top gear
- For all the essentials you need for worry-free

*See also:* **BASICS, ELEMENT**

**ESTABLISH**
- Now firmly established in
- Helping to establish you as
- Establishing our superiority for all to see

**ESTEEM**
- Enhance your self esteem with
- The most esteemed establishment in the city
- We hold our customers in the highest esteem

*See also:* **PRIDE**

**ESTIMATE**
- Free in-home estimates
- For a free, no obligation estimate, contact your nearest representative

- Call right now for a free estimate
- Call today for a fast estimate
- For a free, no obligation, phone estimate
- Call for our no obligation, in-home estimate

**Estimate:** guesstimate, ball park figure, reckoning, figure, appraisal, estimated value, valuation, assessment, price

## EVALUATION
- Call today for a free evaluation of
- We let you make the evaluation
- Standing highest in the evaluation of all the professionals

*See also:* **ESTIMATE**

## EVENT
- The event you don't want to miss
- Warehouse sale event
- The event of the year is back
- Making every event more successful
- Piggy-back on the success of another event
- This truly inspiring event happens only once
- An event everyone has been waiting for

*See also:* **DEVELOPMENT**

## EVERYBODY
- Everybody's doing it
- Something for everybody
- Join everybody else in
- A superior product not for everybody

## EVERYDAY
- Not an everyday event
- Step out of your everyday life
- A sale every day
- Our today, every day, sale rolls on

## EVERYTHING
- Has everything to do with
- Comes with everything included
- Find out everything you need
- Everything to make your job easier
- You have to have at least one of everything
- Leads to everything else
- Everything to make your home and garden look its best

- Everything you need is here
- Everything is maximized
- Where you'll find everything else too

## EXAMPLE

- Came up with this extraordinary example of
- Just one example of the great many useful items you'll find
- Here's another wonderful example of
- Examples galore
- A fine example of the progress that can be made

**Example:** sample, specimen, test, model, pattern, standard, paradigm, ideal, norm, bench mark
**See also; MODEL, TEST**

## EXCELLENCE

- A tradition of excellence since
- Committed to a higher standard of excellence
- Our goal is excellence
- Your search for excellence ends here

*See also:* **BEST, EXCEPTIONAL, FINE, TOP**

## EXCEPTIONAL

- Producing exceptional, award-winning products
- Providing you with exceptional value at a cost you can afford
- The exceptional will always stand out
- Exceptional quality lets your rest assured

*See also:* **EXTREME, SPECIAL**

## EXCITE

- People are getting really excited about
- It's exciting intense interest from all quarters
- Something exciting is on the way
- More exciting than ever this year
- Guaranteed to excite your interest.
- There's nothing more exciting than
- Exciting news is about to break

**Exciting:** thrilling, electrifying, galvanizing, spine-tingling, hair-raising, far out, rip-roaring, rip-snorting, stimulating, stirring, bracing, rousing, inspiring, invigorating, moving, impelling, compelling, affecting, soul-stirring, heart-moving, overpowering, overwhelming, overcoming, starting, astonishing, mind-boggling, mind-blowing, alluring, inviting, enticing, tempting, tantalizing, irresistible, charming, captivating, provocative, intriguing, fascinating, entrancing, beguiling, intoxicating, bewitching, enrapturing, attractive, interesting, appealing, piquant, seductive, sensuous, desirable, toothsome, mouth-watering, sexy, ravishing, voluptuous, glamorous, luxurious

## EXCITEMENT
- Could it be the sheer excitement of
- Feel the excitement of creating
- Our excitement was been regenerated by
- Caught up in the excitement of
- Can you stand the excitement

**Excitement:** motive, impulse, desire, stimulation, spur, call, urge, infection, exhilaration, thrill, seduction, beguilement, intoxication

*See also:* **ACTION, ADVENTURE, DRAMA, FUN**

## EXCLUSIVE
- Found exclusively at
- Exclusive to better stores everywhere
- Now you can have access to exclusive
- Each comes with an exclusive

**Exclusive:** select, particular, picky, choosy, limited, selective, posh

## EXPAND
- All while letting you expand
- Now expanding to include
- Expanding into your neighborhood
- In the midst of a vigorous expansion phase

*See also:* **GROW, INCREASE**

## EXPECT
- Why expect less from
- You expect the best
- If you've come to expect the most from
- You may not expect

## EXPECTATION
- For those whose expectations are higher than their budget
- Even surpassed the critics' expectations
- Living up to the highest expectation
- We can meet all of your expectations
- The greater your expectations the more you need our service

*See also:* **ANTICIPATE, STANDARD**

**EXPENSE**
- At absolutely no expense to you
- We know you've got to keep expenses down
- Another expense you don't need
- Helping you with your biggest expense

*See also:* **COST, SAVINGS, VALUE**

**EXPENSIVE**
- Feels like a more expensive item
- Are you tired of forking over for expensive
- Need not be expensive at all
- Avoid expensive mistakes with

**Expensive:** costly, dear, high, high-priced, over-priced, steep, stiff, exorbitant, excessive, unreasonable, valuable, precious, lavish, prodigal, extravagant, priceless, rich

**EXPERIENCE**
- No experience necessary
- Protected by unparalleled experience
- Helping people with no experience to
- An experience that will turn your head around
- Would experience such highlights as
- An exciting, richly rewarding species
- Bringing your personal experience on
- Giving you hands-on experience
- You've never experience anything like this
- Introducing a totally new experience
- We have immense experience in
- Come to us for an experience like no other
- Come on in today and experience
- My experience has been terrific
- We've banked a lot of experience
- Delivers a much more personal experience
- You'll find a wealth of experience in
- Your own experience proves it special
- For a truly unique experience
- Join us for a genuinely new experience
- Duplicate the experience without leaving home
- We have the people with experience
- Experience the reward you deserve
- Trust our experience
- Building on fifty years of experience

**Experience:** wisdom, knowledge, perception, observation, common

sense, sophistication, enlightenment, learning, cognizance, know-how, savoir faire, understand, discover, realize, discover, appreciate, absorb, take in
*See also:* **FEEL, FEELING**

## EXPERT
- Get expert help immediately
- More than a hundred experts on call just for you
- Our experts can enhance your home with a complete new
- Meet experts who will challenge, instruct and inform you
- We have carefully chosen and trained our experts
- Experts available to work with you at your request
- Here's a sample of what the experts have to say
- Our experts have carefully studied the
- We have experts in every department
- Our experts provide you with the highest level of customer service
- Our expert associates are ready to help
- Ask the experts
- Our experts will show you how
- Experienced experts can help you choose
- Let our experts show you
- Experts agree that

*See also:* **ASSOCIATE, PROFESSIONAL, STAFF, SALESPEOPLE**

## EXPERTISE
- Has combined many years of expertise to bring you
- Giving you real-world expertise
- We possess the expertise and sophisticated capability that is truly essential
- A lot of expertise has gone into this wonderful product
- A whole new world of expertise

*See also:* **EXPERIENCE, KNOWLEDGE**

## EXPLORE
- Cut you loose to explore
- Explore a powerful new way of
- You'll want to explore this vibrant, fascinating product
- Come and explore

*See also:* **DISCOVER, SEARCH**

## EXPOSURE
- Providing ultimate exposure
- A delicious way to extend your exposure to

94

- Increased exposure has resulted in increased
- More exposure for a fresh idea

**EXPRESS**
- Express yourself with
- A very useful means of expressing
- Our records show you have expressed an interest in
- Express your wildest desires

**EXTRA**
- Could you use an extra
- Giving you the extra attention you require
- Enjoy all the thoughtful extras we provide

*See also:* **INCREASE, MORE**

**EXTREME**
- Get extreme
- Extreme comfort, extreme delight
- Not afraid to go to extremes

*See also:* **EXCEPTIONAL**

**EYE**
- Delights the eye and the mind
- The apple of your eye
- Sure to catch your eye
- You won't believe your eyes

*See also:* **SEE**

**FACE**
- A great way of saving face
- There's more to a flawless face than
- Wakes your face all over with a tingle
- At last, a fresh face
- Behold the new face of
- The face of our service has been changed forever
- Let's face it, you need a change
- Squarely facing the future

*See also:* **ASPECT, LOOK**

**FACT**
- Just the facts, ma'am
- That fact remains unchanged today
- For more facts, call

- When you're thinking of buying, you want the facts
- Laying out the hard facts of
- Get the facts you need before you negotiate
- All the facts, please
- First, you want the facts
- Get the facts and get them fast

*See also:* **INFORMATION**

## FACTOR

- A distinguishing factor
- The factors that make us a wise choice for you
- More than all other factors combined
- The biggest factor of all is

*See also:* **ELEMENT**

## FACTORY

- Continues to sell below factory prices
- We manufacture everything in our state-of-the-art factory
- Direct from the factory
- Factory direct
- Rushed from the factory to your door

*See also:* **MANUFACTURER**

## FAIL

- You cannot fail when you follow this path
- Fail-proof
- For those of you who have failed to notice
- When other systems fail, ours soldiers on
- Will never fail you in a crunch

## FAIR

- It's easy to play fair
- If life were fair, we'd all have one of these
- Fair to say that ours is the best

*See also:* **RIGHT**

## FAITH

- Renewing your faith in
- Put your faith in us
- A lot more than just blind faith
- Take a flying leap of faith

*See also:* **TRUST**

## FALL
- Last call for fall
- Making it all fall into place
- Fabulous fall fashion
- Those first days of fall really make you come alive
- The news in products this fall is
- It's what's in store for fall

*See also:* **SEASON**

## FAMILIAR
- A seductively familiar
- Comfy and familiar as your favorite slippers
- The name that's familiar to you

*See also:* **COMFORT**

## FAMILY
- Will keep your whole family busy
- A family to serve your family
- We're just like one of the family
- Far transcends basic family requirements
- For the entire family
- Something for everyone in the family
- We understand how important the time your family spends together is to you
- Discover an investment in family fun
- One all the family can enjoy
- Perfect for all your family's growing needs
- Room for the whole family
- Foremost family product
- Your family has been cooped up to long
- For you and your whole family
- You're like family to us
- Helping families find what they need

## FAMOUS
- Famous name, famous value
- For the most famous name in
- We're famous for our
- You don't have to be famous to be good

*See also:* **KNOW, REMARKABLE, RENOWN**

## FANCY
- Fancy free and open to the world

97

- How does this strike your fancy
- Indulge your fancy
- For something a little fancier

*See also:* **IMAGINATION, WISH**

## FASCINATION

- Encouraging an ongoing fascination with
- Become an object of fascination
- Increasing fascination every day with

*See also:* **EXCITEMENT, INTEREST**

## FASHION

- Here's your fashion secret
- Giving you fabulous fashion and more
- Selected fashions for the whole family
- A way for fashion's new wave
- Will you follow fashion's lead away from
- Join the fashion revolution

*See also:* **ELEGANCE, STYLE**

## FAST

- Faster and easier than ever before
- Go as fast or as far as you wish
- You move fast
- They really move fast
- Fast track your life
- They'll go fast
- It's as fast and easy as
- These babies are really going fast
- First, fast and fun
- Is fast becoming the standard for
- It's never been easier or faster to
- Get it faster an at half the cost
- Get it faster with
- Bringing it to you faster through

**Fast:** quick, rapid, swift, speedy, express, expeditious, accelerated, fleet, nimble, spry, brisk, light-footed, hasty, post-haste, expeditious, lickety-split, with dispatch

*See also:* **INSTANT, SPEED**

## FAT

- Think low fat
- Fat is not where it's at

- Melts fat quickly
- More delicious, with less fat than any other

## FATE
- More than just a twist of fate
- You are fated to succeed
- Now that fate has brought us together

## FAVOR
- Do yourself a favor and
- As a personal favor to you
- We have a favor to ask
- Ask any favor you like

## FAVORITE
- A perennial favorite
- The world's favorite
- Dig into this honest-to-goodness favorite
- An all-time favorite
- We hope our favorites will become yours too
- With so many choices, it's hard to pick a favorite
- Everybody's favorite
- Traditional favorites
- We stock all your old favorites
- Favorites any time of the year
- Here's more of your favorites

## FEATURE
- Feature of the month
- Another specified feature is
- Having this feature doesn't hurt either
- A specific feature is built to conform to the recommendations of
- Featuring a full year of
- Check out the outstanding performance features that make
- Gives you even more key features to
- Features we personally think are the best in the business
- Added standard features
- Plus value-added features and applications
- With many luxury features such as these
- Other famous features include
- You'll find plenty of other fine features, too
- A superior collection of standard features
- A dazzling number of standard convenience features

- The great features add up to a truly outstanding product
- Includes additional features that quite simply blow you away
- Have unique features that make them virtually wear-proof

*See also:* **HIGHLIGHT**

## FEEL

- Think about what feels good
- You'll feel better every day you
- Another chance to feel
- Feel the way you want to feel
- At your best when you feel most comfortable
- Nothing else feels like
- Feel good about what you do
- Just the feel of it will tell you
- Just feel the relaxing pleasure of it
- Nothing feels better than
- You can feel it instantly
- Feels good in every way
- Feels simply fabulous
- You can feel the difference
- Feel the difference for yourself
- Such a spirited feel of
- Keep on feeling great
- Now you can have that same happy, healthy feeling
- Has a very pleasant feel

*See also:* **EXPERIENCE, TOUCH**

## FEELING

- A sensational feeling
- Feeling is believing
- There's always been a feeling that
- For those of us at our company, it's a feeling we hold dear
- A feeling that's part of who we are
- Nothing compares to the feeling of
- A delicious feeling of tranquillity and order
- Let the feeling wrap around you
- For a more sensuous feeling
- You know the feeling

**Feeling:** sensation, emotion, ardor, sense, impression, intuition, inkling, hunch, hint, premonition, tingle, quiver, throb, palpitation, vehemence, heat, attraction, affection, warmth, response, reaction, consciousness, awareness, perception, sensibility, sensitivity, consideration, discrimination, tact, empathy, sympathy, fellow feeling, identification,

vibe, notion, idea, sentiment, conception, thought, estimation, theory, opinion, outlook, viewpoint, point of view, attitude, stance, position, posture, way of thinking, intense, ardent, passionate, receptive
*See also:* **EXPERIENCE, OPINION, THINK**

## FEMININE
- Basics with a really feminine feel
- A surprisingly feminine mix
- For your feminine side
- Experience all the deliciously feminine joys of
- Fabulously, fascinatingly feminine

## FESTIVE
- It's easy to make your home look festive with
- The real joy of the festive season
- Feisty, festive and full of fun
- For that truly festive feeling
- Everyone loves a festive occasion

*See also:* **CELEBRATION, CHRISTMAS, EASTER, HOLIDAY**

## FIELD
- Leading in the field
- Because this is a new, fast-growing field
- A field that's wide open to you
- Get ahead of the field with a boost from
- Our company is best in the field of

## FIGHT
- Helps fight problems
- Fight back with
- We're on your side on the fight to
- Ready to help you fight the fight
- When you know you've got a fight on your hands
- Fights even the worst

*See also:* **BATTLE, WAR**

## FIGURE
- Full figure value
- Enhances you figure like no other
- Figure on our help with
- Letting you figure out how

*See also:* **RELY, SHAPE**

## FINAL

- Final ten days
- All sales final
- Your final chance to
- It's final, we're the best
- Now you can finally find

*See also:* **END, FINISH, LAST**

## FINANCE

- Finance it in ten easy payments
- We arrange financing for you
- Don't worry about how to finance
- When it comes to finance, we're out front
- Just look at the simple financing
- No matter what your record, you can finance
- Let us help you finance
- Finance is no problem
- Gives you a chance to finance something even bigger
- High finance made easy

*See also:* **COST, ECONOMIC, MONEY, PAY, PAYMENT, SAVINGS, VALUE**

## FINANCIAL

- Taking financial responsibility for ourselves
- You can't afford to leave your financial future to someone else
- Now, all your financial needs taken care of
- Taking good care of you financially
- Make out your own financial success
- Invest precious financial resources on other priorities
- And we've got top financial ratings to back us up
- The financial world is a jungle
- Makes the greatest financial sense
- Financially speaking, we're the best
- The end of financial worries for you
- Talk to us about all your financial concerns
- The best financial decision you could make

*See also:* **COST, ECONOMIC, MONEY, PAY, PAYMENT, SAVINGS, VALUE**

## FIND

- We can help you find
- What better place to find out than here
- Find out from the pros themselves

- Definitely worth finding out
- We'll help you find what you need
- What a find
- Need help to find it
- Find it fast
- Helping you find just about anything
- Only here will you find exactly what you're looking for
- Call to find out about
- To find out how to save on
- Finding the item you want has never been so easy
- Looking for a product and can't find it
- We'll find it for you easily
- Where else would you find
- When you fiind yourself in unfamiliar waters
- Why don't you find us
- Only here will you find great
- Find exactly what you're looking for and save money too
- You can find out more fast

*See also:* **DISCOVER, EXPLORE, SEARCH**

## FINE
- For lovers of fine quality everywhere
- The fine difference between good and superb
- Those who appreciate the finer things in life will understand
- Finer than all others
- The finest product we've ever made
- When only the finest will do
- The finest products come from
- It's what makes our products unquestionably the finest

*See also:* **BEST, EXCELLENCE, PREMIUM, SUPERIOR**

## FINGERTIPS
- Now you can have it at your fingertips
- Putting more at your fingertips
- Complete information at your fingertips

## FINISH
- You're not completely finished without
- Finished off with
- And to finish, the grand finale
- And we're not finished with you yet
- Buffed to a lasting finish

*See also:* **END, FINAL, LAST**

## FIRST

- We've placed first among all
- Always think of us first
- Call us first for a successful
- Now we bring you another first-of-its kind
- Be one of the first to get
- Come to the people who place you first
- As well, our company was one of the first to
- The world's first and only
- Make sure we're the first people you call

*See also:* **FOREFRONT, LEADER**

## FIT

- Beauty, comfort, fit—they're all here
- Combined, they ensure an extraordinary fit
- Designed to fit perfectly
- Engineered to fit smoothly into all sorts of
- Fitting into your plans no matter how
- You'll love the fit
- The individual fit makes them the most comfortable for you
- You've never experienced fit like this
- It's only fitting that you have the finest
- The fit that counts
- Fit is everything at
- Fit for a queen, fit for you
- Fits nicely into a compact space

*See also:* **COMFORT**

## FLAVOR

- Loaded with good old-fashioned flavor
- Adding a continental flavor to
- A whirlwind of flavor
- More than just the flavor of the month

*See also:* **TASTE**

## FLEXIBILITY

- But also gives you that little extra flexibility to
- Flexibility to meet individual requirements
- The flexibility to accommodate your needs, whatever they are

## FLEXIBLE

- Flexible enough to meet your demands tomorrow
- You want a company that's really flexible

- A flexible plan to suit your every need

**Flexible:** adaptable, adjustable, comfortable, malleable, tractable, compliant, cooperative, docile, biddable, obedient, mangeable, easy, willing, yielding, ready, amenable, agreeable, receptive, predisposed
*See also:* **ADAPT, CHANGE, VERSATILE**

## FLIGHT
- Let your imagination take flight
- More flights to more places than any other
- Indulge in a wonderful flight of fancy

## FLYER
- Look for your flyer in
- This week's flyers tell it all
- Plan your shopping around these great flyers

## FOCUS
- Future-focused
- Are you out of focus
- Also happens to be the focal point for
- Intensely focused on bettering

*See also:* **CONCENTRATE**

## FOLLOW
- Then we follow through with complete service
- All you need to do is follow each step
- Great follow up with
- The leader others follow

## FOOT
- Starts you off on the right foot
- Helps you put your best foot forward
- Puts you on a solid footing to
- More than just a foot in the door
- We can help put you on an equal footing with
- On an equal footing with the big girls

*See also:* **BASE, FOUNDATION**

## FOREFRONT
- Remaining at the forefront of
- Puts you in the forefront where you belong
- We've always been in the forefront

*See also:* **FIRST, LEADER**

## FORGET
- We should not forget that
- Don't forget about these evocative
- Don't forget to check these out first
- How could anyone forget

## FORM
- Exquisitely formed
- Just complete the attached form
- Stay in top form
- Great form, great substance, all for you

*See also:* **SHAPE**

## FORMULA
- It's patented formula lets you
- This naturally balanced formula
- Have created the most advanced formula possible
- We challenged ourselves to develop a formula that
- It's our most effective formula ever
- The proven formula for success
- Amazing new breakthrough formula

*See also:* **INFORMATION, PLAN, SYSTEM**

## FORMULATE
- Specially formulated to
- Formulated to today's demanding standards
- A plan formulated specifically for you

See also; **CREATE**

## FORTUNATE
- We're very fortunate to have
- An extremely fortunate find
- When you just can't believe how fortunate you are
- You can be one of the fortunate ones who

*See also:* **CHANCE**

## FORTUNE
- Discover a secret that could make you a fortune
- An investment that's already worth a fortune
- Better than fame and fortune
- Good fortune is right in front of you

*See also:* **WEALTH**

## FORWARD
- Fast forward
- Looking forward to
- The treat the whole family looks forward to
- Always moving forward to

*See also:* **AHEAD**

## FOUND
- Found only in four exclusive locations
- Now that you've found us, you'll stay with us
- Founded by people who believed that excellence pays off
- Staunchly true to our founding principles

*See also:* **DISCOVER**

## FOUNDATION
- Provides a foundation for
- Acquire a solid foundation for
- You've got the foundation for
- Always start with a firm foundation

*See also:* **BASE, FOOTING**

## FREE
- Try it for free
- Now you're free to
- Get your free sample today
- Buy one, get one free
- You will receive a second one free
- You've finally broken free
- Free tryout
- Never have you felt so free
- Is absolutely free to you
- Yours free with
- And you get all this free
- Feel free as a bird with
- Like getting every third one free
- A freebie too good to ignore

**Free:** independent, autonomous, at leisure, uninhibited, relaxed, unbound, unchained, untrammelled, unimpeded, unhampered, unbridled, unrestrained, unrestricted, laissez-faire, no holds barred, wild, unconditional, released, exempt, clear, generous, liberal, lavish, unstinting, gratis, on the house, without cost, free of charge, for free, for nothing, at no cost, let loose

## FREEDOM

- Namely, freedom
- Giving you total financial freedom
- Finally, the freedom to take charge of your future
- Making freedom roar
- The freedom you're looking for
- Listen to the call of freedom
- The freedom machine
- Freedom can be habit-forming
- Experience real freedom
- Gives you true freedom of expression

**Freedom:** liberty, autonomy, independence, self-determination, self-direction, emancipation, release, relief, discretion, right, privilege
*See also:* **LIBERTY, OPPORTUNITY**

## FRESH

- Alway new, always fresh
- Fresh products every day
- Giving you a fresh new outlook
- You can't get fresher than this
- Fresher by far than
- You can always use a fresh angle on
- The freshness you want in
- Seals in quality and freshness

*See also:* **NEW**

## FRIEND

- A girl's best friend
- Say hello to an old friend
- You probably know friends or neighbors who love
- Friends will want to know your secret
- Ask your friends and family about
- With a little help from your friends
- Meet new friends
- Come where your friends are
- We want to make a friend out of you

## FRIENDSHIP

- Join a whole world of friendship
- Make hundreds of new friendships
- Your friendship means a lot to us
- A lasting friendship based on trust

## FUN

- Time to have fun
- So you can have fun even faster
- The fun's not over yet
- The fun's just beginning
- Fun, natural and you
- Have fun without worrying about
- Having fun never goes out of style
- Or if you just want to have fun
- Plenty of fun for everyone
- Just for the fun of it
- If you're looking for fun
- What could be more fun
- The package spells fun
- Interested in having a little more fun
- Simple, affordable and fun
- Life is fun
- Makes living fun
- If it's not fun, why do it
- Everything you need to know about having fun

*See also:* **ENJOYMENT, PLEASURE**

## FUNCTION

- Discussing how you will function in the new
- You'll be impressed with how well it functions
- Many more functions than you expect
- Helping you function in a tough situation
- Fun and functional

*See also:* **USE**

## FUSS

- To see what all the fuss was about
- Without the fuss of
- No fuss, no bother
- Find out what all the fuss is about
- Enjoy them with a minimum of fuss

*See also:* **HASSLE**

## FUTURE

- Gives you the tools you need to design a solid future
- Give them the future you didn't have
- Get your future rolling
- For the past fifty years, we've been delivering the future

109

- Welcome to the future
- It's not hard to predict the future
- The future is here–and it's yours
- The future starts today
- The future is now
- The future is in the bag
- But the real future is waiting before you
- If you want to see the future, visit us
- Investing in your future
- Helping to position you for the future
- One of the ways we're keeping our eyes on the future
- Your future depends upon it
- Decision that have your future in mind
- Don't gamble with your future
- To better anticipate your future needs
- New for the foreseeable future
- Unlocking the future for you
- A bright future to come
- Ensuring a strong future for
- Products of the future
- Call today for all the answers to your future
- Better value, brighter future

**Future:** time ahead, tomorrow, prospect, offing, expectation, outlook, anticipation, probability, likelihood
*See also:* **AHEAD, ANTICIPATE, PREVIEW**

## GAIN
- A net gain for all
- Just look at what you stand to gain
- All gain, no pain
- The gains are all yours.
- With so much to be gained by
- You have nothing to lose and everything to gain by

*See also:* **BENEFIT**

## GAMBLE
- You don't even have to gamble a stamp
- It's not a dangerous gamble
- Don't gamble with your health
- Choosing doesn't have to be a gamble
- A gamble you know you can win

*See also:* **CHANCE**

110

**GAME**
- Beat them at their own game
- Join the ultimate game
- We're part of the game
- We've changed the way the game is played
- Improves the way young athletes play the game
- It's more than just a game

**GEAR**
- The most important piece of gear you have is
- Gear up for the new season
- Watch us go into high gear
- Always operating in top gear
- If you've got the game, we've got the gear

**GENERATION**
- Celebrating a generation of
- For generation after generation of
- Call the greatest of this generation
- Simply the best of its generation
- A new generation takes over
- Join the smart generation
- You'll discover a whole new generation of
- Quality has been passed on from generation to generation
- A new generation works to renew

**GENERIC**
- There's nothing generic about
- Name quality in a generic brand
- Save on excellent generic products

*See also:* **BRAND**

**GENIUS**
- Genius at work
- Challenge our resident genius to
- A stroke of genius
- It doesn't take a genius to figure out what's best
- Your friends will think you're a genius
- Turns you into a genius overnight

*See also:* **ABILITY, CAPACITY, SMART**

**GENTLE**
- Gentle enough for

111

- A gentle boost could be all you need
- Gentle and soft to surround with cosiness
- Gentler on your system than

*See also:* **SOFT**

**GET**
- What you get at this location
- Here's what you get when you
- Get it easily from us
- Get in on the savings, get in on the fun
- Get the best while the getting is good

*See also:* **ACHIEVE**

**GETAWAY**
- This summer, treat yourself to a getaway
- For a fast getaway, call us
- Great getaways are waiting

**GIANT**
- We're the product giant
- A giant of a sale
- One of the giants of the industry at your service
- You can walk with giants

*See also:* **BIG**

**GIFT**
- Give a gift and save up to
- Our biggest gift ever
- Give it as a gift
- A gift means so much more when
- Our gift to you
- Call today and get your free gift
- Select the gifts you want from
- Come to us for all your gifts
- Gift boxed or wrapped at no extra charge
- Choose a gift with spirit
- Give a gift that will be enjoyed for years
- Great gift ideas that work for everyone in the family
- A great gift idea
- Gifts and comforts from near and far
- We offer gifts a special someone would enjoy
- The gift that sparkles all year
- The more you buy, the more gifts you may select

- We will give you one of these valuable gifts
- Free gifts and prizes
- Great gifts in store for all the family
- Gifts to entertain

**Gift:** present, favor, endowment, bequest, legacy, heritage, inheritance, bounty, largess, prize, giveaway, contribution, donation, benefit, blessing, boon, gratuity, honorarium, grant, aid, allowance, subsidy, presentation,
*See also:* **BONUS, BOUNTY, PREMIUM**

## GIMMICK

- No catch, no gimmicks
- Don't fall for gimmicks
- This is no gimmick
- We have no gimmicks, only solid value

## GIVE

- It not only helps give you a better
- No other product gives you
- With more to give than
- Giving you the very best
- Giving you more for less
- Give a helping hand with

**Give:** present, bestow, donate, contribute, turn over, award, hand over, vouchsafe, grant, leave, supply, shell out, pay, dish out, allot, allocate, mete out, distribute, apportion, dispense, off, manifest, yield, consign, surrender, relinquish, furnish, endow, entrust, provide, afford, impart, communicate, deliver, confer, empower, enable, authorize, expend, put out, pass on

## GIVEAWAY

- Enter the dream giveaway
- Don't miss this huge giveaway
- The biggest giveaway in our history

*See also:* **GIFT**

## GLAD

- You'll be glad you did
- Always glad to be of service
- Our staff is glad to see you

*See also:* **HAPPY, JOY**

## GLAMOUR

- Add that touch of glamour to your home

- A metaphor for modern glamour
- Glamour shimming under the moon
- The passionate search for real glamour

*See also:* **ELEGANCE**

## GLITTER
- Come to glitter paradise
- All that glitters may not be gold, so ask our experts
- Glittering with beauty
- Spreading a glittering promise before you

## GLOBAL
- A global response to a global problem
- Competing successfully with other global centers
- Able to seize global opportunities with confidence
- It's all about global commerce
- Poised to meet global needs

*See also:* **WORLD**

## GLORY
- These are the glory days
- Relive the glory
- Shoot for glory while you can
- Share in the glory of

## GO
- We're just rarin' to go
- Never go anywhere without it
- Go were no other product has gone before
- Go for it
- With some real get up and go
- When you're on the go, it goes with you

*See also:* **MOVE**

## GOAL
- To help you safely achieve your goal
- Working with only one goal in mind
- Our goal from the beginning was to provide you with the best
- Set goals for yourself
- You'll discover new ways to reach your goals
- We take the time to understand your goals

*See also:* **AIM**

## GODDESS
- Looking like goddess
- Like a gift from a goddess
- Turning yourself in a goddess

## GONE
- Get them before they're gone
- Soon they'll be gone for good
- Going, going, gone
- Once they're gone, they're gone

*See also:* **END, FINISH**

## GOOD
- A product can only be as good as its
- We've come up with something pretty good
- Good for so much
- You'll discover plenty of good things about us
- Nothing else looks and feels quite as good
- So good to your
- Good as gold

*See also:* **FINE**

## GOODNESS
- Bursting with natural goodness
- Gets all the goodness to you
- You can just see the goodness
- Goodness that really satisfies
- Goodness to keep you healthy

## GOODS
- Get the goods here to
- Get your hands on the goods
- The finest of goods and services
- A wide selection of goods

*See also:* **PRODUCT**

## GRAB
- Grab hold of the ultimate
- Grab all the pleasure your can
- Grabs you and holds you
- What better way to grab attention

*See also:* **GET**

## GRACE
- A wonderful saving grace
- Adds grace and charm to any
- This lovely piece can grace your home for only

*See also:* **BEAUTY, ELEGANCE**

## GRADE
- Really makes the grade
- Want to make the grade in style
- Top grade service says it all
- Only the best grade makes the grade
- Grade A all the way

*See also:* **RATE**

## GRATIFY
- Working to gratify your every wish
- Gratify your desire to
- Gratifying more customers than ever before
- Instantly gratifying

*See also:* **SATISFY**

## GREAT
- Great on its own or combined with
- Goes great with everything
- The greatest yet
- Greater than anything you've ever seen before
- A brush with greatness

*See also:* **BIG**

## GROOVE
- A new groove
- Get in the groove
- Groovier than ever
- And lots of groovy new

## GROUND
- Start from the ground up
- Breaking new ground every day
- Get in on the ground floor
- With feet firmly planted on the ground
- Stay grounded in reality

*See also:* **BASE, FOUNDATION**

## GROUP

- A very select group of
- Our group has an outstanding record of
- Choose from our large group of
- Grouped together for easy access
- Join an advanced group today

*See also:* **CHOICE, SALESPEOPLE, SELECTION, STAFF, TEAM**

## GROW

- Grow with us
- One of the fastest growing
- Join the most rapidly growing group in
- Helping you grow more rapidly
- All of which has made us one of the fastest growing companies in the world
- Helping you grow your business
- We grow on you
- The appeal grows on you fast
- It's how we've grown to become
- That's the way we've grown to cover

*See also:* **BOOM, EXPAND, INCREASE**

## GROWN-UP

- Grown-up value
- Fun for grown-ups too
- Designed just for grown-ups
- Join the grown-ups
- Play like a kid, save like a grown-up
- You're really grown-up when you can finally appreciate

## GROWTH

- Getting excited to see the growth
- So future growth is all gain, no pain
- Identified tremendous growth potential in
- Giving the highest growth rate
- Be part of a growth industry
- A sign of personal growth is your increasingly discriminating taste
- No end in sight to the phenomenal growth of
- One of the reasons for this phenomenal growth is
- Take advantage of the explosive growth of
- Poised for further growth

*See also:* **INCREASE**

## GUARANTEE

- Money-back guarantee
- Guaranteed by law
- Remember, we guarantee it
- With our unconditional guarantee there's absolutely no risk on your part
- We guarantee it no matter what happens
- Unconditionally guaranteed for one full year or your money back
- We guarantee that every item has been made to the highest standards
- A ninety-day lowest price guarantee
- Lower prices guaranteed
- Our price guarantee lets you relax
- Price match guarantee
- Satisfaction guaranteed
- Lower prices guaranteed
- Best prices guaranteed
- Your complete satisfaction guaranteed or your money back
- Unconditionally guaranteed for
- We guarantee your satisfaction
- Great low prices guaranteed
- Remember, everything is backed by our famous guarantee
- We offer an unconditional one-year guarantee
- Guaranteed to please
- No-nonsense guarantee
- Each item guaranteed to provide satisfactory service
- Unconditional guarantee
- Backed by our guarantee
- For guaranteed success
- Lifetime guarantee comes with it
- Best guarantee in the business
- Unparalleled guarantee with written references
- Money back guarantee if automatic
- You're guaranteed to find what you need
- Our guarantee is your satisfaction
- The best price guarantee you'll ever find
- Our products are guaranteed for life
- Unconditional money-back guarantee
- Our guaranteed savings
- You're guaranteed to benefit from

*See also:* **ASSURANCE, CERTAINTY, WARRANTY**

## GUESS

- Guess what that can lead to

118

- Takes the guessing out of
- Now you don't have to guess about
- Guess what you can do to
- Don't you hate it when you have to guess
- It's anybody's guess how
- Keep them guessing with
- You don't want to have to guess about something this important
- Get rid of the guesswork

*See also:* **CHOOSE**

## GUEST

- You're always an honored guest at
- All our guests are pampered shamelessly
- We invite all our guests to
- A product your guests will love
- Extends and invitation to guests from all over the world.

*See also:* **VISITOR**

## GUIDANCE

- You need expert guidance from the people who
- Guidance is provided free
- Look to us for guidance
- Always under the firm guidance of our professionals
- Search no further for the guidance you need to

*See also:* **ADVICE, EXPERT, HELP, PLAN, PROFESSIONAL**

## GUIDE

- Gently guides you through difficult
- An excellent guide to achieving
- An invaluable guide to finding success
- A common sense guide to
- Your guide to the best new products
- Let us be your guide
- A really handy guide to
- Your easy-living guide
- It's your guide to new delights
- Your complete shopping guide to
- Using this indispensable guide, you can
- Full-color, troubleshooting guide based on the advice of experts

**Guide:** lead, lead the way, conduct, usher, pilot, drive, navigate, hold the reins, take the helm, direct, steer, show the way, head toward, show the way, put on the right track, escort, advice, counsel, teach, supervise, oversee, preside, manage, superintend, handle, govern, rule, control,

119

example, model
*See also:* **COUNSEL, LEADER**

## GUY
- For the big guy
- It's a guy thing
- For that special guy in your life
- Guys go for it
- Here's one guy who won't let you down

## HABIT
- Make it a habit to visit our
- Our service can be habit-forming
- Shake off old habits, get a sharp new
- Your habits will change forever

*See also:* **CUSTOM**

## HALF
- It's a half and half deal
- And then there's the other half of the benefit
- Don't go home half-satisfied
- Deciding which store is half the battle

## HALLMARK
- Our hallmark is on it
- Look for this famous hallmark
- Look for these hallmarks of
- The hallmark of success stands out
- One of the hallmarks of a successful leader

*See also:* **BENCHMARK**

## HAND
- Give yourself a helping hand
- Giving you a hand up
- Reaching out a hand to you
- All you have to do is hand us your
- The benefit is handed directly to you

*See also:* **HELP**

## HANDLE
- Handled beautifully by
- You'll love the way it handles
- We know you can handle it

- Can you handle this much fun

## HANDS
- If you've got your hands full
- It's in your hands
- Join hands with
- You can't beat hands-on experience
- Build it with your own two hands
- We understand the importance of what you've placed in our hands
- Don't be afraid to place your future in our hands

## HANDSOME
- It also happens to be remarkably handsome too
- You can make a very handsome profit by
- We do handsomely by you
- Handsome is as handsome does

*See also:* **BEAUTIFUL**

## HAPPEN
- Make it happen
- When it comes to happening
- It could happen to you too
- We help it happen for you
- We're seeing it happen throughout the country
- You can see what will happen when
- Showing you how it really happens
- That's what happens when you experience the comfort of

## HAPPINESS
- Turns into pure happiness
- We love to see the happiness on your face when
- We're the happiness store
- The happiness of our patrons is our first concern

*See also:* **JOY, PLEASURE, SATISFACTION**

## HAPPY
- You'll always go away happy
- We want to make you happy
- We're always happy to help
- Whatever makes you happy makes us happy
- We won't stop until you're happy with our product
- They all make someone, somewhere happier

**Happy:** delighted, glad, pleased, contented, gratified, satisfied, thrilled,

elated, well-pleased, tickled, euphoric, cheerful, cheery, gay, sunny,
blithe, in high spirits, blithesome, light-hearted, buoyant, optimistic,
positive, upbeat, debonair, free and easy, happy-go-lucky, carefree,
breezy, easy-going, jolly, mirthful, hilarious, laughing, smiling, joyful,
joyous, jubilant, rejoicing, gleeful, exhilarated, lucky, fortunate,
auspicious, favorable, beneficial, profitable, opportune, valuable, gainful,
lucrative
*See also:* **GLAD, JOY, PLEASURE, SATISFACTION**

## HARD
- It isn't as hard as you think
- We're playing hard to get
- Such a little thing shouldn't be this hard
- We don't make things hard for you
- If you think it's hard to do, think again
- We work harder than anybody else to

*See also:* **DIFFICULT**

## HARMONY
- Creating a harmony of color and form
- We've created the perfect harmony of
- Living in harmony with
- Always in harmony with your wishes
- Working in harmony with you

## HARVEST
- Country harvest in the city
- Time to harvest the benefits of
- When your investment yields a bountiful harvest of
- Come harvest the profits of
- Straight from the harvest to you

## HASSLE
- Hassle-free
- Who says it has to be a hassle
- Yours to use without the hassle of
- Saves time and money and hassles
- No more hassles with
- Say goodbye to hassles forever

*See also:* **FUSS**

## HEAD
- Head-spinning value

122

- Puts you at the head of the line
- Go straight to the head of the class
- Straightens out your head about
- Finally, your head and your heart can agree
- If you've got a head for business, you'll know

**HEADACHE**
- Will take you away from the headache
- No more headaches on account of
- Gets rid of the headache of
- Banish the headache of

*See also:* **DIFFICULT, HARD, HASSLE**

**HEADQUARTERS**
- Your improvement headquarters
- Headquarters for value
- Come the headquarters for
- Make us your headquarters for

**HEALTH**
- In blooming good health
- Widely used by people who are health conscious
- Protecting the health of your family
- Better health for your pocketbook
- Healthy choices for a healthy life
- Particularly important for healthy functioning of
- Deserves to be kept healthy
- Another chance to feel healthy

**HEAR**
- Get ready to hear praises
- We hear what you want
- You've heard it all before
- You haven't heard news this exciting before
- Make yourself heard
- We heard you and we acted fast
- Heard all across the land
- Here's why you may not have heard about it before

*See also:* **LISTEN**

**HEART**
- Will always hold a special place in your heart
- Is there room in your heart for

- At the heart of this success is
- At the heart are professionals who thrive
- Open your heart and have fun
- Go with your heart
- To your heart's content
- Real people, making decisions of the heart
- Designed to take your heart

*See also:* **FEELING**

## HEAT

- Lick the heat
- Now your item can take the heat
- Give heat the cold shoulder
- Turning up the heat with
- The savings are heating up
- Beat the heat and be cool

*See also:* **HOT**

## HELP

- We helped get it there
- A rare gift for helping people to
- With a little help from
- Well, it's part of our job to help you
- Needa little help in livening up
- Nothing helps like
- Actually helps prevent
- To help you, we've introduced
- How can we help you
- Helping to make your day
- Let us help you
- Looking for some help
- We're standing by, ready to help
- Help yourself to
- We've been helping people like you for years
- Will be pleased to help you with all your needs
- Helping people, one at a time
- Need help, come to us
- Our representative is there to help you
- In short, you may need a little help
- We'll help you to
- We've made calling for help easier than ever
- We're ready to help you any time
- When you really have to have help with

- We are committed to helping you

**Help:** aid, assist, accommodate, oblige, abet, befriend, contribute, join in, chip in, lend a hand, boost, lift, cooperate, team up, take part, join forces, support, combine, sustain, maintain, endorse, stand by, save, rescue, deliver, facilitate, ease, expedite, accelerate, speed up, quicken, clear the way, underwrite, enhance, promote, advocate
*See also:* **ACCOMMODATE, BOOST, IMPROVE, SERVE, SERVICE**

## HELPFUL
- Friendly and helpful
- Our helpful staff is always on hand to
- Always striving to be more helpful
- It's always helpful to compare
- Tell us how we can be even more helpful
*See also:* **USEFUL**

## HERE
- Here when you need us
- Everything you need is here
- It's all right here close to you
- Here's how you get your copy
- Here's what you need to

## HERITAGE
- A racing heritage that translates from track to traffic
- Come into your true heritage
- Adding to your heritage with
- Part of your heritage, part of your birthright
*See also:* **LEGACY**

## HERO
- You'll be a hero when you
- Fit for a hero
- Truly heroic in proportion
- Giving you heroic portions of
*See also:* **DAREDEVIL**

## HIGH
- Just about as high as you can get
- High quality, high value
- Helping you get as high as you can go
- Held up to the highest standard

125

- Taking you higher than ever before

*See also:* **BEST, GOOD**

## HIGHLIGHT
- Highlight on savings
- We just want to highlight one of the better
- Style highlighted by
- One of the highlights of

*See also:* **FEATURE, SPOTLIGHT**

## HISTORY
- Making history as you watch
- The rest is history
- Just look at our history and be reassured
- Create some history with
- Opening up a whole new chapter in product history
- You're attending a historic occasion

*See also:* **HERITAGE, LEGACY**

## HIT
- A hit on the runways
- Get the quality you need without taking a financial hit
- A really big hit with the little people
- Hit the pavement running
- You'll be a hit when you show up with
- Now hitting the stores
- Hot hits for hot people

*See also:* **ARRIVE, JOY, PLEASURE**

## HOLIDAY
- Holiday gift offer
- The holidays are for making people happy
- The holidays are right around the corner
- Enjoying the warmth and goodwill of the holidays
- Spend less time preparing for the holidays
- You can find everything you need for the holidays right here
- You'll see just how easy holiday shopping can be
- Fill your home with a holiday atmosphere
- In the joyful spirit of the holidays
- Our warmest wishes for the holidays
- Super holiday specials
- In the spirit of the holidays, we're offering you this special
- You'll find a lot of holiday cheer at

- Take it easy during the holidays
- For the most important holiday of the year
- Take a break from the holiday rush
- Check your store for holiday hours

*See also:* **FESTIVE, CELEBRATION, CHRISTMAS, EASTER**

## HOLIDAY SEASON

- Joy throughout the holiday season
- The holiday season is about to get a lot easier
- Just in time for the holiday season
- Bringing you the best for the holiday season
- Our warmest wishes for a happy holiday season

*See also:* **CELEBRATE, FESTIVE**

## HOME

- Brighten your home
- What you need for your home—for less
- To meet the needs of every home
- It's what makes a house a home
- Come home to value
- A need just now hitting home
- Now you can shop without leaving home
- To help your house feel like a home
- Enhance your home with
- Help is close to home
- Welcome to our home
- Take it home with you today
- Free shop-at-home service
- Do it in your own home
- Another home run from

**Home:** dwelling, residence, domicile, residence, habitation, accommodations, quarters, hearth, family circle, home sweet home, household, homestead, shelter, retreat, refuge, environment, hometown, destination

*See also:* **ACCOMMODATION, DOORSTEP, ENVIRONMENT**

## HONEST

- We're being completely honest
- Nothing but honest value and hard work
- You want the honest truth
- Always honest about the real costs

**Honest:** upright, upstanding, incorruptible, ethical, moral, principled, high-minded, truthful, veracious, trust-worthy, trusty, reliable, dependable, tried and true, faithful, loyal, staunch, steadfast, true-blue, honorable, worthy, right, decent, good, fair, impartial, equitable, fair and square, level, square-dealing, plain-dealing, square-shooting, straight-shooting, unbiased, open-minded, valid, legitimate, rightful, proper, candid, frank, forthright, foursquare, direct, straightforward, straight-from-the-shoulder, genuine, sincere, aboveboard, up front, unequivocal, real, sterling, bona fide, sure enough, authentic, reputable, creditable, straight-arrow, unvarnished

## HONESTY
- Our honesty and patience serve you, year after year
- Honesty is like gold to us
- Above all, we value honesty and integrity

## HOOK
- Designed to get you hooked on
- Get hooked on the best
- You'll be hooked from the start
- Swallowing it hook, line and sinker

*See also:* **INTEREST**

## HOPE
- Sharing your hope that
- Everything you hoped for and more
- Your best hope for

**Hope:** expectation, longing, desire, want, fancy, wish, eagerness
*See also:* **DESIRE, WANT, WISH**

## HOT
- Give a red hot welcome to
- Hot doings in the old town tonight
- Hot off the
- Look hot, feel cool
- For a product that's really hot
- Any more and it would be too hot to handle
- It's the hottest thing going
- Here's the hot spot

*See also:* **HEAT**

## HOURS
- There just aren't enough hours in the day to
  - To provide our customers with the most convenient hours possible
- You'll save the hours and hours it takes to

- Now on extended hours for your shopping convenience
*See also:* **TIME**

## HURRY
- But hurry because they won't last
- Hurry on over and take a look
- They're going in a hurry
- See what the hurry is all about
- Hurry in today before they're all gone
*See also:* **FAST, SPEED**

## IDEA
- One of the nicest things about the whole idea is
- It's your idea of what really matters
- Everything about this idea is perfectly simple
- Now all of this should give you a pretty good idea of just what it takes to
- Here's a crazy idea
- That's why we took the idea beyond
- A classic idea of
- An idea whose time has truly come
- An idea you should consider seriously
- Perhaps it's time you heard an entirely new idea
- The heart of the idea behind
- Add our latest idea to your repertoire
- Does more than just give a general idea

**Idea:** notion, thought, belief, concept, conception, perception, surmise, observation, theory, conjecture, guess, plan, design, dream, vision, intention, object, end, aim, goal, impression, assumption, opinion, view, feeling, conviction, persuasion, philosophy, outlook, principle, teaching
*See also:* **AIM, BELIEF, CONCEPT, DESIGN, FEELING, GOAL, NOTION, OPINION, PHILOSOPHY, PLAN, PRINCIPLE, SYSTEM**

## IDEAL
- Turning it into more than just an ideal
- Ideal for all your needs
- Firmly committed to these ideals
- Living up to the very highest ideals
*See also:* **PERFECT**

## IDEAS
- Offers beautiful and creative ideas for

- Bright ideas don't come cheap
- Encourage people from different disciplines to interact and exchange ideas
- Brilliant ideas cost more
- Enjoy great ideas for
- Ideas you can use immediately
- You supply the ideas, we'll
- Connect with powerful ideas
- Good ideas for you
- Here are even more inspired ideas
- The source of pioneering ideas
- Get some great ideas for
- We've got all kinds of great ideas and smart solutions for
- Need more ideas
- Dozens ideas to get you going
- For more ideas, visit our store

*See also:* **IDEA**

## ILLUSION

- You might think it's an illusion
- It's certainly no illusion that
- The reality behind the illusion
- More than just a beautiful illusion of

## IMAGE

- You don't have to spend millions to give yourself a million dollar image
- Your chance to fashion a spiffy new image for yourself
- Will enhance your business image
- Create an image with impact
- When image is everything
- Living up to our image every day
- Intensify your image
- Your image is key to your success

**Image:** appearance, semblance, aspect, form, shape, idea, concept, likeness, symbol, type
*See also:* **ASPECT**

## IMAGINATION

- Exercise your imagination and have more fun
- It takes real imagination to
- Facing the future with imagination and insight

*See also:* **CREATIVITY**

# IMAGINE

- How could you have imagined that
- Imagine one of these in your home
- Now imagine what we'll do for an encore
- Imagine the time and money you'll save
- Just imagine for a moment
- Take the time to imagine a different reality

**Imagine:** picture, envision, dream up, conjure up, visualize, rhapsodize, envisage, guess, conjecture
*See also:* **THINK**

# IMITATION

- Accept no imitations
- Not just another tacky imitation
- It's the real thing, not an imitation
- Imitation is the sincerest form of flattery

# IMMERSE

- You can be completely immersed in
- Immerse yourself in sheer luxury
- For years, people have been immersed in the idea of

# IMPACT

- A major impact on a material world
- High-impact thinking
- Increase our personal impact with
- We're making a major impact on

**Impact:** force, shock brunt, pressure, impetus, momentum, energy, slam, bang, knock, blow
*See also:* **ENERGIZE, PUNCH**

# IMPORTANCE

- Communicating the value and importance of
- Attesting to its importance
- Your importance to us is enormous
- We understand how much importance your place upon

# IMPORTANT

- It is extremely important that
- We all know how important
- Just as important
- What's the most important thing you put on

**Important:** significant, critical, momentous, weighty, serious, grave,

sober, crucial, urgent, pressing, imperative, necessary, essential, major, principal, prime, primary, big, major, main, substantial, considerable, formidable, imposing, commanding, high-level, superior, big-time, eminent
*See also:* **BIG, SUPERIOR**

## IMPRESSION
- The fast way to make a lasting impression
- Make a great first impression with
- There's no second chance to make a first impression
- The kind of impression you want to make
*See also:* **IMAGE**

## IMPROVE
- Always changing, always improving
- The time when you can most improve
- It's possible to improve on a good thing
- New and improved
- Always looking for ways to improve your shopping experience
- With an aim to expand and improve service through
- Improving through a joint initiative
*See also:* **BENEFIT, BETTER, BOOST, HELP**

## IMPROVEMENT
- The improvement that pays you
- Adding improvement after improvement to an already excellent product
- Helping you make improvements to
- Committed to constant improvement and success
- To find out how you can make improvements

## IMPULSE
- Give way to a totally revolutionary impulse
- More than just an impulse buy
- Your impulses are right to
- Let your wildest impulses out
*See also:* **DESIRE**

## IN-STORE
- Just a sample of what you'll find in-store
- Don't miss our in-store specials
- Great in-store values for the entire family

## INCENTIVE
- Incentive to start saving early
- Providing the buying incentives you need to
- Your business is our greatest incentive
- With even greater price incentives, you win all round

## INCOME
- Generating income for you from day one
- Preserving more of your income to personal use
- You have to stretch your income a long way

**Income:** revenue, returns, receipts, gross, annuity, pension, subsidy, allowance, profits, gain, yield, interest, winnings, take, proceeds, net, gravy, pickings, wages, salary, pay, payment, hire, remuneration, stipend, fee, benefits, extras
*See also:* **MONEY**

## INCREASE
- Increasing your efficiency, your customer base, your bottom line and your growth
- Before it has a chance to increase in value
- You'll notice a dramatic increase in
*See also:* **BOOM, EXPAND, GROW**

## INDEPENDENCE
- The easiest way to get the independence and satisfaction you want
- Helping you keep your hard-won independence
- What real independence is all about

## INDEPENDENT
- Your independent store
- You want to make an independent decision about
- Get the best service from you independent agent

## INDUSTRY
- Remaking an industry
- Helping to make our industry a better one
- The finest in the industry
*See also:* **BUSINESS**

## INFLUENCE
- Including all the new influences
- A far-flung, lasting influence
- Influenced only by the very best

# INFORM

- So you can always be well informed
- While keeping you fully informed at all times
- Makes sure you are informed of the very latest
- Informed with a haunting beauty
- Informs you every time a more advanced model comes in

**Inform:** advise, notify, let know, tell, relate, impart, acquaint, brief, proclaim, publish, broadcast, report, communicate, instruct, teach, enlighten, blow the lid off

*See also:* **ANNOUNCE, COMMUNICATE, TELL**

# INFORMATION

- Finding the right information takes time
- Our information specialists will
- Filled with valuable information
- You'll get full product information so you can compare
- Receive up-to-date information on
- Assuring you accurate information
- Please check with your dealer for current information
- You'll have access to the most current business information and resources
- No one keeps vital information safe like
- Keep this information handy in case of
- Keeps information at your fingertips
- Your trusted retailer has more information
- For more information and reservations, call
- Handy for organizing information
- I'd like to send you more information about
- Providing practical information on
- For even more information visit the store nearest your
- Information is just a phone call away
- Complete information at your fingertips
- Featuring the best ideas and information
- Now you can access a wealth of information on
- For twenty-four hour information, just dial
- Information becoming more and more useful to you every day
- Call now for full information
- If you're interested in some amazing information
- Providing the information you'll need to do just that
- Reorganize the information universe
- Call us and ask for free information about
- Making it possible for you to send for more information
- When you need information right now

- Information is moving fast these days
- The key to your success is the best up-to-date information
- The information you need is right here

**Information:** data, facts, knowledge, intelligence, background, report, communication, message, account, counsel, pointer, lowdown, inside story, details, material, word
*See also:* **ADVICE, ANALYSIS, EXPERT, GUIDANCE, HELP, PLAN, PROFESSIONAL, REPORT**

## INGREDIENTS
- Combined with the purest, mildest, most natural ingredients possible
- Wholesome ingredients to
- Made of several highly effective ingredients

## INHERITANCE
- Preserving a fine inheritance
- An inheritance of excellence
- Taking care of your precious inheritance

*See also:* **HERITAGE, LEGACY**

## INITIATIVE
- A high degree of initiative
- To succeed, you need to take the initiative
- We've been taking the design initiative for years
- Just take a look at this price initiative

*See also:* **BEGINNING, START**

## INNOVATION
- Innovation means looking boldly ahead
- Innovation is about looking forward
- Making the leap from need to innovation
- Tradition meets innovation right here
- Innovation in design and production methods are setting the pace for
- Fifty years of innovation

*See also:* **ADVANCE, FRESH, NEW**

## INNOVATIVE
- Innovative designs for creating and updating your
- One of the finest and most innovative
- This innovative product will put you away ahead of your competition

## INPUT
- We want your input

- Give you the input you want
- We took your input and created this fine product

*See also:* **INFORMATION, SUGGESTION**

**INQUIRY**
- Inquiries invited from
- Quickly answer your inquiries
- In answer to your inquiry

*See also:* **ASK, QUESTION**

**INSIDE**
- Inside, you'll find
- Reaches deep inside you
- Take advantage of inside information

**INSIGHT**
- Providing you with the experience and insight to
- Insight and research has provided this
- Priceless insights struggling to get out

**INSIST**
- Insist on the best
- You insist on our closest attention
- We insist on serving you
- We insist on providing only the finest

**INSPECTION**
- Customer inspection prior to delivery is our long standing possible
- Standing ready for your inspection
- Inviting your closest inspection

**INSPIRATION**
- Suits almost any inspiration you can have
- When you need inspiration, come to us
- Your needs provided the inspiration to create

*See also:* **CREATIVITY, IMAGINATION**

**INSPIRE**
- Inspired and influenced by
- Inspired by the goodness of
- Something to inspire you

*See also:* **ENERGIZE, IMAGINE**

## INSTALL
- Save money by installing it yourself
- So easy to install a child can do it
- Ready to install immediately
- We can install it right away
- You can install it easily yourself
- We can special order and install

*See also:* **BUILD**

## INSTALLATION
- Making installation quick and easy
- Installation services available by professionals
- Complete instructions for easy installation
- Fast and easy installation anyone can do
- Will arrange installation by qualified contractors in most areas
- Installation has been made super simple

## INSTALLMENT
- Buy it on the installment plan
- You'll be able to handle the installments easily
- Payable in convenient monthly installments

*See also:* **STAGE, STEP**

## INSTANT
- Instant value
- Designed for instant gratification
- Get results instantly

*See also:* **FAST, SPEED**

## INSTRUCTIONS
- Always comes with step-by-step instructions
- All you need is the ability to follow simple instructions
- If you can follow these moderate instructions for four weeks
- Follow simple instructions to get started
- Comes with complete instructions included

*See also:* **INFORMATION**

## INTEREST
- In the midst of this flurry of interest
- Brought to you in the interest of
- Showing a healthy interest in
- Is quickly attracting world-wide interest
- Taking a real interest in you

- No interest, no payments for

*See also:* **HOOK, INCOME, MONEY**

## INTERNATIONAL

- We start you thinking internationally
- Think international, think rich, think success
- Fortunate to have an internationally recognized
- Internationally known

*See also:* **WORLD**

## INVENTORY

- Get everything you need from our huge, in-stock inventory
- Huge inventory clearance
- More inventory than ever before
- We just have to clear all the extra inventory
- Too much inventory means big savings for you
- We must reduce our inventory of

*See also:* **STOCK**

## INVEST

- We invest under a microscope
- Invest an hour of your time—get a great return
- Before you invest your money, let us invest our time
- Be careful how you invest your hard-earned money
- Investing in your future
- We invest in you first
- Investing in the most dynamic sectors

**Invest:** put money into, fund, subsidize, back, support, provide capital for, spend, expend, supply, contribute, equip, outfit

## INVESTMENT

- For a very low initial investment you can
- Your investment starts at
- For a low initial investment
- All for a low investment
- Geared for a quick return on your investment
- Make a wise investment in yourself
- Make your investment back and then some
- Achieve the most mileage from your investment
- We look closely at our investments
- Investments that will help your money grow over time
- Protect your investment from the start
- Make an real investment in quality

- The best investment in today's economy
- Make you biggest investment your smartest investment
- For more information on this unique investment please call
- A growth investment with tax savings waiting for you

**Investment:** venture, speculation, risk, endowment, empowerment
*See also:* **MONEY, VENTURE**

## INVITATION
- Your invitation to special trades shows and seminars
- We continue to extend a warm invitation to you
- An invitation from the house of
- An invitation that's hard to resist

## INVOLVE
- Get involved with the future
- Most often involve the best
- You are involved in every aspect of development

*See also:* **JOIN**

## ISSUE
- Often a critical issue
- We know what your issues are
- A special issue filled with ideas
- A very important first issue
- Issued to you immediately upon

*See also:* **CONCEPT, GIVE, IDEA**

## ITEM
- Not all items, colors and sizes in this circular have been offered for sale in all stores
- Buy any item, get one at half price
- Many items are also available in our catalogue
- Among our most popular items this year

## JOB
- Can do the job handily
- For relaxing on the job
- Ensuring the job is done properly
- The job has never been easier
- Get the job done right
- It's a job for our company
- Cuts the job down to size
- Always on the job

**Job:** work, undertaking, business, proceeding, task, chore, activity, exercise, performance, project, affair, venture, enterprise, effort, contribution, accomplishment, achievement, role, function, concern, duty, office, mission, trust, employment, occupation, livelihood, living, pursuit, vocation, calling, profession, field, metier, area, province, trade, craft, grind, contract
*See also:* **BUSINESS, MISSION, TRUST, VENTURE, WORK**

## JOIN
- Join today, it's free
- There's never been a better time to join
- So join the millions who have already
- Join now and win
- Join us for all the excitement

*See also:* **CONNECT**

## JOURNEY
- This journey begins here
- With you every step of your journey
- Sometimes the journey can be long and tiring

## JOY
- A joy to behold
- All the joy of the season to you
- Plunge into the joys of
- Discover the joy of
- There's a certain joy that comes from

*See also:* **COMFORT, HAPPY, PLEASURE, SATISFACTION**

## KEY
- Your key to a successful future
- The key which unlocks
- Your key to peace of mind
- We put the key in your hand

*See also:* **SECRET**

## KICK
- With additional kick
- Get some extra kick
- Something with some kick to it
- Are you kicking yourself for not doing it when you had the chance

*See also:* **HAPPY, JOY, IMPACT**

## KID

- Kid stuff is our business
- Not just kid stuff
- Kids love it
- Bring the kids, they're welcome
- Plenty of fun for the kids
- Our best buys for kids
- Kids can have fun being kids
- Just for kids and a delight for you

*See also:* **CHILD, CHILDHOOD, YOUNG**

## KIDDING

- Who are you kidding
- We're not just kidding around
- Are you kidding yourself that

*See also:* **FUN**

## KIT

- Ask for our free information kit
- This clever kit shows you how to
- Comes with a complete kit
- This kit is all you'll ever need to
- We kit you out completely

*See also:* **GEAR**

## KNOW

- The ten things you need to know before you buy
- Find out what you don't know about
- We invite you to get to know us better
- It's nice to know that we'll take care of you
- Let us know how we did
- We always want to know we are satisfying you
- Just let us know how we can help
- Created by people who know about
- So you'll always know exactly how much
- Nobody knows it better
- Providing just what you need to know
- We really know the product
- Everything you need to know about
- At your fingertips, everything you need to know
- When you want to know more
- Did you know that our product can do all these things
- Care to know more, just call

141

- Know it all right now
- We know a thing or two about
- No one ever has to know
- Only you will know
- The more you know about it, the more you'll want to
- You probably already know
- Everyone knows it works
- But you have to know what you want
- Includes everything you need to know about

*See also:* **UNDERSTAND**

**KNOWLEDGE**
- An unmatched knowledge of local conditions
- You also get years of accumulated knowledge along with your purchase
- It takes knowledge to win
- All our knowledge is at your service

*See also:* **EXPERIENCE, EXPERTISE, INFORMATION**

**KNOWN**
- That's known as intelligence
- Highlights a little known fact
- You've known it all along
- You've always known what you wanted

*See also:* **KNOW**

**LANE**
- Puts you in the fast lane
- Won't leave you coasting in the slow lane
- The slow lane just turned into a superhighway

*See also:* **PATH, ROAD**

**LAST**
- For longer lasting performance
- Lasts and last for hours
- Saving the best for last
- Designed to last a lifetime
- Your last chance to save big

*See also:* **END, FINISH**

**LAUGH**
- Now you can laugh at worries about
- Giving you a reason to laugh

● The last laugh is on
*See also:* **FUN, HAPPY, JOY**

**LAUGHTER**
● Just like a burst of laughter
● Brimming with laughter and enthusiasm
● Just to see the laughter in your eyes
*See also:* **FUNNY, HAPPY, JOY**

**LAUNCH**
● And with the enthusiastic launch of
● Back in the market with the launch of
● With the launch so close, excitement is building
*See also:* **BEGINNING, START**

**LEAD**
● Only natural that we should take the lead in providing
● Will be on hand to lead you through it
● Taking the lead in providing you with the finest
● Making sure we're always in the lead
● Widely regarded as one of the leading
*See also:* **GUIDE**

**LEADER**
● Always a leader in the field of
● We got what it takes to be a world leader
● There's only one world leader
● Is the acknowledged leader in
● Be the leader of the pack
● We're the new leader in
● The acknowledged leader in
● Leaders in award-winning
● Join the leaders in
*See also:* **FIRST, FOREFRONT, HEAD**

**LEAGUE**
● In a league of their own
● Now that you've moved into the major leagues
● Big league success with little league costs
*See also:* **GROUP**

**LEAP**
● This is the way to leap forward

- Making the leap from need to innovation
- We here when you're ready to make the leap

*See also:* **ADVANCE**

## LEARN
- To learn more about how you can become part of
- We learn everything we can
- Learning more every day about
- Learn firsthand what you need to know about
- If we've learned anything, it's that
- Learn everything you need to know about
- Learn the ins and outs of
- Introduce you child to a lifelong love of learning

*See also:* **UNDERSTAND**

## LEASE
- We lease for less
- For sale or lease, it still makes sense
- It makes more sense to lease

## LEGACY
- Inheriting an unparalleled legacy of
- Carrying a proud legacy of quality
- Our legacy is at your service

*See also:* **HERITAGE, INHERITANCE**

## LEGEND
- Glamour befitting a legend
- Make them into local legends
- What legends are made of

## LESS
- Get the best for less
- Bringing you the finest for less
- You simply can't get it for less
- Nowhere else where you get it for less
- Don't settle for less
- Less is more
- You won't get it for less anywhere else
- Get less of the things you don't need
- You'll pay a little less for it

*See also:* **REDUCE**

**LET**
- It's all about letting go
- There's no letting up
- You won't ever want to let it go
- Practically impossible to let go of

**LEVEL**
- Conducted at the most efficient level possible
- Provides its owner with an exceptional level of
- A level of luxury previously unheard of in this class

*See also:* **STANDARD**

**LIBERTY**
- The exhilaration of liberty
- Taking the liberty of offering you
- Gives you more liberty to
- Experience more liberty than you've even known before

*See also:* **FREEDOM, OPPORTUNITY**

**LIFE**
- Dress for real life
- Take control of your life
- Get your life back to normal
- A celebration of life
- Put some life in your
- Life can be a real challenge
- You don't need that in your life
- Has a vigorous life of its own
- Giving new life to thousands of
- Has it changed your life yet
- Uncompromising quality helps you enjoy life to the fullest
- The quality of modern life depends upon
- New lives begin here
- Learn how to add life to your years
- The essence of life
- Makes life so much simpler
- A place where life happens
- Places value on how you choose to live your life
- Determine how you will live your life for years to come
- Like is a series of choices
- For once in you life, take a chance on
- There's more to life than

*See also:* **ENERGIZE, REJUVENATE, REVITALIZE**

## LIFESTYLE
- Increase your ability to enjoy a healthier, more active lifestyle
- Contributes to a healthy, active lifestyle
- Finally, the lifestyle you've always dreamed of
- Helping you meet the demands of today's fast-paced, hectic lifestyle
- You've worked hard for this lifestyle
- Changing your lifestyle can be easy and exciting

## LIFETIME
- Try it just once in your lifetime
- A once-in-a-lifetime chance to
- Providing you with a lifetime of productive

## LIFT
- Anyone in need of a lift can choose
- Give yourself a lift
- Gives your style a lively lift
- And doing other heavy lifting

*See also:* **IMPROVE**

## LIGHT
- Making light work to your advantage
- In harmony with light
- Super  light, super strong
- Spreading a little light in the world

## LIKE
- If you like last year's model
- Chances are you'll like
- You'll take a liking to
- Nothing else like it
- We pay close attention to your likes and dislikes
- There's nothing quite like a good
- If you're someone who likes to live to the fullest

*See also:* **CHOOSE, PREFER**

## LIMIT
- We reserve the right to limit quantities
- This flyer contains limited-time sale values, special buys and items at our everyday low prices
- Limit is one per family
- There are no limits to where you can go

*See also:* **END, FINISH**

**LINE**
- Get the inside line on your favorite
- A new product line now available in all our stores
- We manufacture a complete line of quality products
- Drop us a line
- It all starts with an entirely new line of
- The most complete line of high quality products
- Proud to present a complete line of
- Be first in line
- The lean, sleek lines of
- The latest in a long, proud line of
- Helping you hold the line on
- A full line of products to let you make better use of
- It's time you discovered the full line of

*See also:* **CHOICE**

**LINK**
- Provides the missing link
- Your chance to link up with
- Links you quickly to

*See also:* **CONNECT**

**LIQUIDATION**
- Bankruptcy liquidation
- Don't miss our big liquidation sale
- Everything is in liquidation

*See also:* **SALE**

**LISTEN**
- We do it by listening carefully to your needs
- Listen every day for news of
- Actually listens to you
- We're listening every day
- You talk, we listen
- We listen to you and then we act

*See also:* **HEAR**

**LITTLE**
- A little or a lot, you do the choosing
- All this for as little as
- Giving you just that little bit more
- A little goes a long way

**Little:** small, tiny, teensy, pint-size, wee, mini, short, itty-bitty, itsy-bitsy, peewee, baby, bantam, child size, toy, lightweight, petite, dainty, slender, slim, thin, skinny, midge, miniature, minute, atomic, infinitesimal, microscopic, brief, abbreviated, rarely, seldom, infrequently, snip, scrap, trifle, iota, modicum, smidgen, pinch, dash, tad

## LIVE
- It doesn't matter where you live
- Give so that others may live
- Makes it a whole lot easier to live with

*See also:* **ACCOMMODATION**

## LOAD
- Taking the load off your shoulders onto ours
- Fully loaded at a great price
- When the load is just too much
- Now don't have to carry the whole load by yourself

*See also:* **LOAD**

## LOCAL
- Buy products made locally
- Look what these local businesses are offering you
- Now one of our local stores can provide

*See also:* **DOMESTIC**

## LOCATION
- A friendly but upscale location
- A prime location for
- A wide range of products and services available at one convenient location
- Combining an excellent location with
- Watch for our new location to serve you
- Great savings at three convenient locations
- Check your phone book for the location nearest you
- Check the white or yellow pages of your phone book for the location nearest you
- At one location only
- Now at a convenient new location just round the corner from you
- Selected as the finest location for

*See also:* **PLACE**

## LOCK
- So you don't find yourself locked out of

- Locks in vital goodness
- Our door is never locked
- We have a lock on value

## LOOK

- Take a second look at
- Take a real close look at
- You'll never look twice at anything else
- Look for them in better stores nationwide
- Look for these terrific savings and buys throughout the store
- This season's most wanted look
- Look less forbidding
- Look to us for value
- Take a closer look
- Just look around you
- Two ways to look at
- Create the look you desire
- Great looks every day
- Worth looking into
- Also, be sure to look for our
- You don't have to look any further than
- Look no further
- Sure to have just what you're looking for
- Get the right look at the right price
- Look one way, change it the next
- They'll always know how good you look
- You look your best when
- A look defined by you
- You'll have a look that's very real
- The look of the moment
- The winning look is all about style
- Looking better is only part of it
- Looking smart is easy when
- Fun colors, fun looks
- You'll see the latest looks for
- Great looks at great prices
- Somebody to look up to
- All the hottest looks
- We invite you to take a look
- Take a look at the endless possibilities of
- Look for more new products
- Take a good second look at
- So you can create whatever look you want
- Accentuate your look

- Look forward to looking better
- We look forward to seeing you
- Just can't resist the urge to take a closer look
- Made to give that professional look
- The sleek new looks feel right
- Looks aren't everything
- Look good while you do it
- A naturally beautiful look
- The look and feel of genuine
- Looks are everything

*See also:* **APPEARANCE, ASPECT, SEE, SEARCH**

**LOSE**
- There's no way you can lose
- You just can't lose when you shop at
- Lose the blahs, come to us

*See also:* **END, FINISH**

**LOVE**
- There are many things to love about
- But you'll love the very look of it
- For those of you who really love life
- Improve your love life
- You love it, it loves you
- For when love blossoms
- Gotta love the

**Love:** affection, fondness, warmth, cherishing, adoration, devotion, liking, adulation, esteem regard, attachment, regard, closeness, intimacy, passion, fancy, infatuation, concern, sympathy, caring, amity, concord, harmony, accord, relish, savor, enjoy, long for

*See also:* **DESIRE, EMOTION, FEELING, PASSION, WISH, WANT**

**LUXURY**
- The finest luxury offer
- A benchmark of our commitment to classic luxury and sophistication
- Looking for luxury and savings
- A long list of thoughtfully provided luxuries
- Offers a full measure of luxury and comfort
- A whole new level of luxury

**Luxury:** luxuriousness, luxe, sumptuousness, lavishness, opulence, splendor, abundance, profuseness, excessiveness, indulgence, ease, easy street, well-being, sufficiency, bed of roses, wealth, affluence, richness,

epicureanism, sybaritism, hedonism, voluptuousness, sensuality, high
living, *dolce vita*, pleasure, enjoyment, delight, extravagance, refinement
*See also:* **ENJOYMENT, RICH, PLEASURE, WEALTH**

## MACHINE
- More machine for your money
- People have often described us as a well-oiled machine
- Thrill to a magnificent machine

## MADE
- Tell them you made it yourself
- You've got it made
- Better made, better price
*See also:* **BUILT**

## MADNESS
- Midnight madness
- Super special madness
- Inventory madness give you unbelievable prices
*See also:* **FEELING**

## MAGIC
- It seems like magic but its good old fashioned hard work
- Magic moments have a way of happening here
- Do you believe in magic
- Makes you believe in magic every day
- There's always something magical about seeing

## MAILBOX
- Look for it in your mailbox
- Look for upcoming issues in your mailbox
- As close as your mailbox
- A whole new world in your mailbox
- Just open your mailbox and find

## MAINSTREAM
- Now gaining a mainstream following
- Challenging the mainstream
- A far-out idea now entering the mainstream

## MAINTENANCE
- Easy maintenance
- Lowest maintenance of all

- And it's all maintenance free
- Which means it's extremely low-maintenance
- You can do a little preventative maintenance

**Maintenance:** preservation, upkeep

## MAKE

- Everything we make is now available a great prices
- You can make as much as
- We stand behind everything we make
- Has the makings of something big

*See also:* **BUILD, CREATE**

## MAKER

- Makers of fine products for five decades
- Brought to you by the makers of
- For years, the makers of the very best products

*See also:* **MANUFACTURER**

## MANAGE

- Helps you manage your time and your schedule
- Just when you're wondering how you'll manage
- Helping you manage your most valuable asset

*See also:* **AFFORD, CONTROL**

## MANAGEMENT

- Achieved through careful management
- Now under the new ownership and management of
- Our management team personally meets with

*See also:* **GUIDE, GUIDANCE**

## MANDATE

- Our mandate is to please you
- Your confidence is our mandate to serve your needs
- You've given us a mandate to
- For years, our mandate has been to

## MANUFACTURER

- Buy direct from the manufacturer
- Manufacturer's suggested retail prices
- Direct from the manufacturer
- Quality begins with the manufacturer

*See also:* **FACTORY, MAKER**

## MARKET
- If you're in the market for
- You can cash in on a vast, untapped market
- Successful in a very exciting market
- If you're in the market for excellence
- Heralding our entry into the market
- The best value on the market
- Reach your goal in an increasingly demanding market
- The market is hot
- Judging from our number one market share
- Best on the market

**Market:** marketplace, mart, exchange, trading center, shopping center, commercial resort, mall, emporium, supermarket, trade, traffic, sale, transaction, commercialism, jobbing, brokerage, truck, dealing, barter, negotiating, husting, quotation, appraisal

*See also:* **BARGAIN, MONEY, PRICE, SELL**

## MARKETING
- A marketing giant at your service
- Put our guaranteed marketing plan to work for you
- Join us in marketing this product across the country
- A marketing team outclassing all others

## MATCH
- You get a better match by
- Mix and match with joyous abandon
- The perfect match for you
- We can help you find the right match
- Matching as closely as possible
- We're the matchmakers

*See also:* **PAIR**

## MATERIAL
- Quality materials at exceptional prices
- Utilizing only the very best materials
- The finest of materials goes into making

*See also:* **STUFF**

## MEAN
- What does this mean for you
- Gives new meaning to
- Providing a safe, clean, efficient means of

*See also:* **UNDERSTANDING, WAY**

153

## MEET
- Come in and meet the whole team
- A wonderful meeting place
- A meeting of great minds
- We look forward to meeting with you to discuss

*See also:* **VISIT**

## MEMBER
- You are a valued member of our client group
- The easy way to become a member
- You become an instant member when you buy
- All the advantages of being a member are yours

*See also:* **PARTNER**

## MEMBERSHIP
- Membership is absolutely free
- Applications and membership cards available to for immediate access to the program
- A lifetime membership is an added bonus
- Your membership is highly valued

*See also:* **PARTNERSHIP**

## MEMORY
- Far more than just a beautiful memory
- Memories are made of this
- Share special memories
- Helping you build a precious memory

*See also:* **MEMORY, REMIND**

## MERCHANDISE
- For quality merchandise, we are unequalled
- A wide selection of merchandise throughout the entire store
- Merchandise may vary by store
- Please touch the merchandise
- Top quality merchandise at bargain prices

**Merchandise:** goods, commodities, stock, stock in trade, vendibles, produce, staples, supplies, dry goods, yard goods, cargo, shipment
*See also:* **INVENTORY, STOCK**

## MESSAGE
- A product with a message
- We want you to get the message
- Our message to you is a pretty exciting one

- A golden opportunity to get your message out there
- Lets you rush messages anywhere

*See also:* **COMMUNICATION**

**METHOD**

- Others have succeeded quickly using this exact method
- There's still the tried and true method of
- We have developed the best method for
- Using only the most modern methods

*See also:* **PROCESS, WAY**

**MIND**

- It's a glorious state of mind
- When you've got one thing on your mind
- Comes with built-in peace if mind
- Take your mind off other matters
- We take everything off your mind
- Mind power is best
- Where designing minds meet
- You should make up your own mind about
- Tomorrow's finest minds are right here
- Bright minds at your service

**MINIMIZE**

- Really helps to minimize
- Minimizing the risks and maximizing results
- When you want to minimize

*See also:* **LESS, REDUCE**

**MINUTE**

- It takes only a minute to find out how
- Take a minute right now to
- Just minutes away

*See also:* **INSTANT, MOMENT**

**MIRACLE**

- Everyone said only a miracle could
- An amazing miracle you've been waiting for all your life
- Some call it a miracle
- Now, the miracle of
- Thanks to the miracle of

**Miracle:** wonder, marvel, phenomenon, wonderwork, prodigy, curiosity, spectacle, portent, rarity

## MIRROR
- Now look in the mirror and see the change
- You only have to consult your mirror to see the difference
- Your mirror will tell you the truth

## MISS
- This is not a hit or miss
- Don't miss out on
- You're missing out on something great
- Don't miss a minute of it
- You don't know what you're missing until you
- Look at what you're missing

*See also:* **OUT**

## MISSION
- Everything we do is part of our mission to improve the world around us and help more people to
- Gain the ability to focus on your mission
- Our sole mission has always been

*See also:* **AIM, GOAL**

## MISTAKE
- Make no mistake about how good we are
- Don't worry if you made a mistake
- It would be hard to make mistake if you tried
- No more expensive mistakes

## MIX
- No mixing required
- Mix and match
- Now here's a clever way to really stir up the mix
- Really mixes it up
- Creating a  really nice mix of

*See also:* **BLEND**

## MODEL
- All major makes and models available
- Each is a working model of
- Have developed a model whereby

*See also:* **EXAMPLE, PROTOTYPE**

## MODERN
- Make a major modern impact

- Join the modern world with
- Using the most modern methods to
- Turn it into the most modern in

## MOMENT

- Never a dull moment with
- Relive the moment again and again
- Shining moments in
- At a moment like this
- Life is full of such special moments
- Make this moment golden
- A defining moment in
- Take a moment right now to call for details

*See also:* **INSTANT, MINUTE**

## MONEY

- There's big money to be made
- Are you saving enough money
- How to get more for your money
- Helping you save time and money
- And, of course, you want real value for your money
- Has a healthy respect for money
- Money can flow out as easily as it flows in
- Earning more money than ever before
- Making your money work harder for you
- When you want to save money
- Don't you think it's time to save some money
- Committed to saving you money
- Send no money now
- The best for your money anywhere
- Save money, make money
- You'll be amazed at how much further your money will go
- Ask about our no-money-down option
- Watch your money
- It's a money machine
- Helping your money grow over the long term
- Saves you money every day
- Save your money the easy way
- When you want to save money
- Now that's easy money
- Offering you the finest money can buy at an affordable price
- Now, make all the money you need
- Money will roll in fast

157

- Gets more spendable money into your hands
- Make money the easy way
- We'll show you how to save more money
- Make big money with our simple plan
- Solve all your money problems
- Start making money right away with
- You can make this money with very little investment

**Money:** medium of exchange, standard of value, note, cash, cold hard cash, legal tender, greenbacks, coin, change, chickenfeed, folding money, almighty dollar, dough, moolah, mazuma, bread, loot, do-re-mi, gravy, wampum, bucks, mint, boodle, bundle, bill, capaital, funds

*See also:* **CASH, DOLLAR, FINANCE, INVEST, INVESTMENT**


## MONITOR
- Now you can monitor results instantly
- Designed to closely monitor
- We monitor you long after you've

*See also:* **SEE, WATCH**


## MONTH
- Deal of the month
- This month only
- This is savings month at
- Don't pay for six months


## MOOD
- Puts you in the mood for
- Reflects your every mood
- Are you in the mood for savings
- Celebrate all of your moods

*See also:* **EMOTION, FEELING**


## MORE
- For whole lot more
- Expect to get a lot more than you pay for
- And start getting more out of your
- To find out more about any of our advanced
- More is better
- More is definitely more
- Need we say more
- To find out more about the new
- More than just a
- More for less

- Expect more from our store
- No more when these go
- Get more of the things you need
- Count on us for more
- Gives you more everyday
- We came up with more
- More please
- If it means more to you than something just to
- More than just
- Able to do more with less
- More than any other
- Made for a whole lot more than
- Giving you all this and more

**More:** additional, extra, plus, supplemental, supplementary, spare, fresh, new, added, addition, increment, increase, adjunct, again
*See also:* **EXTRA, INCREASE**

## MORNING

- Jump start your morning with
- A morning sort of thing
- A new morning for you

*See also:* **BEGINNING, DAWN, START**

## MOST

- When it comes to making the most of
- The most for the least
- That gets the most out of
- Squeezing the most from every
- Showing you how to get the most from your
- Make the most of
- Get the most for yourself out of

**Most:** greatest, largest, utmost, ultra, extreme, maximum, farthest, furthest, summit, ceiling apex, pinnacle, climax
*See also:* **EXTREME**

## MOVE

- Gets things moving fast
- The wisest move you'll ever make
- The smartest move you could make
- Get a move on
- Make your move today
- It's your move
- Make the right move now

- The right move at the right time
- Can get you moving again
- Every move you make will be a success
- The best move you ever made
- Why it's the right move for you

*See also:* **ACTION, ACTIVITY, CHOICE**

## MUSCLE

- Easy, affordable ways to build marketing muscle
- We've added considerably more muscle
- Put some muscle into your

*See also:* **POWER, STRENGTH, STRONG**

## MUST

- A must for anyone who contemplates
- A must for those wanting to make it as independent entrepreneurs
- They're definitely must-haves
- It's a must for anyone planning to
- An absolute must

**Must:** necessity, requirement, need, prerequisite, essential

*See also:* **ESSENTIAL, NEED**

## MYSTERY

- Taking the mystery out of
- Still remains a mystery
- Thrill to the mystery of
- Do you crave that touch of mystery

*See also:* **SECRET**

## NAME

- The best place to promote our name
- You'll see how the business got its name
- The most recognized name in
- Most trusted name in
- Just to name a few
- From the name you trust for quality
- No other name is so trusted
- A name you can trust
- Everyone loves to see their own name
- Certain names register better than others
- Our name registers better
- The number one name in
- A name that is accepted by

- Remember the name
- It won't be the last time you hear this name
- More name recognition than ever
- It's already got you name on it
- Looking for names you can trust
- Taking on some of the biggest names in the industry

*See also:* **REPUTATION**

## NATURAL

- For a smooth, natural look
- A natural high
- Looking your best, naturally
- It's the natural thing to do
- Only natural that
- Made of all-natural materials for your comfort
- What a natural
- A great natural way to promote
- Making it the natural center for
- So natural, in fact, that
- Naturally, it's the best

*See also:* **ENVIRONMENTAL**

## NATURE

- Discover the true nature of
- Experience the power of nature
- Nature's most valuable gift to us is
- Only nature could inspire so perfect a
- The way nature intended
- Back to nature the easy way

*See also:* **EARTH, ENVIRONMENT**

## NEED

- This is what you need
- What you may need the most is
- We have everything you need to
- We have what you need most right now
- Needed on a daily basis
- You don't need special equipment or an office
- It will give you whatever you need to
- That's all you need to
- We designed it to meet the needs of
- The answer to all your needs and more
- Tailored to your very special needs

- To better identify and respond to your needs
- Committed to meeting the unique needs of
- Our products are designed to meet all of your needs
- We cover all your needs
- Save on everyday needs
- Finding services to fill your unique needs
- As we continue to meet your ever increasing needs
- Addresses your unrecognized needs
- Depending on your needs
- With us, your needs always come first
- After careful study of your needs

**Need:** demand, requirement, necessity, requisite, obligation, charge, duty, essential, indispensability, shortcoming, urgency, desire, hope for, desire, crave, yearn for, long for, want, wish, require
*See also:* **DESIRE, ESSENTIAL, WANT, WISH**

## NEIGHBORHOOD
- Do it without even leaving your neighborhood
- Close to neighborhood shopping
- Right in your neighborhood
- Your neighborhood center for

*See also:* **LOCAL**

## NEIGHBOR
- We want to be your best neighbor
- Offering special prices for our neighbors
- What your neighbors are saying
- Meet your new neighbors

*See also:* **FRIEND**

## NETWORK
- A network that grows with you
- Support for your entire network
- Delivering more on your network
- A network of more than
- A network of people at your command
- Become part of the network by filling in the enclosed reply form
- The most extensive network available today
- Part of a worldwide network
- Nobody knows networks like we do

## NEVER
- Will never be the same again

162

- There's never been anything like this
- You've never seen an offer like this before

**NEW**
- Also new are
- Get the amazing new
- Look what's new
- Something new in the business of
- The brand new product you want
- A sensational new feeling
- Here's all the new stuff
- The newest and the best
- The shock of the new
- Why buy new
- Introducing the all-new
- Gets you into a brand new product fast
- Can allow you to move up to a new product more frequently
- New this year
- New on the market

New: modern, late, recent, advanced, contemporary, topical, twenty-first century, present-day, hot, hot off the press, abreast of the times, up-to-the-minute, up-to-date, spanking, brand new, mint condition, late-model, newly arrived, futuristic, revolutionary, ahead of its time, far out, new-fangled, pristine, fresh, smart, current, hip, fashionable, stylish, all the rage, the latest thing, novel, original, untried, experimental
*See also:* **BEGINNING, FRESH, MODERN, START**

**NEWS**
- News that could have a big impact on your
- Keeping pace with the latest news
- What's the news
- The good news is
- Surprising news revealed inside
- Getting the news to you instantly
- The really good news is
- Good news for everybody
- Terrific news about
- I have some great news for you
- Here's yet more wonderful news
*See also:* **COMMUNICATION, INFORMATION**

**NICE**
- Doubly nice for

163

- The very nicest
- Doing nice things for nice people like you
- A very nice touch is
- The nicest thing you can do for yourself right now
- What nicer way to

**Nice:** agreeable, pleasant, attractive, winning, winsome, delightful, likable, cheering, amiable, friendly, amusing, cordial, genial, charming, gracious, generous, sympathetic, understanding, gratifying, pleasing, pleasurable, good, enjoyable, satisfactory, proper, suitable, appropriate, decent, decorous, precise, accurate, detailed, flawless, scrupulous, careful, great, dandy, crackerjack
*See also:* **ENJOYMENT, PLEASURE**

## NICHE
- Has captured a specialized niche
- Niche marketing is coming into its own
- Now that you've found your niche
- Move to a better niche
*See also:* **LOCATION**

## NORMAL
- Gets your life back to normal
- Nothing could be more normal than
- Excellence is just normal for us
- Will not disrupt your normal activities

## NOTE
- We also took care to note
- People are sitting up and taking note
- Make a note to
- One of the most noted
- Has just issued several noteworthy
*See also:* **NOTICE, SEE**

## NOTHING
- Nothing does it better than
- Nothing like the old way of doing things
- There's absolutely nothing like it
- We hold nothing back
- You ain't seen nothing yet
- There's nothing else as good
- Nothing remains the same

**NOTICE**
- A special notice to all
- Serving notice that the best is here
- Make them sit up and take notice
- Everyone will notice when you

*See also:* **NOTE, SEE**

**NOTION**
- Puts to rest the notion that
- Someday, should you take a notion to
- A truly splendid notion that deserves attention

*See also:* **CONCEPT, IDEA**

**NOW**
- When now actually means now
- Speaking of right now
- Do it now
- Now is the time to
- It's now or never
- There's no time better than now to
- Now you see it , now you don't
- Now, for a short time only, available at

**Now:** immediately, at once, instantly, at present, at this time, right now, just now, nowadays, right away, straightaway, without delay, soon, presently, promptly, instantly, forthwith, directly

*See also:* **ALREADY, INSTANT**

**NUMBER**
- This little number is strictly for the daring
- You've got our number
- We've got your number
- A smart little number going places fast
- Our number is in the book
- Go ahead, check out the numbers
- The numbers don't lie
- Not just a numbers game

**NUTS**
- You'll go nuts for
- Your friends might think you're a little nuts, but
- Getting right down to the nuts and bolts of it
- Watch them going nuts over your brand new

## OASIS

- A hidden oasis of rare and wondrous beauty
- Come to an oasis of pleasure
- A quiet little oasis in the midst of the hurly burly

## OBJECTIVE

- Truly essential to achieving your long-term objectives
- If your objective is to improve
- Our biggest objective is to ensure your satisfaction

*See also:* **AIM, GOAL, MISSION**

## OBLIGATION

- And you are assured, at no obligation
- No obligation to you now or ever
- Call today for a no obligation demonstration
- Taking care of your obligations can sometimes be difficult

*See also:* **PRESSURE**

## OFFER

- Limited time offer
- We are pleased to offer our customers a wide range of
- Take advantage of this free trial offer
- We're happy to oblige by offering new
- One cool offer for one cool customer–you
- Incredible offer you can't afford to miss
- Special designer offer
- Doorcrasher offer
- In-store bonus offer
- Cannot be combined with any other offer
- Some specified items not included in this offer
- This great offer ends soon
- You two can take advantage of this offer
- Incredible one-time offers
- On special offer for this week only
- Offers much more than just
- Free trial offer
- Take advantage of this unique offer
- Simply an offer no one can refuse
- Offers something that's been sorely missing in
- Always has more to offer
- An exclusive offering of
- The offerings are spectacular
- Plus, you can save even more with these additional offers

166

- These special offers are exclusive to
- Offers available to our valued retail customers only

*See also:* **SALE, SAVINGS**

## ONE

- There's only leader in this field
- The one and only
- Right away, you know it's the one for you
- This is one magnificent product

## ONE-STOP

- Providing one-stop service
- The result is one-stop shopping
- When you want one-stop convenience, come to us
- All at a one-stop service center

*See also:* **CONVENIENCE**

## ONLY

- Only at these outlets
- The only product in existence that
- Only here can you find your dream
- Your only consideration should be

*See also:* **EXCLUSIVE**

## OPEN

- Open up to value
- Always open to new ideas
- Open more hours than our competitors

## OPENING

- Our grand opening continues with
- Grand opening full of savings for you
- Incredible savings, free gifts and prizes to celebrate the opening of
- Thrilled to be opening our biggest

*See also:* **BEGINNING, START**

## OPERATE

- Easy to operate
- Allows you to operate even further afield
- All operating instructions included
- If this is how you operate, take a look at our product

*See also:* **FUNCTION, USE**

## OPINION

- We care about your opinion
- In our opinion, the best
- Changing opinions all across the country
- We have a different opinion of value

*See also:* **BELIEF, CONCEPT, FEELING, IDEA, PHILOSOPHY, PRINCIPLE**

## OPPORTUNITY

- Don't let this exciting and profitable opportunity pass you by
- The result is a unique an financially powerful opportunity
- Nothing to lose, everything to gain by learning about this brand new and unique opportunity
- Offering you this splendid opportunity for success
- Providing a tremendous opportunity for your whole family to
- Only those who realize this golden opportunity is waiting
- An opportunity to build a truly independent
- Knock on opportunity's door today
- Opportunity knocks but once
- Don't miss this glorious opportunity to
- This is your best opportunity to
- Offering you the perfect opportunity to stop and take advantage of
- Once-in-a-lifetime opportunity
- Giving you the optimal opportunity to enjoy
- Offering visits and residents alike an opportunity to view
- A red-hot opportunity only available here
- Don't let the opportunity fly away
- To find out more about the opportunity of
- Opportunities abound
- International opportunities available
- Allows you more opportunities for
- Crank up the opportunities to
- Business opportunities opening up all over
- Making opportunities easier and easier to identify

**Opportunity:** accident, serendipity, possibility, prospect, opening, likelihood, occasion, time, right occasion, favorable moment, good time, golden chance, contingency, chance, right circumstances, once-in-a-lifetime chance, break, stroke of luck, twist of fate, turn of events
*See also:* **CHANCE, OPTION**

## OPTION

- If you wish to take advantage of this option
- You also have the option to

- Giving you the option to
- Take a look at all these options
- Explore interconnected options
- More options than you ever imagined possible
- You've got a lot of options to consider
- As you examine the options more closely
- Come to us for an even bigger menu of options
- Now you have more options
- There's plenty of sophisticated options around

*See also:* **CHANCE, CHOICE, CHOOSE, OPPORTUNITY**

## ORDER

- Order today and see
- Order right away and find out how easy it is to
- Order yours direct from
- Ordering is so simple
- Return the order card and write to
- Ask about our special order items
- We can special order virtually everything
- All special order items
- May we take your order
- Complete and mail the attached order form
- Everything is made to order
- Order at your store's customer service desk
- Order today for fastest service
- Please order today
- It's so easy to order

*See also:* **BUY, PURCHASE, SELL, SALE**

## ORDINARY

- Not your ordinary product
- This is no ordinary product
- Anything but ordinary
- Doesn't look or feel like ordinary items
- Go beyond ordinary

## ORIGINAL

- The originals just got stronger
- If you're an original, you need us
- The original product, not an imitation
- Come to the original source of

*See also:* **UNIQUE**

## OTHER
- Accept no other
- There just isn't any other that can perform this well
- Working with others is all-important to us
- What it's done for others, it can do for you
- Wait until you've seen how it has helped others

*See also:* **ALTERNATIVE**

## OUT
- Don't be left out
- Find out what's in, what's out
- Do you find yourself out in the cold

*See also:* **MISS**

## OUTDOORS
- Indoors or outdoors, you can use it everywhere
- Celebrate the great outdoors
- Outdoor fun for the whole family
- Spend more time outdoors with

## OUTLET
- Value and quality at outlet prices
- Coming soon to an outlet near you
- Factory outlet
- The biggest outlet yet

*See also:* **FACTORY, STORE**

## OUTLOOK
- Always a fresh outlook
- Time for a change of outlook
- It all depends on your outlook

*See also:* **FEELING, IDEA, VIEW**

## OUTPERFORM
- Will greatly outperform any other
- We manage to outperform
- Outperforms conventional products three to one

## OWE
- You owe it to yourself to
- You'll be surprised at how little you owe
- You won't find yourself owing huge amounts

*See also:* **DESERVE, DUE**

## OWN
- Don't miss this chance for you to own your own
- You'll be proud to call your own
- Own your own territory
- Locally owned and operated by
- Easy to own, easy to use
- You can own it today
- For your very own

*See also:* **BUY, PURCHASE**

## OWNER
- Helping you feel more like an owner
- We work hard to take good care of our owners
- Once you become an owner, you'll never again go back to leasing
- More proud owners because of us

## OWNERSHIP
- Experience the pride of ownership
- Providing a lower cost of ownership
- Time to take ownership of your future

## PACE
- The pace is picking up
- You set the pace
- At whatever pace you want
- Keeping up with your pace

*See also:* **RATE, SPEED**

## PACESETTER
- If you're a pacesetter
- We're the pacesetter for
- Keeping up with the pacesetters

## PACK
- Packed with savings
- Always ahead of the pack
- Packed with exciting
- Packing in more value for less money

## PACKAGE
- Good things come in small packages
- After you've read our detailed information package
- A part of your service package

- This excellent package features
- Means so much more when it's packaged beautifully
- So nicely packaged and presented
- Choosing the best package for you

*See also:* **KIT**

## PAINLESS

- Looking for a painless way to
- Now borrowing money is completely painless
- Not just painless, but pleasant as well

## PAIR

- Pair the pieces with everything
- The power pair
- Pair up with us and see
- Get the pair for the price of one

*See also:* **DOUBLE**

## PALATE

- Sure to delight any palate
- Even the most finicky palate will be pleased
- Created to appeal to your palate
- Discriminating palates all over the country enjoy

*See also:* **TASTE**

## PAMPER

- Sit back, be pampered, and watch the world go by
- In pampering you, no detail has been overlooked
- Pampering you with relaxing comfort
- Pamper yourself
- Pamper your family with love and attention
- A little romantic pampering is definitely in order
- You've never been pampered like this

*See also:* **CARE**

## PARADISE

- A paradise awaits you
- Cruising paradise is now so easy
- Shoppers' paradise
- Enjoy a little touch of paradise
- You'll think you've found paradise

*See also:* **OASIS**

## PART

- Always a part of the landscape
- Part of who we are
- And now you can be part of it all
- We want you to be part of it
- Look the part for less
- Something you'll never have to part with
- We're excited to be part of

## PARTICIPATE

- Hundreds of participating items
- Visit your nearest participating store or dealer
- Here's how you can participate
- The best way to participate is
- Look what you get when you participate in
- The whole neighborhood is participating

*See also:* **JOIN**

## PARTNER

- When you're looking for a partner to
- Your partner in success
- Partners you can trust
- In something this important, you need partners you can rely upon

*See also:* **MEMBER**

## PARTNERSHIP

- Establishing a solid partnership with you
- Another benefit is the result of our partnership with
- Our ongoing partnership helps you in every way
- A respected partnership for years

*See also:* **MEMBERSHIP**

## PARTY

- Bringing the rest of the world to the party
- We're having a party and you're invited
- Let's have a party tonight
- Join the party
- Brings the party to your home
- This country's largest party

*See also:* **FESTIVE**

## PASS

- You can't pass it up

- Don't pass this one up
- Passing savings value on to you
- Gets more than a passing grade

## PASSION
- Passion wins out
- Join the passion for
- Passion and mental stimulation
- We have a passion for
- Surrender to your passion for

*See also:* **DESIRE, EMOTION, FEELING**

## PATH
- Setting you on the path to successful and fulfilling
- Offers an uncomplicated path to
- The path to financial and personal success
- Setting the path for the rest of your life

*See also:* **METHOD, ROAD, WAY**

## PATIENCE
- Patience goes a long way toward
- Now your patience is about to be rewarded
- Developed with infinite patience and care to detail
- We'll never try your patience with

## PAY
- Nothing else to pay
- Does it pay to wait
- Are you paying too much
- Pay off your investment in less than
- Always pay yourself first
- You pay for only what you use
- Why pay more
- Pay now or pay later, but pay you must
- Don't pay until
- Don't pay for one full year
- Why pay for a costly new
- An easy way to buy now, pay later
- Choose from these easy ways to pay
- Doesn't it feel good to pay less
- Nothing to pay for six months on all our inventory
- Are you paying too much for
- You'll never pay less for

- A way to really make it pay
- Finally paying off for you
- Pays for itself the first time you use it.

**Pay:** compensate, remunerate, reward, recompense, refund, settle, satisfy, liquidate, discharge, clear, honor, square, meet, spend, expend, hand over, shell out, lay out, cough up, ante up, contribute, chip in, advance, yield, return, profit, avail, benefit, help
*See also:* **COST, MONEY, PROFIT, REWARD**

## PAYMENT
- No interest, no payments for twelve months
- One payment plan
- No down payment, no monthly payments
- So you can maintain an affordable payment
- Easy payment plan
- You won't even notice these low payments
- Your payments can be significantly lower
- The affordable payments allow you to

## PEACE
- Here to give you the peace of mind you need
- It's a little extra peace of mind
- When you just want peace and quiet
- Complete comfort and peace of mind
- You'll have peace of mind just knowing
- Providing maximum peace of mind

## PENNY
- Pinching pennies till they holler
- We look after your pennies too
- For just pennies a day, enjoy
- Finally available for pennies
- Just pennies each

## PEOPLE
- We're looking for people like you to
- A service people want
- A service that smart people are willing to pay for
- Charming people make this a hit
- People are all different
- We care about people
- People are our business
- Naturally, its from the people who know about

175

- Everyday people are the best of all
- There to ensure the people you care about are provided for

*See also:* **ANYBODY, CUSTOMER, SHOPPER**

## PERFECT
- Perfect for all your needs
- The search for the perfect
- You always feel perfect in
- That's perfect in every way
- We've spent years perfecting

*See also:* **BEST, IDEAL**

## PERFECTION
- The search for perfection ends here
- The myth of perfection exploded
- The relentless pursuit of perfection
- It all depends on how you view perfection

## PERFORM
- Ready to perform
- Just watch the way it performs
- Able to perform even more services for you
- You will perform better when you have the help of

*See also:* **ACHIEVE, ACCOMPLISH, ACT, DO**

## PERFORMANCE
- For peak performance
- For style and performance in one beautiful package
- Anticipating long-term performance
- Delivers legendary performance
- Unbeatable combination of power and performance
- Three ways to look at performance
- Treat yourself to a command performance
- Advanced performance never stops
- A really sporty performance
- It embodies quality and performance
- Good performance, good economy
- The perfect harmony of inspired performance
- Experience the exhilarating performance of
- For longer performance life
- Performance you can trust down the road
- If you demand the ultimate performance
- With years of peak performance to offer

- Now that same performance can be found in

**Performance:** entertainments, show, drama, representation, spectacle, happening, execution, doing, accomplishment, attainment, completion, realization, achievement, work, deed, feat, act, exploit, enterprise, endeavor, undertaking, task, procedure, production, operation, transaction

*See also:* **ACCOMPLISHMENT, ACHIEVEMENT, JOB, TASK**

## PERK

- Want to perk up your life
- Enjoy one of the perks of
- Watch them perk up when you walk in with

*See also:* **BONUS, REJUVENATE**

## PERSEVERANCE

- A combination of hard work and perseverance
- Your perseverance is finally paying off
- When perseverance really counts

**Perseverance:** endurance, steadfastness, persistence, continuance, patience, stamina, courage, grit, pluck, zeal, ambition, application, tenacity, resolve, determination, decision

## PERSONAL

- The personal touch in everything
- Your choice is a very personal thing
- Personalized, confidential service
- We take excellence very personally

**Personal:** individual, private, secret, close to one's heart, particular, exclusive, especial, special, intimate, familiar, chummy, one-on-one

*See also:* **CONFIDENTIAL, SECRET, SPECIAL**

## PHILOSOPHY

- We have dramatically re-interpreted our philosophy
- A company with a global philosophy
- Working to fit in with your personal philosophy
- Shaped by a daring new philosophy of

*See also:* **AIM, BELIEF, DESIGN, FEELING, GOAL, OPINION, PHILOSOPHY, PLAN, PRINCIPLE, SYSTEM**

## PHONE

- The only cost is the phone call
- As easy as picking up your phone
- Last day to order by phone

- Shop by phone and save time and money
- Please phone for availability
- Visit your local store or shop by phone
- Just pick up the phone and it's yours

*See also:* **CALL, TELEPHONE**

## PICK

- Come in and pick up your windfall
- Fresh picked for maximum freshness
- The pick of the crop
- Simply pick up a product today
- Let us be the one you pick

*See also:* **CHOICE, CHOOSE, DECIDE, SELECT**

## PICTURE

- Think about the big picture
- A critical part of the picture too
- Will stay in the picture for years
- Can you picture it
- Just picture yourself doing this
- Helping you get the picture

*See also:* **VIEW**

## PLACE

- Coming to a place near you
- It seems fitting that the best place in town is ours
- Always a very popular place
- A rather nice place to be
- Always placing you first
- The most charming place to be
- Perhaps no other place evokes such stirring images
- A friendly local place to visit
- You can reach more places from more places
- You'll never feel out of place
- Discover the people and places of

*See also:* **LOCATION**

## PLAN

- A detailed, A to Z plan to
- The plan is great
- It's always best to plan ahead
- You do the planning, we do the work
- It's time for a custom marketing plan

- Start planning today for
- Helping you determine which plan is best
- Make us part of your plans
- To get ahead, you've got to have a plan
- We have a better plan anyone else
- Planning carefully for the future
- Sensible, long-range planning is essential to
- Detailed plans designed for you and you alone
- Your plans tell you how to
- Success is your when you follow these simple plans
- Follow simple, step-by-step plans
- Just follow the plans with their detailed instructions

**Plan:** scheme, arrangement, design, grouping, layout, organization, pattern, configuration, proposal, project, prospect, conception, purpose, view, intent, ambition, intention, hope, aspiration, map, ground plan, model, sketch, draft, chart, look ahead, arrange, line up, work out, schedule, block out, propose, strategize, devise, develop, frame, construct, envision, mastermind, contemplate, outline, draw up, plot, shape, connect, intend

*See also:* **INFORMATION, STORY, STRATEGY, SYSTEM**

**PLAY**
- Something the kids can play with for hours on end
- Would you rather play catch-up
- Are you ready to play
- Play time for everyone
- We don't play around with value
- Make it into child's play
- Play with the best
- Playing around with
- Play to your heart's content

*See also:* **ENJOY, FUN, HAPPY**

**PLAYER**
- We help you look like a player
- Some of the biggest players come to us for
- Now you can be a real player

*See also:* **PARTICIPATE, PARTNER**

**PLEASE**
- You'll be especially pleased with
- Our only goal is to please you
- A decidedly pleasing product

179

- Developed specifically to please you
- Please the whole family with
- We've been pleasing customers for years

*See also:* **GRATIFY, SATISFY**

## PLEASURE

- A product that will keep on giving pleasure
- Blended with the smooth pleasure of a legendary
- The delightfully unsettling pleasure of
- The ultimate pleasure principle
- Discover the pleasures of being free
- Bringing pleasure to everyone
- Alive with pleasure
- What a pleasure to share with
- So many pleasures at your fingertips
- The tempting allure of forbidden pleasures

*See also:* **AMENITY, COMFORT, DESIRE, ENJOY, JOY, NICE**

## PLEDGE

- Our pledge to you has always been
- Keeping the pledge
- We never go back on our pledge
- Making a solemn pledge to you

*See also:* **COMMIT**

## POCKET

- You needn't stretch this month's pocket money
- You don't need deep pockets to buy this product
- Now you can keep more money in your pocket
- Puts savings in your pocket as soon as you walk in the door
- Pocket money right away

*See also:* **SAVE, SAVINGS**

## POCKETBOOK

- Suits everyone's needs and pocketbook
- Goes easy on your pocketbook
- Light on the pocketbook, heavy on value
- Hang onto your pocketbook, here we come

*See also:* **BUDGET, WALLET**

## POINT

- Which, of course, is exactly the point
- This could be the turning point

- People are beginning to get the point
- You've made your point
- The point is big benefits for you

*See also:* **REASON**

## POPULAR

- Has never been more popular
- Once again the most popular item in
- That's why we've become so popular with so many
- One of our most popular items
- Giving you the perennially popular
- Popular, year after year

**Popular:** in demand wanted, desired, favored, in fashion, in vogue, fashionable, stylish, all the rage, *au courant*, well-liked, successful, beloved, easily understood, everyday

*See also:* **DEMAND, DESIRE**

## PORTFOLIO

- Best fits your investment portfolio
- A portfolio of value for you
- Expanding your portfolio in unexpected directions

## POSITION

- Putting you in a great position to
- Uniquely positioned to
- You couldn't be in a better position to
- An excellent  competitive position that translates into

*See also:* **LOCATION, PLACE**

## POSITIVE

- Positively painless for everyone
- Just wait until you see the positive results
- A very positive move for you all round
- Very positive, very popular

*See also:* sure, certain, sound, definite, unequivocal, categorical, indisputable, confident, assured, real, veritable, optimistic, hopeful, cheering, sunny, heartening, inspiring, encouraging, promising, favorable, propitious, profitable, good, affirmative, salutary, genuine, authentic, solid, substantial

*See also:* **SUCCESSFUL**

## POSSIBILITY

- Change it from a possibility to a reality now
- Think of all the possibilities

- Imagine the unlimited possibilities of
- Discover the mind-boggling possibilities of

*See also:* **CHANCE, OPPORTUNITY**

## POSSIBLE

- Now makes it possible for you to
- Suddenly, anything is possible
- Making it possible for the very first time

**Possible:** likely, probable, liable to, odds-on, feasible, workable, doable, practicable, achievable, within reach, attainable, affordable, thinkable, credible, conceivable

## POTENCY

- The highest potency yet
- Increase the potency of
- Have bumped up the potency to the highest levels yet
- Test the potency of

*See also:* **POWER, STRENGTH**

## POTENTIAL

- Helping people achieve their potential
- Leaving you free to reach your full potential
- There is a huge potential for
- All this incredible potential can be yours for only

*See also:* **OPPORTUNITY**

## POWER

- Designed to give you the power to do more
- Puts the power in your hands
- Delivers all the power and flexibility of
- Experience the sheer, exhilarating power of
- Powered by personal style
- Put all this power to work for you
- Feel the surge of power
- Along with increased value power
- Take the restorative powers of

*See also:* **ABILITY, CAPACITY, MUSCLE, STRENGTH, STRONG**

## PRACTICAL

- Tough, bright and practical
- Offering a practical solution to your
- A purely practical decision
- It's what practical people do

- The smartest, most practical thing you can do

*See also:* **USEFUL**

## PREFER

- For those who prefer
- Or, if you prefer
- More people prefer our product than any other
- Most preferred product
- You'll prefer it to all others
- Preferred above all others

*See also:* **CHOOSE, LIKE**

## PREFERENCE

- We're glad to alter our product according to your preference
- Your preference dictates everything we do
- Simply express your preference and the deed is done
- The number one preference is

*See also:* **CHOICE**

## PREMIUM

- The industry calls it premium
- Premium products always on hand just for you
- We put your patronage at a premium
- Premium values for premium customers
- Always at a premium

*See also:* **BEST, FINE, EXCELLENCE, SUPERIOR**

## PRE-OWNED

- Great pre-owned specials
- Pre-owned but still in premium condition
- Get a fine pre-owned product for a fraction of the cost of new
- A great pre-owned item is waiting for you

## PREPARE

- You've got to prepare now for
- Takes only minutes to prepare
- Fully prepared, oven ready
- Helping you prepare for an unpredictable future
- We've spent years preparing for this moment
- Not just well-prepared but tasty too
- Prepare yourself for a savings blowout
- The way is already prepared for you to

**Prepare:** make ready, set up, fix up, lay the groundwork, set the stage,

take steps, warm up, rehearse, practice, whip into shape, tune up, review, go over, outfit, equip, furnish, supply, provide, fit out, rig out, deck out, dream up, brew up, arrange, organize, frame, set up
*See also:* **PROVIDE, READY, SUPPLY**

## PRESENT
- Our company proudly presents
- Presenting the number one, most awaited product
- Makes great presents
- Always present your best side

*See also:* **GIFT, SHOW**

## PRESENTATION
- Dazzling presentation of a brand new
- Our feature presentation
- Come and let us make a presentation to you of
- Excellence and exquisite presentation is reflected in all our services

## PRESERVE
- In addition to preserving your precious things beautifully
- Some things are really worth preserving
- Preserving tradition and respect for

## PRESSURE
- Put some pressure on
- Today, the pressure is building to
- Pressure to squeeze out more productivity than ever before
- If you're feeling the pressure to

*See also:* **OBLIGATION**

## PRESTIGE
- It's not just about prestige
- Do you want the prestige, satisfaction and security of
- Increase your prestige with
- Our prestige is very high in our community
- The most prestigious

## PRETTY
- Has you sitting pretty
- Pretty and popular
- Will save you a pretty penny
- A lot more than just pretty good

*See also:* **BEAUTIFUL**

**PREVIEW**
- Free preview invitation
- You are invited to preview
- Don't miss this rare preview of
- Call for an exclusive preview
- Free preview
- See this special preview

*See also:* **ANTICIPATE, FUTURE**

**PRICE**
- At a price you can afford
- And not only through price
- Offered at a sweeter price
- The lowest price you've ever seen
- Irresistible, especially at this price
- At last, priced right
- No-haggle price
- Non-negotiable bottom line price
- Big in everything but price
- Our best-priced products
- At a price that's too good to pass up
- Three great items at one great price
- Lower priced guaranteed
- Value priced for quick sale
- Unbeatable quality and price
- At an amazing low price
- Everyone has their price
- Our price is just less
- Priced not to cost the shirt off your back
- Lowest price ever
- Price chopper values every day
- Blowout price
- At a price you just can't afford to overlook
- A price you can live with
- A price that's hard to copy
- A truly affordable price
- Low price leader
- Best price, best advice
- Huge price drops this week
- The lowest price is right here
- We'll meet the price and beat it
- Our price guarantee means
- At an uncommonly affordable price

- For a price that won't cut into your
- Listed at a fabulous price
- It's competitively priced at

**Price:** cost, expense, charge, fee, rate, check, tab, bill, payment, hire, rent, fare, toll, tax, levy, duty, assessment, consideration, recompense, remuneration, compensation, outlay, expenditure, value, worth, amount, figure, valuation, appraisal, quotation, demand, asking price, bounty, reward, prize, stipend, consequence, result, loss, cost, damage
*See also:* **BUY, CASH, COST, MONEY, PURCHASE, SAVINGS, VALUE**

## PRICES
- We have the lowest prices
- Where low prices are just the beginning
- Best prices in town
- Everyday low prices made better
- Prices guaranteed until
- At prices you just won't believe
- You'll find all the greatest prices at
- Nobody beats our prices
- Great low prices guaranteed
- Everyday low prices
- Great prices, quality guaranteed
- Amazing miracle prices
- Really really great prices
- Calls for special prices on
- New low prices on
- Prices in effect until
- Heavenly results at down-to-earth prices
- Rock bottom sale prices
- Low low prices that just won't stop
- Everyday low prices made better
- Prices are low today and everyday
- Prices guaranteed until
- Prices will never be lower
- Best prices guaranteed
- A low introductory prices
- Nobody beats our prices
- Prices you can afford
- Putting our prices where our mouth is
- Sale prices in effect until
- Prices will be lots of fun
- New lower prices

- Best prices, superior quality
- For some of the best prices yet
- Has it all—and for low low prices
- The highest quality at the lowest prices
- If we advertise our low low prices, the competition will have a fit
- Excellent prices on
- Sale prices in effect this weekend only
- Low, low prices on
- Lowest prices every day
- Just great prices every day
- Prices will be lots of fun
- At highly competitive prices
- At prices you won't mind paying

*See also:* **PRICE**

## PRICING

- Power pricing for power people
- Competitive pricing at all our locations
- We've put a lot of thought into pricing
- Downright enticing pricing
- And our pricing shows it

*See also:* **COST, PRICE**

## PRIDE

- Take pride in the fine quality of our
- Something you/we do with pride
- Built with pride
- Our staff takes pride in the fine service they provide
- We take great pride in what we create

*See also:* **BOAST, CONFIDENCE, ESTEEM, FEELING, PROUD**

## PRINCIPLE

- The principle behind it is simple
- We stand firmly in the principle that
- Our founding principles remain the same
- Sticking to tried-and-true principles

*See also:* **BASE, FOUNDATION, STANDARD**

## PRIORITY

- What's your priority
- People like yourself are always our highest priority
- We have no other priority
- Always in line with your priorities

**Priority:** urgency, precedence, seniority, rank, preference, primacy, preeminence, superiority, supremacy, importance, consequence
*See also:* **CHOICE**

## PRIVACY
- With complete security and privacy within your own home
- Your privacy is guaranteed
- Offering complete and total privacy
- Protect your privacy with ironclad secrecy

*See also:* **CONFIDENTIAL, SECRET**

## PRO
- Go straight to the pros
- Find out from the pros themselves all about
- What the pros urge you to do
- Let's you perform like a pro
- The name pros trust
- Be treated like a pro

*See also:* **EXPERT, PROFESSIONAL**

## PROBLEM
- No problem
- Not only addresses these problems but
- Now you can solve problems the same way—right in your own home
- Tired of covering up your problem
- You're looking at the end of all your problems
- Helps you solve specific problems
- More than just solving problems in a routine way
- Alert you to your problems

**Problem:** riddle, poser, question, mystery, predicament, quandary, plight, pickle, hornet's nest, difficulty, trouble, affliction, handicap, disadvantage, inconvenience, nuisance, pest, headache, bother, vexation, hassle, annoyance, intractable
*See also:* **CHALLENGE, CONCERN, HASSLE, MYSTERY, QUESTION**

## PROCESS
- We can quickly and easily guide you though the entire process of
- The process of turning your dreams into reality
- An evolutionary process that's a combination of
- Puts you in charge of the whole process

*See also:* **METHOD, WAY**

## PRODUCT

- A valuable product or service that's always in great demand
- Our product is already used by most manufacturers of
- Do you have energy, imagination and a great product
- We make it easier for customers to get hold of our product
- People love our product
- To help you choose the best product
- A product best suited to your needs and lifestyle
- Selected as the most desired product
- Our latest product improvement
- It's products like these that help
- Products you need in the colors you want

*See also:* **SAMPLE**

## PRODUCTIVITY

- Maximizing productivity and minimizing downtime
- Just watch productivity shoot up
- Productivity has increased every year with
- High productivity means savings on

*See also:* **ACTIVITY, MAKE**

## PROFESSIONAL

- Do it like a professional
- A really professional level
- Designed with the professional in mind
- Help you to obtain professional results
- Committed to providing prompt, professional service
- We're listening to the professionals
- Now you can select the industry's most professional company
- Fast, professional service
- Let an experienced professional take care of everything for you
- Give yourself the professional advantage
- You need a professional to help you
- Find out what the professionals are thinking and doing
- Staffed by experienced professionals
- Our professionals believe that serving a client means more than just a lot of talk
- Should only be done by professionals
- Knowledgeable service professionals guarantee expert advice and superior customer service
- Our world-wide team of professionals is waiting to help you to
- Demands the highest degree of professionalism

**Professional:** skilled, knowledgeable, experienced, pro, veteran,

seasoned, trained, adept, dextrous, adroit, accomplished, able, apt, gifted, talented, polished, expert, proficient, masterful, masterly, topnotch, top-flight, crack, best, virtuoso
*See also:* **EXPERT, PRO, SKILL**

## PROFILE
- Giving you a higher profile in
- When you're ready for a higher profile
- Increase your profile where you need it most

*See also:* **RECOGNITION**

## PROFIT
- Translates directly into profit for you
- An opportunity you can profit from immediately
- High profit margins with less effort
- How would you like an even bigger profit
- Profit from inside information
- Your partner in profit
- Everyone can profit from
- Incredible profits can be yours
- Now your profits are your own
- Adds up to profits for you
- How to develop profitable

**Profit:** gain, return, yield, interest, income, revenue, net, bottom line, winnings, proceeds, remuneration, recompense, surplus, excess, gravy, advantage, benefit, help, aid, service, good, efficiency, use, usefulness, furtherance, improvement, betterment
*See also:* **BENEFIT, BOTTOM LINE, BOUNTY, SAVINGS, VALUE**

## PROGRAM
- We tailor our program to meet your specific needs
- We have designed this program specially for you
- Ask about our program to
- We offer a self-starting program
- Examine the entire program to see
- Discover why we offer a complete program
- One of the most comprehensive programs ever introduced
- The diversity of programs available
- Programs to meet your individual performance requirements
- Our most popular, full-featured care program
- Consider the economical, effective programs offered by
- Properly designed programs are the key to controlling

*See also:* **DESIGN, INFORMATION, PLAN, SYSTEM**

## PROGRESS
- We've made great progress to date
- Join the march of progress today
- Riding the leading edge of progress
- Progress has arrived

*See also:* **ADVANCE, CHANGE, FUTURE**

## PROJECT
- For every project, big or small
- Taking care to plan the project in every detail
- We manage and complete the entire project for yu
- Now you can complete your project with
- Our associates can help with your projects
- Plus exciting new projects

## PROMISE
- Deliver on the promise of quality and value every day
- That's a promise we deliver
- Our promise to you
- So much more than just a visionary promise
- Fulfilled the promise that
- No longer just a promise, but a dazzling reality

**Promise:** pledge, assurance, word of honor, vow, oath, declaration, testimony, affirmation, obligation, guarantee, warranty

*See also:* **GUARANTEE, PLEDGE**

## PROMOTE
- Promoting itself as the highest standard in
- There's really only one place to promote
- Rightfully promoting this product as the very best in

**Promote:** encourage, hearten, boost, build up, raise, lift, support, sanction, back, sustain, uphold, hold up, maintain, improve, strengthen, amend, make better, upgrade, help, develop, enrich, enhance, augment, contribute to, benefit, advance, facilitate, foster, nourish, nurture, aid, help, abet, advocate, advertise, introduce, make known

*See also:* **ADVERTISE, BENEFIT, ENHANCE, HELP, RECOMMEND, SELL**

## PROMOTION
- The biggest promotion ever
- As part of our brand new promotion
- Our most exciting promotion of the year
- Take advantage of this huge promotion

- The best value promotion

*See also:* **PROMOTE, SALE**

## PROOF

- Here's proof from people who have succeeded
- Offers solid proof that
- Giving you the proof you need to choose us
- If you need any more proof, just watch
- Simply proof that we're the best

## PROTECT

- Protects beautifully
- Nothing protects better
- Protect yourself and your family
- Nothing else protects your investment quite as well
- Protect it with
- To preserve and protect
- Now you'll be fully protected

## PROTECTION

- A professional level of protection
- There's no better protection than
- For the protection you've been looking for
- The protection you need to
- For added protection
- When you need fast protection against
- Provides quality protection for
- This research has led to one of the most powerful protection programs
- And you gain the added protection of
- Total body protection
- For more concentrated protection
- Delivers excellent protection
- Giving you all-season protection
- Take protection with you wherever you go
- In short, if you still don't have proper protection
- Protection against the inevitable
- Offering the highest level of protection possible

**Protection:** preservation, conservation, care, safekeeping, maintenance, upkeep, safety, security, defence, guard, safeguard, shield, bulwark, barrier, wall, cover, screen, sanctuary, asylum, safety zone, shelter, refuge, haven, harbor, precaution, preventative measure, insurance

*See also:* **SAVE**

**PROTOTYPE**
- Developing better prototypes in shorter time
- The very prototype of
- Springing from the most advanced prototype ever to

*See also:* **BEGINNING, MODEL, START**

**PROUD**
- Proud to help keep it that way
- You'll be proud of what you're doing
- You have every reason to be proud
- As much as we are proud of our service and product
- Make them proud of you
- Always proud to serve your every need
- That's why we're so proud of

*See also:* **BOAST, CONFIDENCE, PRIDE**

**PROVE**
- Prove it yourself
- Let us prove to you what our professionals can do
- Over and over again, our customers prove that
- Now you can prove conclusively that our product is better

*See also:* **TEST**

**PROVEN**
- We've proven it with quality
- The proven one
- Proven time and time again
- One of nature's most proven

**PROVIDE**
- Always pleased to provide
- Providing the finest service to valued customers like you
- We can provide you with instant
- Taking care to always provide the best

**Provide:** furnish, supply, contribute, accommodate, equip, outfit, afford, yield, produce, present, serve, give, bestow, endow

*See also:* **GIVE, SERVE, SUPPLY**

**PROVIDER**
- The leading provider of
- Welcome to the world's premier provider of high-quality
- The most qualified provider in business today

*See also:* **SUPPLIER**

## PROVING GROUND
- Think of it as a proving ground for
- A proving ground for the future
- Has long been a proving ground for the toughest

*See also:* **PROVE, TEST**

## PUNCH
- More punch than ever
- Just punch out this number
- The punch delivered in everything from
- Pumped up to give it some punch
- Adds some real punch to your
- Punched-up value

*See also:* **IMPACT, STRENGTH**

## PURCHASE
- Call this number now to purchase
- With every purchase you make
- Purchasing our products is convenient and secure
- Free with your every purchase of
- Take advantage of this special purchase
- A huge special purchase on
- Now you can purchase it so easily
- Actually available to you for purchase
- Save on all your purchases

*See also:* **BUY, OFFER, SALE**

## PURPOSE
- We have products for every purpose
- Designed with a purpose
- Our purpose is to please you
- Have never wavered from our set purpose of

*See also:* **AIM, FUNCTION, GOAL, MISSION**

## PURVEYOR
- The exclusive purveyor of
- For a hundred years, purveyors of fine products
- Now your local purveyor of
- Your neighborhood purveyor will be glad to help you

*See also:* **PROVIDER, SELLER, SUPPLIER**

## QUALIFY
- Find out if you qualify at

- Listen to discover whether or not you qualify
- You qualify instantly for
- Listen to find out if you qualify
- As one of an exclusive few qualified to
- You may be already qualified for

## QUALITY

- The quality you want at the price you need
- Providing you with the best quality at great prices
- The ultimate in quality
- Now offering a wide range of quality products
- Quality you can trust at the nation's lowest price
- Quality you can rely upon
- Exudes quality in every respect
- Preferring quality over quantity
- Quality guaranteed
- Experience the difference quality makes
- Quality manufactured from
- Quality from start to finish
- Quality products at warehouse prices
- We have all the top quality products you're looking for
- Because quality always takes precedence
- You'll love the homemade quality of
- Quality is a non-negotiable concept
- Best quality ever
- Our concern for quality can be seen in our customer service
- Exceptional quality at an amazing low price
- Compare our quality and price anywhere
- Quality and value are guaranteed
- Unbeatable quality and price
- Quality you can trust at the country's lowest prices
- Committed to quality, value selection and service
- Full line of quality
- Quality you can trust
- You'll love the quality
- Finest quality ever
- Enables us to provide you with a top quality product
- Handcrafted quality at factory prices
- Far less than what you would expect to pay for this great quality
- Start at an unprecedented-for-quality price of just
- For consistent quality insist upon the best
- Now you find all the same qualities in our exciting new

**Quality:** characteristic, property, attribute, distinction, note, cachet,

feature, trait, virtue, quirk, nature, kind, grade, sort, style, particular, element, personality, disposition, tendency, bias, leaning, penchant, predisposition, innate, endowment, gift, talent, genius, faculty, knack, badge, earmark, trademark, forte, strong point, selling point, merit, advantage, superiority, excellence, class, eminence, preeminence, greatness, nobility, fineness, worth, value, supremacy, perfection, status, standing, notability, elite, privilege
*See also:* **BEST, EXCELLENCE, NATURE, VALUE**

## QUANTITY
- Always putting quality before quantity
- Limited quantities available
- Due to anticipated high demand, quantities will be limited to
- While quantities last

**Quantity:** amount, substance, measure, extent, content, capacity, sum, whole, lot, lots and lots, share, portion, quota, batch

## QUESTION
- Now on hand to answer all your questions
- Happy to answer any questions you may have about
- If you have any questions, you can just call
- Ask these key questions to help you choose
- Your local center will be happy to assist you with any questions you may have
- A question of doing the very best for yourself
- If you have any specific questions, ask to speak to
- Ask yourself these questions

**Question:** query, inquiry, problem, issue, enigma, puzzle, riddle, mystery
*See also:* **ASK, DEMAND, INFORMATION, INQUIRY, MYSTERY**

## QUOTATION
- Phone for a free quotation
- We'll beat any written quotation
- Always the most competitive quotation
- We'll match and better any quotation you bring us

*See also:* **ESTIMATE, EVALUATION, PRICE, VALUE**

## RAIN CHECK
- We are pleased to provide a rain check on any item not available during this promotion
- You can always get a rain check
- If an item is out of stock, take a rain check

*See also:* **ALTERNATIVE**

# RANGE
- This is made possible through a range of
- We offer an even wider range of
- Only our product comes with a full range of
- Enjoy a full range of
- The most far ranging selection of top quality products
- Choose from our vast range of
- That's why we've developed a range of premium quality products

*See also:* **ALTERNATIVE, CHOICE**

# RANK
- Ranked as one of the best
- Constantly ranked as the top
- We've earned top rankings in
- When you're ranked among the top
- Call now to join the ranks of successful
- Always in the ranks of the best

*See also:* **POSITION**

# RATE
- Rated number one more times than any other
- Scrambling to keep up with the rate of change
- Our best labor rate is
- Our success rate is well above the average
- Offering more than just competitive rates
- Rates take a tumble
- Hurry—bonus rates available only on
- You get preferred rates

*See also:* **CASH, GRADE, MONEY, PACE, PRICE, SAVINGS, SPEED, VALUE**

# RATHER
- What would you rather be doing
- When you'd rather be golfing
- We know there's a dozen things you'd rather do
- We'd rather be helping you save money
- Rather than wait, call us now

*See also:* **ALTERNATIVE**

# RE-OPENING
- Grand re-opening party
- Re-opening after extensive renovations to better serve you
- Re-opening bigger and sassier than ever

- Re-opening under new management
- You're invited to our grand re-opening

**REACH**
- Reach us fast
- Reach for the best
- Reach more people faster with
- It's all within your reach
- If your reach exceeds your grasp, we can change all that
- Reaches you faster than any other
- Reach out and take hold of
- You only have to reach out

*See also:* **COMMUNICATE, TOUCH**

**READY**
- Ready to go
- Get ready for
- We're getting ready to
- Are you ready for this
- Ready to rock and roll
- We'll be happy to get you ready now for
- Primed and ready to
- You've been ready for this for a long time
- Now you're ready for anything

*See also:* **EXPECT, PREPARE**

**REAL**
- Just real products for real people
- Make it real by getting a
- Get real with
- When you're looking for real value and savings, come to us

*See also:* **REAL**

**REALITY**
- Get used to the new reality
- Making your dreams a reality
- Is it time for a reality check
- Now it can be a reality for you
- It's often a hard reality that

**REASON**
- Seeming to defy reason
- One more reason why

- The reason is simple
- All these things add up to some very good reasons why
- People tell us the number one reason is
- Just another reason people trust us
- Seeming to defy reason
- As good a reason as any
- There's no reason to let
- The number one reason why
- It stands to reason that it's the one thing you shouldn't scrimp on
- Now there's no reason to worry
- Ten reasons why we're number one
- Three great reasons to
- The top ten reasons to
- Giving you more reasons to buy
- More convincing reasons to shop at
- It's for these reasons and many more that we've
- Do it for all your own reasons
- Here are just a few of the reasons why people buy

*See also:* **CHOICE**

## RECIPE
- A surefire recipe for success
- The recipe is simple
- Spectacular in your favorite recipes

*See also:* **INFORMATION**

## RECOGNITION
- Increasing the recognition factor
- The opportunity to gain recognition
- Basking in international recognition
- We've earned the recognition of

*See also:* **PROFILE**

## RECOGNIZE
- Widely recognized in the industry
- You may not even recognize the new, improved
- Something you'll recognize instantly
- Recognized as the best

*See also:* **UNDERSTAND**

## RECOMMEND
- Recommended by professionals
- More experts recommend our product

- Very proud to recommend
- Highly-recommended everywhere

**Recommend:** approve, commend, promote, speak well of, put in a good word for, sanction, favor, plug, tout, cry up, endorse, uphold, second, vouch for, underwrite, back, guarantee, suggest, offer, propose, advance, prescribe, endorse, encourage, advocate, praise, support

*See also:* **ADVANCE, PROMOTE**

## RECORD

- Make it one for the record books
- A proven record for quality and reliability that assures
- An impressive record spanning three decades
- Record savings are waiting for you
- Nobody can compare with our proven track record

*See also:* **INFORMATION**

## REDESIGN

- We have completely redesigned everything
- Every component has been redesigned to increase
- Now you can redesign your life today
- Redesigned into a brand new

*See also:* **CHANGE**

## REDUCE

- Some models reduced up to
- Goes straight to work reducing
- Prices reduced yet again to save you money
- Now we're able to reduce costs even more

*See also:* **LESS, MINIMIZE, SAVE**

## REDUCTION

- Further reductions now in effect
- Drastic reductions
- Don't miss these huge price reductions
- Unbelievable reductions of up to

*See also:* **SAVINGS**

## REFINEMENT

- It's all about the refinement of things
- A further refinement is
- For people of refinement and taste

*See also:* **ELEGANCE**

## REFLECTION
- Get an honest reflection of
- There's no more accurate a reflection than
- A reflection of your tastes and needs
- A reflection of today's hottest trends in

## REFRESH
- Have helped to refresh the body and the mind
- Wake refreshed, not tired
- Always refreshing, always fresh
- Refresh your point of view

*See also:* **REGENERATE, REJUVENATE, RENEW, REVITALIZE**

## REFUND
- We'll issue you a complete refund
- If you are not satisfied for any reason, just return the product for a complete refund
- We'll refund your money on the spot
- Return it for a refund on
- We'll not only refund your money, we'll also
- Prompt refunds for your convenience
- Always a guaranteed refund if you're not satisfied in any way

**Refund:** restore, replace, return, repay, give back, pay back, recompense, compensate, remunerate, reimburse, remit, make compensation, satisfy, adjust, settle, square, make amends, redress, make good, make restitution, cover, indemnify, redeem, rebate, repayment, reimbursement, allowance, cut, discount, reward, indemnify, restore

*See also:* **PROFIT, SALE, VALUE**

## REGENERATE
- Able to regenerate growth quickly
- Regenerating interest in a big way
- Thanks to natural regeneration

*See also:* **REFRESH, REJUVENATE, RENEW, RENOVATION, REVITALIZE**

## REGISTER
- Register now and get a gift coupon
- As soon as you register, you get all this
- Register and win
- Register all your friends too
- Thank you for registering

## REJUVENATE
- Because it helps rejuvenate
- Watch it rejuvenate your
- A wonderful rejuvenating influence
- We all need a little rejuvenation now and then

*See also:* **REFRESH, REGENERATE, RENEW, RENOVATION, REVITALIZE**

## RELATIONSHIP
- Plans include a relationship marketing program
- The relationship can seem almost mystical
- We value our relationship with you enormously
- Hope this will be the start of a longstanding relationship

*See also:* **FRIEND, FRIENDSHIP, PARTNERSHIP**

## RELAX
- Why not relax
- Relax in a quaint and cosy atmosphere
- Just sit back and relax and leave the rest to us
- When you really want to just relax and have fun
- Now you can be relaxed about

*See also:* **COMFORT, EASE, FREE, FREEDOM, REDUCE**

## RELEASE
- Releases extra burst of
- Just released this week
- Announcing the release of a spectacular new product

*See also:* **FREE, UNLOCK**

## RELIABILITY
- Over a century of rock-solid reliability
- Improving the reliability of your
- Rest assured about the reliability of
- Reliability is our middle name
- Reliability you can count on

*See also:* **DEPENDABILITY, TRUST**

## RELIABLE
- Nothing proves so reliable as
- Everything should be this reliable
- The most reliable in the business of
- Designed for people who depend on reliable
- You just can't get more reliable than this

## RELIEF
- Bringing instant relief for
- Natural relief within reach
- Transform discomfort into blessed relief
- Puts natural relief within reach
- For fast-acting relief
- Giving you quickest relief
- For speedy relief from
- You won't believe the relief
- What a relief to let us do it all

*See also:* **COMFORT, EASE, FREEDOM**

## RELY
- You can always rely on us
- Someone you can rely on
- That's why so many successful people like you rely upon
- One thing you can always rely upon
- We're the company folks have always relied on to take care of
- Thousands rely on us every day

*See also:* **BANK, DEPEND, TRUST**

## REMARKABLE
- Truly remarkable
- Now creating truly remarkable changes in
- It's remarkable that so many
- Making all the difference between the ordinary and the remarkable
- For a remarkable change in circumstances

*See also:* **FAMOUS, NOTE, NOTICE, SPECIAL**

## REMEMBER
- Why not remember this day by doing something special
- Remember your loved ones with the best
- Remember how lovely it was to
- Be someone people remember
- Always remembering your individual tastes and needs

*See also:* **MEMORY, REMIND**

## REMIND
- We don't need to remind anyone of the need for
- Will always remind you of your happiest moments
- Take a moment to remind yourself about the importance of
- There to remind you to have some fun

*See also:* **REMEMBER**

## REMINDER

- A constant reminder that no matter how far you go
- When you need a little reminder of
- Give them a beautiful reminder that you care

*See also:* **REMEMBER**

## RENEW

- Renew your acquaintance with an old friend
- Renewed just for you
- Time to renew your membership benefits
- Renew yourself with
- Treat yourself to a very renewing experience

*See also:* **REFRESH, REGENERATE, REJUVENATE, RENOVATION, REVITALIZE**

## RENOVATION

- Your quality renovation specialists
- When complete renovation is called for
- Low-cost renovations with topnotch quality

*See also:* **REFRESH, REGENERATE, REJUVENATE, RENEW, REVITALIZE**

## RENOWN

- Internationally renowned
- A quickly spreading renown for
- Renowned for quality and service

*See also:* **FAMOUS, NOTE**

## REPEAT

- Repeat of a sell-out
- There's certainly no need to repeat the importance of
- And now back for a repeat performance
- We're about to repeat the miracle
- An even grander repeat of last year's blowout

## REPLACE

- Replaced, free, with no time limit
- We'll replace any damaged item with no cost to you
- If it breaks, we'll replace it fast
- Now is the time to think about replacing
- It's time to replace your clunky old product with something new

*See also:* **REFUND, RENEW**

## REPORT
- We're happy to report that
- Here's what you'll discover inside this invaluable report
- Our customers are reporting a lot of pleasure and satisfaction
- When you report back to us, we pay attention

*See also:* **INFORMATION, RECORD**

## REPRESENT
- Always representing the best
- Represented a breadth of products and services unequalled by any other retailer
- There is no better way to represent your business
- Representing ourselves as exactly what we are—the best

*See also:* **SHOW**

## REPUTATION
- Built a reputation for excellence over the years
- Our reputation keeps customers coming back
- Reputation based on an unchanging formula
- Living up to its reputation is this splendid
- Nothing can tarnish our reputation for
- We put our reputation on the line every day
- With a reputation as solid as your own
- A reputation built on solutions

*See also:* **FAMOUS, RENOWN**

## RESEARCH
- Take advantage of our outstanding research team
- Extensive research is an absolute necessity
- Our research never stops
- Enhancement through ongoing research
- Through this extensive research, we find
- Advances in research now enable you to do something about

**Research:** investigation, inquiry, analysis, study, scrutiny, fact-finding, probe, exploration, assessment, appraisal, search, quest, survey, review, examine, seek

*See also:* **ADVANCE, BREAKTHROUGH, INFORMATION, REPORT, SEARCH**

## RESERVE
- Always reserved for you
- Reserve yours now
- Hurry, you must reserve before

- Call now to reserve
- Continually keeping something in reserve for you

**RESIST**
- Sometimes you just can't resist
- Resist if you can
- Don't even try to resist
- Won't be able to resist you when you wear

**RESOURCE**
- The largest resource for
- Your resource guide to
- Your own personal resource center
- You can't afford to be without this invaluable resource any longer
- Link up to a national resource
- Discover the latest in resources and services
- Providing the kind of resources you'll find valuable
- Telling us about the kind of resources you'll find valuable

**Resource:** asset, support, help, reserve, source, cache, storehouse, savings, wealth, property, real estate, goods, possessions, holdings, income, revenue, profits, gains, money, bucks, funds, finances, belongings, capital, cash, wherewithal, effects, estate, accounts receivable, securities, bonds, stocks, notes, inventory, goodwill, skill, know-how, knowledge

*See also:* **ADVANTAGE, MONEY, INFORMATION, KNOWLEDGE, PROFIT, SKILL**

**RESPECT**
- A highly-respected
- The world's most respected
- Determined to gain your respect
- Someone the competition respects
- With some of the most respected products in the world

*See also:* **REPUTATION**

**RESPOND**
- Responds instantly
- Responding to all your needs
- We respond faster than anyone else
- We respond to what you want
- Watch people respond to you in a whole new way

*See also:* **ANSWER**

## RESPONSE
- To instantly select the optimum response
- Elicited a boisterous response
- Measuring success by the huge response to
- Everything depends on your response
- Giving you a better, quicker response to
- Your response is important to us
- You also get the improved responsiveness you need

*See also:* ANSWER

## RESPONSIBILITY
- Bearing full responsibility for
- We see this as a great privilege and responsibility
- You don't have to carry the responsibility all alone when we're nearby to help
- We'll take all the responsibility for

## RESPONSIBLE
- Has been consistently responsible for
- Responsible for your success
- We're the responsible party
- Responsible directly to you
- Responsible for more happy customers than any other

*See also:* ANSWER

## RESULT
- Produced a truly amazing result the first time out
- For top results
- Helping you achieve great results
- Visible results begin in
- Blazing fast results
- Providing immediate results
- To measurably increase results
- Compare our performance results with that of
- We are results-oriented
- You can swear by the results
- For optimum results
- Helps give you professional results
- You'll be very satisfied with the results
- Best possible results will be achieved
- Simply heavenly results
- There simply isn't a more cost-effective way of obtaining guaranteed, professional results

- You get great results
- Results that pull ahead of the pack
- Guaranteed permanent results
- If you want results, come to us
- Promising early results indicate
- With truly extraordinary results

**Result:** outcome, conclusion, effect, issue, end, upshot, consequence, spin-off, development, harvest, crop, resolution, feedback
*See also:* **PROFIT, RETURN**

## RETURN

- You may return it to us if you're not satisfied
- If you're not happy with any item you order from us, simply return it
- Return it for a full refund or replacement, whichever you prefer
- Satisfied people are returning again and again to
- How to get a huge return on your investment

*See also:* **BACK, COMEBACK**

## REVENUE

- Increasing your self-generated revenue
- Each year, increasing revenue has show the value of
- Watch revenues shoot skyward
- More revenues mean more benefits for you

**Revenue:** income receipts, funds, money, remuneration, allowance, yield, gain, return, fee, finances, wealth, substance, means, wherewithal, capital, cash, proceeds, assets, resources, proceeds, earnings, yield
*See also:* **CASH, MONEY, SAVINGS, VALUE**

## REVITALIZE

- Revitalize your skin
- Refreshing, revitalizing, relaxing, wonderful
- You can revitalize your entire self
- Revitalize your body, your spirit and your bank account

*See also:* **REFRESH, REGENERATE, REJUVENATE, RENEW**

## REVIVE

- Helps to visibly revive
- Taking advantage of swiftly reviving interest in
- Reviving a fine old-fashioned idea

*See also:* **REFRESH, REGENERATE, REJUVENATE, RENEW**

## REVOLUTION

- It's a revolution in your

- A revolution that's still turning heads
- A revolution was born
- Thanks to our revolutionary new design
- From the people who revolutionized

*See also:* **CHALLENGE, CHANGE, SHAKE**

## REWARD

- Can be very rewarding for you
- Reward yourself with
- It's only your just reward
- Low investment, big rewards
- The rewards add up
- Free rewards
- You will be able to enjoy the rewards
- To find out how your company can realize the rewards of
- You'll be getting great rewards faster
- Enjoy the rich rewards of
- You can earn rewards every time you
- Bringing you more rewards for less
- Reap the rewards of low prices
- Get your free rewards faster

*See also:* **BENEFIT, CASH, MONEY, SAVINGS, VALUE**

## RICH

- Rich enough to arrive in a limosine
- Your own ideas can make you rich
- A rich array of choices and benefits
- Get rich quick
- An experience this rich

*See also:* **MONEY, WEALTH**

## RIDE

- Ride with the wind
- Enjoy the ride
- Don't let any fly-by-nighter take you for a ride
- When everything is riding on the choice you make

*See also:* **MOVE, SPEED**

## RIGHT

- We're sure to have the right one for you
- The key is knowing how to do it right
- Just right for you
- Do it right the first time

- Finally, you've got it right
- Ask which is right for you
- Offering the right products, the right service and the right price
- That's right
- Delivered right to your door
- The right thing to do
- Choose the one that's right for you
- Right on the money
- Products that are right for
- One is right for you
- It's your right to
- Right place, right products, guaranteed low prices
- You'll know how right you were to choose
- You are right to start early

*See also:* **ACCURATE**

**RISK**

- At absolutely no risk
- We're in business to minimize your risks
- Doing business can be risky
- Minimizing risk takes building relationships
- Leave the risk behind
- The risk is almost zero
- Practically risk free
- Absolutely no risk on your part
- Helps protect you against risk better than others
- Because we understand more kinds of risk
- An arrangement that takes the risk out of
- Without risk to the user or the environment
- The risk and rivalry is fierce

**Risk:** peril, hazard, danger, vulnerability, jeopardy, insecurity, unpredictability, chance, liability, imperilment, unpredictability, plunge, long shot, speculation, endanger, expose, menace, threaten, play with fire, venture, gamble, attempt, go for broke, hazard all, throw caution to the winds, take a flier, speculate

*See also:* **ADVENTURE, CHALLENGE, VENTURE**

**ROAD**

- Get on the road with
- Find your own road
- There are no road maps
- All roads lead to our store

*See also:* **ACCESS, PATH, WAY**

210

## ROLE
- New rules, new roles
- Will play a very big role in
- We'd like to play a bigger role in your life
- Tell us how you see your role in
- Helping to enhance your role in

*See also:* **ACTION, ASPECT, FACE, FUNCTION**

## ROMANCE
- Just the right touch of romance
- For the sheer romance of it all
- Swept away by romance
- Step into a world of romance
- The product that whispers romance

*See also:* **EMOTION, FEELING**

## ROMANTIC
- From the designer of the world's most romantic
- Receptive to romantic possibilities
- When you're in a romantic mood
- So romantic, you could swoon

*See also:* **EMOTION, FEELING**

## ROOM
- Great for any room in the house
- Brighten any room with
- Make room for the new kid on the block
- And, of course, there's plenty of room for
- Standing room only
- Giving you room to breathe

*See also:* **SPACE**

## RULE
- Get ready to rule
- Break the rules and win
- Our rules are pretty simple
- Keep breaking the rules by

*See also:* **COMMAND, STANDARD**

## RUSH
- Experience the ultimate rush
- Rush in today and buy yours
- Everyone is rushing to

- The rush is on

*See also:* **HURRY, SPEED**

## SAFE

- There's never been a simpler way to stay safe
- Remarkably safe for
- When you want to be really save
- Safe and convenient
- Safe and effective for everybody who needs it
- Safe for all uses
- A very safe way to
- Now safer than ever before

*See also:* **CERTAINTY, SECURE**

## SAFETY

- Legacy of safety innovations
- More of a safety net for you and your family
- Increased safety, increased peace of mind
- More built-in safety features than any other

*See also:* **GUARANTEE, SECURITY**

## SALE

- Everything in the store is on sale
- Our entire selection is on sale
- The sale continues, so hurry in today
- Get it for him/her on sale
- Weekly sales never stop
- One sweet sale
- Special sale prices on
- One-of-a-kind sale
- Sale ends before you know it
- Items return to regular price when the sale ends
- Famous brand sale at bargain prices
- Kick-off sale for our new location
- Sale starts today so hurry in
- Plus great weekly sales all year
- Sales have never been better
- For more sales, watch our flyer
- This sale won't be advertised to the general public
- We invite you to join us for a special neighborhood sale
- More for less sale
- This sale won't be advertised to the general public
- We invite you to join us for a special neighborhood sale

- A honey of a sale
- All on sale for less than you've ever paid before
- This is our annual seasonal sale
- Wow, look at all the sales

**Sale:** blitz, clearance, doorcrasher, extravaganza, liquidation, special, selling, vending, trade, traffic, exchange, bargaining, jobbing, auction, reduction, cut, discount, markdown, closeout

*See also:* **BENEFIT, BUY, MONEY, PURCHASE, PROFIT, SAVE, SAVINGS, VALUE**


**SALESPEOPLE**

- The best trained salespeople you'll ever meet
- Our salespeople are the very finest
- Speak to one of our salespeople immediately
- Enthusiastic salespeople are always on hand to help you

*See also:* **ASSOCIATES, EXPERT, PROFESSIONAL, SALESPERSON, STAFF**


**SALESPERSON**

- A knowledgeable salesperson is at your command
- Important to choose the best salesperson for the job
- Easy to judge the professionalism of the salesperson
- A friendly salesperson is always close at hand to

**Salesperson:** salesman, saleslady, shopman, clerk, salesclerk, seller, vendor, middleman, agent, drummer, solicitor, door-to-door salesperson


**SALVATION**

- This could be the salvation of
- The prospects for salvation is closer than ever
- Has been the salvation of small business for the last decade

*See also:* **CERTAINTY, SAFETY**


**SAMPLE**

- Call today for your free sample and discount certificate
- A free sample treatment is yours for the asking
- Provides a splendid opportunity to sample the many different
- We'll even send you a free sample just for asking

*See also:* **MODEL, PRODUCT, PROTOTYPE**


**SATISFACTION**

- Your satisfaction is unconditionally guaranteed
- We guarantee your satisfaction
- Satisfaction is a guarantee

- We simply won't compromise your satisfaction
- Your satisfaction matters to us
- Backed by our pledge of satisfaction
- You are entitled to continuous and complete satisfaction
- Alway to your total satisfaction
- Satisfaction is a must
- Your satisfaction guaranteed or your money cheerfully refunded
- Ensures your satisfaction on all purchases

**Satisfaction:** fulfillment, gratification, contentment, pleasure, enjoyment, joy, delight, happiness, comfort, assurance, belief, acceptance, trust, reparation, compensation, repayment, remuneration
*See also:* **COMFORT, ENJOYMENT, PLEASURE**

## SATISFY
- Experience the joy and pleasure of satisfying your needs
- It's very satisfying for everyone
- We want to be sure you're totally satisfied with
- And if, for whatever reason, you are not satisfied, just return the item
- Our customers are the most satisfied of all
- We've learned how to satisfy

*See also:* **GRATIFY, PLEASE**

## SAVE
- Save an additional percentage on
- Great ways to save and get the most from your
- Save more with
- Now you can save in more ways than one
- Save on everything you need to
- Save on products for the whole family
- You always save more at
- Save, save, save
- Everyone loves to save money
- Come save with us
- Try the intelligent way to save
- Ask us how you can save even more
- Stop and save
- People come here to enjoy themselves and to save
- Shop and save
- Find out how smart shopper save
- Save money by using less
- You can save even more by
- And then save yet more money on
- Save on our super savers

**Save:** rescue, redeem, liberate, protect, safeguard, guard, secure, shield, screen, keep, preserve, conserve, maintain, sustain, carry over, reserve, husband, withhold, save for a rainy day, hold in reserve, set/put/lay aside, put away, lay by/in/aside, stow away, salt away, squirrel away, store, store up, hoard, stockpile, amass, accumulate, pick up, economize, scrimp, scrape, pinch pennies, tighten one's belt, cut costs, cut expenses, buy wholesale

*See also:* **COLLECT, PROTECT**

## SAVING

- Get serious about saving
- See how close you are to saving big
- Now you're saving bigtime
- And you'll enjoy saving additional cash on
- Saving you the trouble of
- Saving you time and money
- We've been saving the best just for you
- Just think about all the money you'll be saving
- When your goal is saving money
- Will provide customers with an additional saving on

*See also:* **SAVINGS**

## SAVINGS

- Helping you identify substantial savings
- Look to us for vital savings on everyday needs
- Savings like you've never seen before
- More savings on the latest
- Direct savings to you
- Opens the door to value and savings on
- You'll see the savings mount
- Aisle after aisle of savings waiting for you
- Carnival of savings, a riot of fun
- Get the savings you want from
- Fill up on savings
- Get in on the savings
- You'll see the savings in
- You'll be astounded at the savings
- Packed with sensational savings
- Unbeatable everyday savings
- It's all about incredible savings
- Super savings
- It's all about great savings for you
- You must shop during our exclusive savings weekend

215

- Joins us as all our stores offer incredible savings
- When you want the biggest savings
- Choose the savings you need
- Locks in savings longer
- Special savings on our complete inventory
- Fill up on savings
- Stupendous savings Saturday only
- Power savings for power buyers
- Big savings over the cost of buying elsewhere
- Super savings on our entire selection of
- Savings available only until
- Day-to-day savings for wise shoppers
- Look inside for more blockbuster savings
- Just look at the potential savings
- Amazing savings keep customers coming back
- Hurry in and check out these savings and values
- Hurry in for hefty savings
- Savings quoted off regular price
- You've never seen savings like this

*See also:* **BENEFIT, CASH, MONEY, PURCHASE, SAVE, SAVING, VALUE**

## SAVVY

- How savvy are you about
- The store for smart, savvy people
- Cool and savvy
- Savvy buyers have known the secret for a long time
- Joins the ranks of the super savvy
- Savvy folks know where to find us

*See also:* **SMART**

## SAY

- We can confidently say that
- You can say that again
- Just say the word
- We listened to what you had to say and we got better
- What you say really counts with us
- Listen to what people are saying
- Which is no more than might be said about

*See also:* **COMMUNICATE, TALK, TELL**

## SCHEDULE

- Now you can work on your own schedule

- Everyone deserves a break from busy schedules
- Our extensive schedule includes
- We scheduled it for your convenience
- We can always fit you into our schedule

*See also:* **TIME**

## SCIENTIFIC

- Backed by major scientific studies
- Proven through rigorous scientific testing
- More scientific studies show our product is best for you
- The scientific way to improve your life
- Behind this gorgeous exterior is a major scientific breakthrough

*See also:* **RESEARCH**

## SCOOP

- Here's the scoop
- Get the scoop on saving money
- Scoop up the value and the savings
- We've got the scoop on our competitors

*See also:* **NEWS**

## SCORE

- Score a winner
- Know the score
- Come to someone who really knows the score
- We want to score big with you

## SCRATCH

- Gets you started from scratch
- Starting from scratch is easy
- Scratch and save
- Does a lot more than scratch the surface

*See also:* **BASE, BEGINNING, START**

## SEAL

- Your seal of approval
- Our seal is excellence is upon it
- Always look for this seal on the product
- Signed, sealed and delivered before you know it.

## SEARCH

- Your final search starts here
- Your search is over

- We've got what you've been searching for
- Have you been searching for
- We'll do your searching for you

*See also:* **DISCOVER, FIND, RESEARCH**

## SEASON

- Smack in the midst of a season of
- This season's most important trend
- There's no better time to prepare for the season ahead
- All-season versatility

## SEAT

- Puts you in the driver's seat
- Fasten your seat belts
- Giving you the best seat in the house
- Taking a back seat to no one

## SECOND

- Right this very second
- Second to none
- There are no second choices
- Don't hesitate another second

*See also:* **BEST, MOMENT, TIME**

## SECRET

- Learn the secret
- It's no secret that
- The secret is incredibly simple
- A secret that will change your life completely
- This secret is incredible
- You can put this simple secret to work for yourself right away
- Discover the sweetest little secret
- This secret will turn your business around
- You'll prove to yourself that this amazing secret can work for you
- Before you buy, you should know this secret
- For the first time, the secret is revealed
- The secret to naturally healthy
- What's the secret to
- Nature's ultimate secret
- Unlocking new secrets of
- Finally yielding up the secrets of

*See also:* **CONFIDENTIAL, INFORMATION, MYSTERY, PRIVACY**

## SECTION
- Special pullout section
- The whole section is packed with savings
- A section completely devoted to your needs

*See also:* **PART**

## SECURE
- All to make sure your investment remains secure
- Very secure, you can be sure
- Secure in the knowledge that
- Doing whatever it takes to make you feel secure

*See also:* **CERTAINTY, GUARANTEE, SAFE**

## SECURITY
- An extra measure of security
- Address security concerns
- When sensible security is your first concern
- Surround yourself with a welcome sense of security
- Enjoy the added security of
- Includes extensive security features to ensure privacy

*See also:* **CERTAINTY, GUARANTEE, SAFETY, WARRANTY**

## SEDUCTION
- Timeless seduction is yours
- It's outright seduction
- Surrender to the seduction of

*See also:* **APPEAL, ATTRACTION, SEXY**

## SEE
- Now's the time to see
- See for yourself
- Don't miss seeing all our
- You have to see it to believe it
- Finally, something you've never seen before
- Drop in and see for yourself
- Seeing is believing
- We have it, even if you don't see it
- See and be seen
- You've got to see it in action

*See also:* **LOOK, SEARCH**

## SELECT
- That's why we won't select just any

- Only a select group of agents carry and sell
- Select quality for special customers
- Every item has been hand-selected
- Will help you select exactly the product you need
- Select the one that's right for you
- Makes it so easy to select
- Now available at selected outlets

*See also:* **CHOOSE**

## SELECTION

- You won't believe the selection—or the savings
- Selection may vary by store
- Nobody comes close to the selection and service offered by
- An unrivalled selection of
- Premium selection and quality
- We have an unbeatable selection
- We've got selection and service
- Nobody beats our selection
- We have a large selection of styles and colors to choose from
- Selection may vary from store to store
- Hurry—for best selection shop early
- You get great selection when you come in
- Our entire selection is now on sale
- Expanded selection just in
- More than just the best selection of
- We have a huge selection of
- With plenty of selection at
- We've got the right selection for you
- Knowledgeable salespeople will help you with your selection
- Choose from an unbeatable selection of
- Come in and see our selection of
- Make you selection from thousands of
- New, extended selection
- Offering a better selection than any competitor
- See our massive selection of
- The most diverse selection of products you've ever seen
- Just one of the many selections our staff is proud to recommend
- Our best selection of
- Widest selection of merchandise in town
- A large selection is waiting for your perusal
- Choose from a comprehensive  selection of
- Widest selection of models and brand names
- Our entire selection is now on sale

- Our selection doesn't stop here
- The largest selection in the area
- The proper selection is very important
- Unrivalled selections of top-quality
- More selections every day at

*See also:* **CHOICE**

## SELL

- Leave the selling to us
- We skip the hard sell
- Hard sell just isn't our style
- And that's exactly what we sell
- We don't do high-pressure selling
- Before we sell anything to you, we make sure
- Almost sell themselves

*See also:* **BUY, PURCHASE, PROFIT, SALE, SAVINGS, VALUE**

## SELLER

- Our top super seller
- We've dropped the price again on our biggest seller
- People are snapping up our best seller
- Such a top seller it will soon be gone

*See also:* **SALESPEOPLE, SALESPERSON**

## SENIORS

- Seniors' day bargains
- Free gift for seniors
- Great advantages for seniors
- Calling all seniors
- Take advantage of our great seniors' discounts

## SENSATION

- A remarkable new sensation
- A sensation you haven't felt before
- The new sensation sweeping town

## SENSE

- Finally, something that makes sense
- A little old-fashioned common sense works wonders
- It makes sense to call us today
- An admirable sense of style and value
- It just makes sense to do it now
- Makes more sense than ever before to

- Simply shows your good business sense
- All you need is a little common sense and the ability to

*See also:* **REASON, SMART**

## SENSES

- A true delight for the senses
- Stirring the senses, stirring the passions
- Let your senses make your decision
- All your senses will thrill to

*See also:* **EMOTION, FEELING**

## SENSIBLE

- Used by sensible people worldwide
- The sensible thing to do
- It's what sensible people do
- A sensible person like you can easily see the benefit

*See also:* **REASON, SENSE, SMART**

## SENSITIVE

- Pampering the most sensitive
- Always sensitive to your needs
- The most sensitive of all

*See also:* **EMOTION, FEELING**

## SERIES

- This exciting series features
- First in a series from
- Get the whole series
- There's never been a series like this
- This best-selling series is
- A creative, stylish series of

*See also:* **SELECTION**

## SERIOUS

- And because we take this matter so seriously
- Now for some serious savings
- Get down to serious satisfaction
- We're serious about helping you to
- Before things get serious

*See also:* **SENSIBLE**

## SERVE

- We look forward to serving you in the year to come

- Proudly serving you with stores across the land
- Just warm and serve
- All we want to do is serve you
- Serving you from coast to coast
- Serving you faster
- Working hard to serve you better
- Waiting to serve you right now
- Serving up savings and value

**Serve:** wait on, attend, minister to, care for, give service, help, render assistance, lend a hand, oblige, accommodate, abet, assist, be of service, work for, respect, honor, perform, function, do the duties of benefit, contribute to, boost, advocate, support, recommend
*See also:* **BENEFIT, HELP, PROMOTE, RECOMMEND**

## SERVICE

- Providing an essential service for
- A new dimension in full and self-service
- Does a real service for all your needs
- Providing you with loyal service wherever your business takes you
- Offering comprehensive services, including
- There is no charge for this service
- City knowledge, country service
- You'll find real friendly service
- All-new service begins now
- Warm, attentive service is as famous as
- Around-the-clock service
- Service that will catch your eye and your attention
- Romantic elegance combines with gracious service
- Service is unquestioned
- Guaranteed service no matter when you call
- You gave your services and staff top marks
- Service in a class of its own
- We hope you will find this an invaluable service
- Service while you wait
- For professional service you can trust
- We service what we sell
- Established as a service to
- Service makes it simple for you to
- Low prices, superb services
- At your service, every day
- Worry-free service
- Keeps giving you the same excellent service you've come to expect
- Great prices, superior services

- Best price and service since
- Information to help you make the most of this new service
- Safe, speedy service seven days a week
- Fast, friendly service
- Not to mention the attentive service one can only find at
- Providing a very valuable service
- Fantastic service seven days a week
- Includes the exceptional service of
- Where service is an art
- The art of fine service
- Providing services in just the areas you require
- Additional products and services you won't find anywhere else
- We also give you value-added services such as
- We'll continue to search for new services to full your needs
- With a broad range of customized service to manage
- Knowing where to go for better services
- An exploding demand for these services

*See also:* **BENEFIT, FUNCTION, HELP**


## SET

- Set includes everything you need
- Get set for a thrill
- Setting the scene for savings
- We're all set to serve you
- This innovative gift set includes

*See also:* **COLLECTION, READY**


## SET-UP

- For a one-time only set-up fee
- You'll love our convenient set-up
- The best set-up for you

*See also:* **ESTABLISH**


## SETTING

- A truly intimate setting
- A great addition to any family setting
- Creating a setting you'll feel comfortable in
- Relax and enjoy yourself in a setting that

*See also:* **ENVIRONMENT, LOCATION, PLACE**


## SETTLE

- If you don't want to settle for just any
- The perfect product to settle down with

- Don't settle for second best
- Whatever choice you settle on, you'll be pleased

*See also:* **CHOOSE**

**SEXY**
- The sexiest products going
- Sleek, sexy and slinky
- A sexier, brasher look

*See also:* **BEAUTIFUL, FEELING, SEDUCTION**

**SHAKE**
- Shake things up a little
- Get down to where things are movin' and shakin'
- We shake up old ideas

*See also:* **ACTION, CHANGE, REVOLUTION**

**SHAPE**
- Shape up now for
- Behold the shape of things to come
- They'll stay in peak shape when you
- And now available in a variety of different shapes and sizes

*See also:* **CONDITION, FORM**

**SHARE**
- Share in these great savings
- Share the benefits
- We want to share all this with you
- Get your fair share of fun
- Sharing is part of our value
- Nothing is more satisfying than sharing
- When you see what we have to share

*See also:* **BENEFIT, HELP**

**SHIFT**
- Whenever there's a massive shift like this
- There's been a major shift recently
- The balance of power has shifted to you
- Keeping you abreast of all the shifts in
- The ground can shift right under your feet

*See also:* **CHANGE**

**SHINE**
- It's your turn to shine

225

- Your reason to shine
- You'll take a shine to our product
- We've taken a shine to you

## SHIP
- Your ship has come in
- Watch your ship arrive in style
- Shipped the same day
- We ship the moment we receive your order

*See also:* **DELIVER**

## SHOP
- Where else would you shop for
- You can shop in style for
- Shop early for best selection
- Shop till you drop
- Why shop anywhere else
- All you have to do is shop
- Find out what shopping is all about
- Shop at your local store for these great values
- You probably know why millions shop at
- The smart way to shop
- Calling all shopaholics
- You'll see just how easy shopping can be
- Plan your shopping around a visit to our store
- Providing you with one-stop shopping

*See also:* **BUY, MONEY, PURCHASE, STORE**

## SHOPPER
- A shoppers' paradise awaits you
- For the discerning shopper
- More shoppers flock to us than to any other
- We strive to make our shoppers happy

*See also:* **BUYER**

## SHOUT
- Shout out loud and clear
- The value shouts at you
- We give you something to shout about
- Shout with joy
- We don't have to shout it out

*See also:* **COMMUNICATE, TALK**

# SHOW

- Showing what we're made of
- Showing once again why
- We can show you how easy it is to
- Showing you how to double your
- Best in show
- Show off
- We'll show you how to dazzle
- We can do it or show you how
- Helps you get on with the show
- Putting in a spectacular show
- Let us show you how

*See also:* **DISPLAY, DEMONSTRATION**

# SHOWCASE

- A stunning showcase for
- A veritable showcase of value and style
- What better showcase for your/our talents than
- Turning your home into a showcase

*See also:* **DISPLAY, SHOWROOM**

# SHOWROOM

- We're your product showroom
- Call now or visit our showroom today
- Visit our showroom for many unique design ideas
- Look past the showroom glitter
- Visit our new showroom and save

*See also:* **DISPLAY, SHOWCASE**

# SIDE

- Show your sensational side
- Lets your wild side come out
- A product with many sides
- Showing another side of you
- We refuse to take sides

*See also:* **ASPECT, PART, PROFILE**

# SIGHT

- We set our sights on a brand new challenge
- Set your sights on something higher still
- It's called love at first sight

*See also:* **AIM, GOAL, SEE**

227

## SIGN

- Sign up today and beat the rush
- Use it at the first sign of
- Sign up now and check out
- Sign up and take advantage of our early bird discount
- A good sign that you've gotten the right
- Visit us and sign up for big value
- Showing all the signs of a sizzling deal
- Reducing the signs of

## SIGNATURE

- Our exclusive signature series
- It's easy to recognize our signature products
- All it takes is your signature to
- As soon as we have your signature, we swing into action

*See also:* **REGISTER**

## SIMPLE

- Such a beautifully simple solution
- It's the simple things that count
- Simple and safe
- Pure and simple value
- Keeping things simple
- Nothing could be simpler
- It's that simple
- The joy the simplest things can provide

*See also:* **EASE, EASY**

## SIMPLICITY

- Designs share an appealing simplicity
- You'll love the elegant simplicity of
- We've reduced it all to a beautiful simplicity

*See also:* **EASE, EASY**

## SIMPLIFY

- Simplified and streamlined
- Simplifies your life for you
- Let us help to simplify things for you

*See also:* **EASY**

## SIZE

- Discover why we've doubled in size
- Huge size range for lots of choice

- In exactly the size you want
- No matter what size you're looking for, we can help
- May be shown larger than actual size
- Just my size, just your size
- With standard and custom sizes available
- Now available in a wide selection of shapes and sizes

*See also:* **BIG, CHOICE**

## SKILL

- You'll also find skills you need to better evaluate
- It takes a certain skill to
- Exhibiting superb problem-solving skills
- Use your valuable skills and experience to work with us
- A company with people skills
- We have all the required skills to

*See also:* **CRAFT, EXPERT, INFORMATION, PROFESSIONAL**

## SKIN

- End dry skin forever
- Imagine your skin actually looking better with time
- Makes your skin more beautiful from the very first time you use it
- Defend skin against exposure that can lead to signs of premature aging
- The moisture in your skin keeps building
- Skin looks better and better
- Designed to minimize visible signs of aging in your skin
- The beauty of healthy looking skin
- Improves skin texture
- Gives your skin just the right amount of moisture

*See also:* **BODY**

## SKY

- We do more than blue sky it
- The sky's the limit
- We're not just offering pie in the sky

*See also:* **IMAGINE**

## SLOW

- Don't let it slow you down
- Sure won't slow you down
- In a slow and leisurely matter
- Time to slow down and take a look around you

**Slow:** unhurried, dawdling, moderate, leisurely, slow-paced, paced,

methodical, deliberate, prolonged
*See also:* **PACE**

## SMALL
- Small is beautiful
- It's small wonder that
- And you can start small
- It's the small things that count

*See also:* **LITTLE, SIZE**

## SMART
- It's so smart it even
- Get smart quick
- It's the smart thing to do
- Found to be the smart way to
- Smart folks shop at
- What may well be the smartest
- Smarter, faster, better-priced
- The smartest move you'll ever make
- Go where the smart people go
- You've got the smarts to recognize

*See also:* **SAVVY**

## SMILE
- Gets you smiling
- Find out why they just keep smiling
- Smiles appear right before your eyes
- You leave with a smile
- Let us put a smile on your face

*See also:* **GLAD, HAPPY, JOY, PLEASURE, SATISFACTION**

## SMOOTH
- Starts to smooth and soften in an instant
- Satiny smooth
- Smooths and refreshes
- Get the smooth moves and the cool duds
- Glides more smoothly
- Elasticity, resilience and smoothness increase significantly
- A smoothness that comes from

*See also:* **EASE, EASY**

## SNACK
- Take a snack break

- When you want a healthy snack
- A snack that satisfies your craving for
- Time out for a snack
- Some snacks just don't cut it

*See also:* **DINE, EAT, TREAT**

## SOAR

- Makes you soar like an eagle
- Get ready to soar
- Really starting to soar
- A burning desire to soar higher

*See also:* **FLIGHT**

## SOFT

- Ultra soft to pamper your whole body
- Softer than soft
- Softer than anything that touches you
- You've never felt anything as soft as this
- Softness that's pure heaven

**Soft:** pliable, pliant, flexible, bendable, plushy, malleable, squishy, tractable, stretchable, plastic, shapable, lithe, supple, smooth, silky, velvety, satiny, creamy, kissable, fuzzy, downy, furry, fleecy, cosy, warm, mellow, muted, understatement, heavenly, tranquil, low, pastel, fluid, curved, gentle, genial, temperate, tender, sweet, mild, indirect

*See also:* **COMFORT, PAMPER**

## SOLD

- Get sold on our service
- Everything must be sold
- Sold to the bare walls
- Must be sold for rock bottom prices
- Sold down to the bare walls
- Before you know it, you're sold on it
- Sold by the dozens every week
- Get sold with
- Just one look and you'll be sold
- You'll be sold on a brand new idea

*See also:* **BUY, CONVINCE, PURCHASE, SELL**

## SOLUTION

- Introducing your newest, biggest solution yet
- Common sense is the best solution to
- An enormously scalable solution

- The most economical solution to
- Willingness to look for solutions wherever they might exist
- A safe, gentle solution
- You can't find a better solution to your needs
- It's the only real solution to
- The number one selling solution worldwide
- A lively, affordable solution
- Be part of the solution
- The easy solution for our
- An array of upgradable, customer-focused information management solutions
- Intelligent solutions for all your needs
- Innovative and practical solutions for all your problems
- In business to find the right solutions for our customers
- Finding the right solutions for you
- Dedicated to finding solutions for you
- Providing solutions for every level of your organization
- Solutions to help you compete and succeed in the years ahead
- Solutions are shaped by the needs of the moment

*See also:* **ANSWER, RESULT**

**SOLVE**
- Perfect for helping you solve your not-so-small problems
- No matter what the problem, we can solve it for you
- Solving problems like this is our business
- When you're looking for someone to solve
- There's nothing you can't solve so long as you try

**Solve:** work out, resolve, figure out, crack, answer, untangle, unravel, translate, decode, unlock, penetrate, fathom, get at, clear up, explain, interpret, elucidate, make clear, account for

*See also:* **HELP, UNLOCK**

**SOMEONE**
- For that special someone
- Someone, right now, is waiting for you to
- When you really want to impress someone

**SOMETHING**
- Something comes over you when
- A little something for everybody
- Something you really ought to know
- The start of something big

## SOON
- Coming soon to a store near you
- Soon to be in your neighborhood
- Getting it to you sooner
- Get yours sooner than anyone else

*See also:* **EARLY, FAST, SPEED**

## SOPHISTICATED
- For the most sophisticated system in the business
- Just a little more sophisticated than
- Sophisticated people know

*See also:* **SMART**

## SOPHISTICATION
- Coming out with a fresh, modern sophistication
- With more sophistication than every before
- You don't see this kind of sophistication just anywhere

## SORT
- Sort it out with
- See the light and sort out your life with
- Products of the better sort
- We have just the sort you're looking for

**Sort:** make, kind, type, class, line, grade, quality, genre, category, list, lot, style, manner, group

*See also:* **BRAND**

## SOUL
- You want something that includes a soul
- Is the guts and soul of
- We haven't lost sight of the heart and soul of

*See also:* **FEELING, HEART**

## SOUND
- Alive with the sound of
- Based on thoroughly sound knowledge
- A really sound idea
- You'll like the sound of it when you hear

*See also:* **RELIABLE, TRUST**

## SOURCE
- We're your source of
- Your source for

- Go straight to the source
- The premier source is now available

*See also:* **BEGINNING, RESOURCE**

## SOUVENIR
- The perfect souvenir for you and your family
- Mecca for souvenir hunters
- A souvenir you'll never part with

*See also:* **REMEMBER**

## SPACE
- You create the space
- Create a great outdoor/indoor space
- Create a brighter, more inviting space
- But space is limited
- Excellent utilization of space
- Space age value
- Limited space available for
- Maximize your space and your savings
- Space is still available
- A space you can really live with
- We have much more to say than we can squeeze in this small space
- Even the smallest spaces have potential for
- Time to head for open spaces

*See also:* **ROOM, STORAGE**

## SPEAK
- Speak volumes
- Our products speak for themselves
- We're not just speaking figuratively
- Speaking up about value

*See also:* **COMMUNICATE, TALK, TELL**

## SPECIAL
- Special pre-release price when you
- We've got the special things you're going to be wanting
- If you'd like to do something special for
- Something very very special
- Makes it just a little bit more special
- Grand opening special
- Yes, we're back with another one day special
- Our special has been extended
- Early bird specials galore

- Check out these early opening specials
- What makes this so special
- This week's specials
- Coming soon is something very special
- You need something special
- Early morning specials. first come, first served
- Super specials on our most-wanted products
- Don't miss these awesome specials

**Special:** particular, specific, certain, distinct, distinctive, individual, singular, one of a kind, different, unusual, uncommon, rare, unique, out-of-the-ordinary, unconventional, unorthodox, novel, new, important, significant, memorable, momentous, great, earthshaking, foremost, predominant, primary, paramount, chief, principal, prime, notable, noted, outstanding, celebrated, well-known, private, select, elite, exceptional, incredible, spectacular, dear
*See also:* **BEST, NEW, SALE, SAVINGS, VALUE**

## SPECIALIST
- Call a specialist
- Your product specialist
- For those times when you really need a specialist
- That's why our teams of specialists get to know you
- Our specialists are waiting to talk to you
*See also:* **EXPERT, PROFESSIONAL**

## SPECIALIZE
- For those who want to specialize
- We also specialize in
- Specializing in the best
- Specializing in everything for the home
- We specialize in providing detailed information
*See also:* **EXPERT, PROFESSIONAL**

## SPEED
- Built for speed
- You'll be awed by the speed at which we can
- Making their way to you at warp speed
- Advanced features for simplicity and speed
- Speediest service in town
*See also:* **FAST, INSTANT**

## SPEND
- Make more, spend less

- Spend the day/night, not your savings
- Do it without spending a cent
- Spend less on the best
- Cuts your spending by half
- Now you don't have to spend a ton of money on
- You'll be enjoying yourself more and spending a lot less
- Not just a convenient way to increase your spending power

*See also:* **BUY, PURCHASE, PAY, SAVE, SAVINGS, VALUE**

## SPIRIT

- A product with spirit
- There's no better place to get into the spirit than at
- It all springs from our unique corporate spirit
- Breathe in the spirit of adventure
- Breathing more spirit into
- Get into the spirit
- In the spirit of our hardy pioneer ancestors
- Our tribute to the spirit of the west
- It is precisely in this spirit that
- Born-to-run spirit
- Our ingenuity and entrepreneurial spirit will keep us reaching out
- Feel a whole new spirit of

*See also:* **ATMOSPHERE, FEELING, FREEDOM, HEART, SOUL**

## SPLASH

- Making a major splash in the world of
- The splash of savings
- Splashdown for excitement
- Make a big splash today

## SPLENDID

- They're splendid on their own
- What a splendid opportunity to
- What could be more splendid than
- A very splendid idea

*See also:* **FINE, GOOD**

## SPONSOR

- Proud to be a sponsor of
- Brought to you by the sponsors of
- Sponsoring the finest
- Just look at who our sponsors are

*See also:* **BACK, SUPPORT**

**SPORT**
- No matter what your favorite sport is
- To counter the wear and tear of high impact sports
- Try it just for the sport of it

*See also:* **GAME**

**SPOT**
- We've got a privileged spot for you
- If you have a soft spot for
- This is the spot
- Saving the best spot for you
- One of the wittiest, most sought-after spots
- Hits the spot
- The new spot for
- Spot-on savings
- Spot check on value

*See also:* **LOCATION, PLACE**

**SPOTLIGHT**
- Leap into the spotlight
- Grabbing the spotlight
- Turning the spotlight on
- Today the spotlight is on you

*See also:* **FEATURE, HIGHLIGHT**

**SPRING**
- Spring into action
- Spring savings
- We spring into action instantly
- New spring colours flatter you best
- Our new spring collection features popular
- Come in for a touch of springtime
- Will once again be hosting a spring celebration of
- Spring spectacular
- Hot spring deals
- Get that happy spring feeling
- Spring into summer
- Say goodbye to winter, hello to spring
- April showers of great spring values
- Bring on spring
- Spring into savings
- Experience an early taste of springtime
- Spring shopping spree

- Spring into action where the savings are
- Get a jump on spring

*See also:* **LEAP, SEASON**

## SQUEEZE

- Squeeze more from you
- Putting the squeeze on you
- Great gifts for your main squeeze
- Squeezes more from your shopping dollar
- Are you feeling really squeezed

*See also:* **PRESSURE**

## STAFF

- Knowledgeable staff
- We have whizzes on staff to help you
- Knowledgeable staff is always on hand to help you with your selections
- The friendly staff is waiting to
- Just ask any member of our staff
- Our staff is always standing by to
- Our helpful staff can show you how
- One of our friendly staff will answer your questions
- With the help of our very professional staff

*See also:* **ASSOCIATE, CREW, EXPERT, PROFESSIONAL, TEAM, SALESPEOPLE**

## STAGE

- For your transitional stage
- No matter what stage you are in
- Come and see the next stage of

*See also:* **INSTALLMENT, STEP**

## STAND

- Stands up to the roughest wear
- We want you to know where we stand
- We stand right behind you all the time
- A product that can stand the heat

## STANDARD

- The true value of establishing unbeatable standards
- Exceeding the highest standards daily
- Sets professional standards for
- Setting the standard for all others

- You choose the standard, we deliver the results
- And control the standard of service you receive
- An exceptional standard of quality and service
- The standard by which the others are measured
- Standards that work hard for you
- A proven approach to developing high standards
- Will be remembered for impressive standards
- The highest standards of excellence
- Working to set the finest standards of

**Standard:** model, pattern, example, paradigm, ideal, mirror, prototype, archetype, rule, principle, guideline, rule of thumb, regulation, precept, order, gauge, guide, touchstone, measure, criterion, axiom, foundation, norm, average, par, rank, median, grade, recognized, accepted, approved, orthodox, official, definitive, classic, authoritative, established, sure, reliable, common, widespread, prevalent, popular
*See also:* **GUIDE, MODEL, POPULAR, PRINCIPLE**

## STAR

- Where stars are born
- Hot stars in a new universe
- The star of our show is
- You be the star
- Here, you're always the star
- Meet the newest star in our galaxy
- Just one of the stars of our
- Reaching for the stars

*See also:* **BEST, CELEBRITY, TOP**

## START

- It's so easy to start
- Don't start until you've seen
- Start your own home-based
- Starting at just
- Getting started is simple with
- To get you started right away
- Just for starters
- The best possible start
- Getting started is easy
- Start smart, stay smart
- A thrilling start to
- And that's just the start
- Get ready for a strong start next year
- Great results start at

- Give yourself a head start
- Try starting over
- Now you can start over with
- It doesn't cost a lot to get started
- We start you off with

**Start:** begin, commence, go ahead, embark, set sail, set about, take off, jump off, kick off, blast off, get going, take steps, get a move on, get on the stick, start off, start out, move out, get the show on the road, plunge in, dive in, get one's feet wet, get down to it, get to it, arise, dawn, break out, spring up, crop up, initiate, instigate, set in motion, start the ball rolling, take the first step, break the ice, open, pioneer, lead off, institute, inaugurate, found, establish, set up, organize, break ground, lay the foundation, introduce, launch, usher in, create, beget, engender, give birth to , give rise to, sow the seeds of

*See also:* **BEGINNING, CREATE, INNOVATION, LAUNCH**

## STATEMENT
- Makes a strong statement
- You can make a statement with
- A cool, confident statement
- An individual statement
- Making a statement without saying a word
- Make a statement with

*See also:* **COMMUNICATE, SAY, TALK, TELL**

## STATUS
- Reserved for those who know there are more important things in life than just status
- Your status just shot up
- A simple, inexpensive way to increase your status
- Everybody could use a little more status

*See also:* **RANK, POSITION**

## STAY
- To make your stay more enjoyable
- Ensure that it stays that way
- And to make sure our customers stay with us, we're offering
- We stay with you all the way

## STEP
- Leads you every step of the way
- Take a big step towards
- You'd better step on it because

- Helping to make a swift step forward
- Two simple steps to help you to
- Taken one step further
- Stay in step with the world of change
- Take this important step today
- Here are some easy steps to
- Ten steps to a cleaner, healthier
- Check out these easy steps

*See also:* **ACTION, INSTALLMENT, METHOD, STAGE**

**STOCK**
- All stock will be sold
- Always in stock, round the clock, day-in, day-out
- Dozens in stock, reserved just for you
- A time for taking stock
- Stock up on these fine items
- Stock up on essentials
- Stock up now before they're all gone
- All new stock on our shelves
- New stock is arriving daily
- Day in, day out–always in stock
- We stock hundreds of
- Not every item may be stocked by
- We stock everything you'll need for
- Stock up now
- Stock up while you can
- Stock up while quantities last
- New stock means new value
- All stock will/must be sold
- Open stock bonanza

*See also:* **INVENTORY, MERCHANDISE, STUFF**

**STOP**
- Hundreds of ways to stop
- Stop by your nearest
- Why not stop by and say hello
- Stop the problem dead in its tracks
- But we won't stop there
- Designed to stop problems before they start
- But we didn't stop at just
- That's why we'll never stop doing our level best to serve you

**Stop:** halt, arrest, prevent, repel, repulse, deny, avert, discontinue, conclude, end, withdraw, knock off, shut down, complete, finish, pause,

cease, desist, quit, slow down, break off, wind up, run out, run its course, rest, terminate, close, silence, subdue, lower the boom, squash, scotch, check, nip in the bud, overpower, cut off, shut off, prevent, delay, postpone
*See also:* **CHANGE, HELP**

**STORAGE**
- Designed for easy storage
- For all your storage needs
- Doubles your storage space
- Everybody needs more storage
- Abounds with convenient storage

*See also:* **ROOM, SPACE**

**STORE**
- Every store guarantees low prices on
- You store's savings are sizzling on
- It's what's in store for
- The company store people look to for the very best
- We want to be your one-stop store
- Celebrate our hundredth store opening
- See store for details
- Now at fine stores everywhere
- A truly unique store for you and your family
- Your savings store
- Your neighbourhood store
- Not only does your store bring you top quality merchandise
- Hurry into your store for this super special on assorted designer items
- Your store brings you only the best
- Coming soon to a store near you
- More surprises in store
- The best in store for you
- Our superstores are now bigger than ever
- Available at selected stores only

*See also:* **MARKET, OUTLET**

**STORY**
- We'll never be without the full story
- Now that's the whole story
- We can tell you a pretty interesting story
- Don't be satisfied with only half the story
- The inspiring story behind

- This could be your story

*See also:* **INFORMATION, PLAN, STRATEGY, SYSTEM**

## STRATEGY
- Conducting strategy sessions
- Helping you develop the right strategy to
- Here's the best strategy
- Whatever your personal financial strategy
- For up-to-date strategies

*See also:* **INFORMATION, PLAN, SYSTEM**

## STREET
- Street smart, street sleek
- The look is street-smart
- Has made its way down to the street
- Street-level glamour
- Word on the street says

## STRENGTH
- Strength is inspiring
- Industrial strength value
- To add strength for within, we have
- Add to your strength by
- Extra strength provided by
- Driven by strength and performance
- Combines the strength of
- Multiplying your strengths
- Increasing your strength of purpose
- Dozens of ways to strengthen your

*See also:* **MUSCLE, POWER, STRONG**

## STRIDE
- The joy of finally hitting your stride
- Find your stride
- Will take it all in stride
- Striding with you boldly into the future

*See also:* **MOVE, STEP**

## STRIVE
- Striving each day to provide our customers with quality service and quality products
- We strive to have the items you want
- Striving every day to please you

- Working longer, striving harder to
*See also:* **EFFORT, TRY**

**STRONG**
- Turn to the strong one
- Strong as steel
- Strong enough for you
- Strong on savings, strong on value
- Getting stronger every day
- Putting a strong emphasis on
- Become stronger than you ever thought possible

**Strong:** mighty, powerful, sturdy, tough, virile, robust, red-blooded, hearty, hale, fortified, durable, heavy-duty, cast-iron, substantial, enduring, long-lasting, permanent, solid, sound, firm, resolute, unyielding, unbending, emphatic, intense
*See also:* **POWER, STRENGTH**

**STUFF**
- Where people know their stuff
- Here's some terrific stuff, and it's free
- Get great stuff for only
- More stuff, better stuff, cheaper stuff
- Showing you some very exciting stuff
*See also:* **INVENTORY, MERCHANDISE**

**STYLE**
- What better way to mix style and individuality
- A real sense or style
- Making a difference in style
- You can create any style with
- Luxuriant texture and style
- Accessorize with style
- Decorate your home with timeless stylings
- Find it at your style store
- Celebrated styles you've admired for excellence
- Come in and see our assorted styles and
- Country style comfort
- Special style features
- It's an energetic style that's all about living well
- The height of style, the very pinnacle of taste
- Now learn what style is all about
- The singular style of
- Your style is real

- Real style, comfort and great colors
- We have many other/more sizes and styles for you to choose from
- Designer styling combines elegance and comfort
- Decidedly stylish in a casual world

*See also:* **CHIC, ELEGANCE, FASHION**

## SUCCEED

- Keeps you succeeding every step of the way
- Get out of your way and let you succeed
- Nothing succeeds like success
- At last, we've succeeded in creating

**Succeed:** accomplish, complete, do, work out, carry through, make good, prosper, thrive, grown, advance, get ahead, succeed with flying colors, triumph over, win, conquer, prevail, luck out, strike it rich, hit the jackpot, make the grade, turn out, be victorious

*See also:* **ACCOMPLISH, ACHIEVE, WIN**

## SUCCESS

- To ensure your success
- Flushed with success
- The opportunity for success you've been seeking
- Sharing the secrets of success
- Guarantee your success by
- Become an overnight success
- Ongoing commitment to your success
- Already a great success
- When your success depends on us
- Have made this week a huge success
- For guaranteed success, talk to us
- The success of your business depends on you
- Join the voyage to success
- Ensuring your success requires clear direction
- Steering you toward success while keeping your costs down
- The real foundation of our success is our people
- Find success right in your own back yard
- We believe in success, pure and simple
- The size of your success is totally up to you

*See also:* **ACCOMPLISHMENT, ACHIEVEMENT**

## SUCCESSFUL

- Working to ensure you remain successful
- Used successfully by thousands
- Successfully serving customers for twenty years

- All the earmarks of a successful business

*See also:* **POSITIVE**

## SUGGESTION
- Please take a few moments to jot down your comments and suggestions
- We listen to every suggestion you give
- We have a few suggestions for you
- Special suggestions are always welcome

*See also:* **COMMENT, INFORMATION, INPUT, PLAN, STORY, STRATEGY, SYSTEM**

## SUMMER
- Summer's here already
- Super values and buys make summer even better
- Put some sizzle in your summer
- Enjoy it all summer long
- Spring into summer
- Summertime fun at big savings
- Great summer value on
- Summer is here and so is super savings
- Shape up for summer now
- With summer just around the corner
- We'll help you keep cool all summer long
- Summer wouldn't be summer without
- Sizzlin' summer deals
- A perennial summertime favorite
- We've got a hot summer deal on a cool
- Lots of summer shortcuts
- Summer spectacular
- Summer's sunsational savings
- Think summer, think relaxation
- Summer value days
- Get set for summertime

*See also:* **SEASON, SUN**

## SUN
- Give yourself some fun in the sun
- Perfect for sun lovers
- Have a good time in the sun
- Discover your place in the sun

*See also:* **FUN, SUMMER**

# SUPER
- It's extra super
- Super values, super savings
- Our service is super
- We thing you are super
- Supercharged with value

# SUPERIOR
- At superior stores everywhere
- A genuinely superior product
- When you see how superior our service really is
- Turning in a superior performance
- First in strength and superiority

*See also:* **BEST**

# SUPERSTORE
- Your superstore just around the corner
- Your new superstore is open and ready
- A superstore with everything you want

*See also:* **OUTLET, STORE**

# SUPPLIER
- We have been a leading supplier for years
- We want to become your exclusive supplier of
- After you've seen what other suppliers have to offer, come to us

*See also:* **SELLER, SUPPLIER**

# SUPPLY
- Supply the industry for thirty years
- Stocks an endless supply of
- The supply is shrinking
- Our supply is limited so hurry in today
- Send in your order now while the supply lasts
- While supplies last

*See also:* **GIVE, PROVIDE**

# SUPPORT
- Providing you with all the support you need
- Support offered at every stage
- Offering full-scale support
- To help support your
- Provides perfect support for
- With unrivalled support to help you explore

247

- Ranks are united in our support for
- Lending real support to your enterprise
- We'll give you the information, guidance and support you need to
- Supporting you every step of the way
- Outstanding support means outstanding performance

**Support:** elevate, bolster, uphold, enhance, buttress, shoulder, keep up, reliever, comfort, sympathize, assure, hold up, hang in, maintain, sustain, cherish, nurture, nourish, foster, provide for, take care of, look after, watch over, tend, mind, finance, subsidize, pay for, fund, sponsor, underwrite, capitalize, put the money up for, set up, meet the expenses, encourage, abet, accommodate, hearten, advocate, promote, vouch for, endorse, make good, adopt

*See also:* **BEHIND, HELP**


## SURE

- That's why we've made sure we have what you want
- You have to be sure that
- When you're not sure what to do, call us
- They'll make sure that everything comes out for the best
- A sure way to success
- When you've never been more sure
- It's a sure thing
- Sure you want to save more money
- To be sure you get exactly what you want

*See also:* **CERTAINTY, GUARANTEE, RELIABLE**


## SURPRISE

- Don't be surprised if you come out on top every time
- Not surprisingly, people choose us first
- You'll be surprised at just how good our product is
- The surprise of
- Surprise him with a top quality
- Someone with everything can still be surprised
- And much to the surprise of many
- No surprise that we are leaders in
- Our excellence is no surprise at all

*See also:* **UNEXPECTED**


## SURVIVAL

- Always worked and planned for your survival
- To you, it means survival
- In today's tough world, it's survival of the fittest

**SURVIVE**
- Surviving beautifully
- Helping you survive in the everyday rough and tumble
- Survived the hardest conditions

*See also:* **LAST**

**SWING**
- You don't have to swing to
- We're swinging
- Opinion is swinging in our direction
- Get into the swing of the new

*See also:* **CHANGE, CHOOSE**

**SWITCH**
- Switch to freedom
- Now you don't have to constantly switch between
- Switch and save
- Switch to a better brand of
- Isn't it time you switched
- More people than ever are switching to
- To convince you to switch to

*See also:* **CHANGE, CHOICE, CHOOSE, TRADE**

**SYMBOL**
- Just look for this symbol
- For years it's been the symbol of quality
- This symbol means the very best
- To symbolize the preservation of

*See also:* **SIGN**

**SYSTEM**
- You can't buy a better system
- Our proven system can quickly adds up to profits
- No other system even begins to come close
- It does just that via an innovative system of
- A system that lives up to everyone's expectations
- All to make sure your system remains intact
- Identify ways to expand your system down the road
- Beating the system is a snap with
- Makes other systems look like ninety-eight pound weaklings
- Works effortlessly with your other systems
- Ask for the system that works fast and easily
- A superior system for

- A totally personal system for you
- All because of our advanced system
- Total systems designed to being people closer together

*See also:* **DESIGN, GOAL, IDEA, INFORMATION, PHILOSOPHY, PLAN, PRINCIPLE, PROCESS, PROGRAM**

## TACKLE
- Now it's time to tackle the big challenges
- When you're ready to tackle the big one
- We can tackle anything you throw at us
- Helping you tackle what life brings

*See also:* **CONQUER, HELP, TRY**

## TAILOR
- We tailor it especially for you
- Custom-tailored to your needs
- Impeccably tailored
- Tailor-made for

*See also:* **FIT, SERVE, SHAPE**

## TAKE
- Who says you can't take it with you
- Something we don't take lightly
- A completely different take on things
- Taking you farther and higher than ever before

*See also:* **ANGLE, MOVE**

## TALK
- We're talking about
- This is a good time to talk about
- We're talking products and services
- We hope to talk to many of you through these venues
- Feel free to talk to our staff about
- Talk of the streets/town/land
- You should be talking to us
- Now you're talking
- And we're not just talking about
- Straight talk on
- We take the time to really talk to you
- Looking for someone you can talk to
- We've got the time to talk
- Can we talk

*See also:* **CALL, CONSIDER, TELL**

**TARGET**
- Don't be a target this winter
- A sale that targets you
- Need not be mutually exclusive targets
- To reach your/our target customers quickly
- Targeting a whole different kind of

*See also:* **AIM, GOAL**

**TASK**
- No longer find the task so daunting
- Multi-tasking is our specialty
- For a product that's really up to the task
- Getting all your tasks done satisfactorily

*See also:* **JOB, VENTURE, WORK**

**TASTE**
- Giving you a taste for the very finest
- Taste the best
- For the cultured taste you crave
- A rich, rewarding taste
- Taste the difference
- Tastes better too
- Put your taste buds on full alert
- Great tasting
- Taste the freshness
- If you have a taste for
- Without taking the bite out of taste
- Low in fat doesn't mean low in taste
- Puts the taste back in
- Get a taste now
- Taste the warmth
- Taste the best of both worlds
- Have you tasted it yet

*See also:* **CHOICE, FLAVOR, PREFER, TRY**

**TEACH**
- We'll teach you the ABC's of
- As you teach us your needs
- Gladly teaching you everything you need to know to

*See also:* **INSTRUCTIONS, LEARN**

**TEAM**
- Join the team

- You can join our leading team
- To join the winning team, call
- Because we've got the best team
- Determining who will fit in best with your team
- A strong team player
- Working with a team of leading people from around the world
- You count on your team to succeed
- Make us part of your team
- The most successful team in history

*See also:* **CREW, GROUP, PARTNER, SALESPEOPLE, STAFF**

## TEAMWORK

- By encouraging respect for teamwork
- For better work and better teamwork
- Excellent teamwork is the key to our success
- You'll be impressed with our teamwork

*See also:* **PARTNERSHIP**

## TECHNICIAN

- An expert technician is always on hand to answer your questions
- Let our technicians do the work do all the work for you
- Trained technicians always here to help
- Our technicians are the best in the business

*See also:* **EXPERT, PRO, PROFESSIONAL, STAFF**

## TECHNIQUE

- The secret techniques of
- Covers step-by-step techniques for creating
- Created using the most advanced techniques
- Developing ever better techniques of
- Spent decades perfecting the technique of

*See also:* **METHOD, TECHNOLOGY, WAY**

## TECHNOLOGY

- Enjoy the challenge of conquering new technology
- Pushing technology to the limit
- We've been advancing technology in the areas of
- Applying technology to some of the world's most difficult problems
- How quickly technology becomes ancient history
- Led us to the development of innovative technologies to help you
- Ensuring today's technology won't be obsolete tomorrow
- Uses the most advanced technology to
- Connects you to the extraordinary technology of

- And this same technology allows you to do much more than just
- The result of a new generation of technology
- An impressive combination of advanced technology and ease of use
- Breakthrough technology
- Compares state-of-the-art technology with
- Integrating new technologies
- To better technology alternatives
- Your lifeline to the latest technology
- As the latest technology becomes available
- The most technologically savvy way to
- Actively involved in the development of new-age technologies

## TELEPHONE
- Limited time only so telephone today
- As close as your telephone
- Order it over the telephone
- All done via your telephone

*See also:* **CALL, CONNECT, ORDER, PHONE**

## TELL
- Let me tell you more about this fascinating secret
- We keep telling you about
- Please tell us what you think
- Telling it like it is
- Tell your friends about the things you've discovered
- Anyone will tell you that

*See also:* **COMMUNICATE, SAY, TALK, TELL**

## TEMPT
- We love to tempt you with
- You can't help but be tempted
- Let us tempt you with this terrific selection of
- More people are tempted by
- A very tempting offer

**Tempt:** entice, allure, seduce, lure, fascinate engage, infatuate, carry away, enamor, excite, captivate, charm, attract, appeal, enthrall, enrapture, bewitch, hypnotize, mesmerize
*See also:* **APPEAL**

## TEMPTATION
- Embrace temptation
- Sweet temptations
- Give in to the temptation of

253

- Nothing but wall-to-wall temptations

*See also:* **APPEAL, SEDUCTION**

## TEST

- Because these solutions have been thoroughly tested
- This product has been clinically tested to be safe and effective
- Give us a test run
- Just wait till you see the test results
- Put us to the test and see how well we do
- Could what you're using now pass this test
- Everything you do has already been tested

*See also:* **RESEARCH, TRY**

## THANK

- Thank you for your business
- Thank you for your order
- We're thanking our loyal customers with this fabulous, limited-time offer
- We have what they'll thank you for
- We've made it big, thanks to you
- Thanks to your support and encouragement
- Thanks to you business is jumping
- Thanks for thinking of us
- Just wanted to say thanks
- Our way of saying thank you
- Thanks to new technological advances
- But thanks to all of you
- Thanks to all who dropped in to say hello

*See also:* **APPRECIATE, APPRECIATION**

## THING

- We think the neatest thing about it is
- It's the real thing
- We've got a thing about quality
- Naturally, you like nice things

*See also:* **STUFF**

## THINK

- You probably don't think about these things very often
- If you're thinking of
- Just think of it
- Just when you're wondering what will they think of next
- Think again about

- Think big
- Start thinking of your future
- Taking the time to actually stop and think
- Why didn't they think of this before
- See what you think
- You probably think you'd never be able to
- Discover a whole new way of thinking
- It's smart thinking like this that's made us the choice of
- A place where all forward thinkers turn

*See also:* **CONCEPT, CONSIDER, IDEA**

## THOUGHT

- You never need to give it a second thought
- Here's some thoughts on
- You probably never thought you'd even need a
- We'd like to hear your thoughts on

*See also:* **CONSIDER, THINK**

## TICKET

- Your one-way ticket to the hottest
- Giving you a ticket to success
- Hurry and get your ticket today
- Just the ticket

## TIME

- An don't waste any more time
- Isn't it time you
- Too much to do and not enough time
- Time is on your side
- Your time together is precious
- So time won't tell
- Just another way to save you time
- Really prime time
- Do it any time you wish
- We invest our time in your happiness
- There's no better time to
- Save time and money
- It's that time again
- Now would be a very good time to do it
- The perfect gift, the perfect time
- For the first time in years
- Just a matter of time
- On time and on budget

- Great if you're really pressed for time
- Limited time only
- Right place, right time for
- The time is right/ripe for
- Do it now, because time is running out fast
- The latest time and money saving service
- We're there when the time comes to
- Just in time for
- Once upon a time
- Before time runs out
- Now is the time to
- Save time and effort
- Limited time only
- For a limited time, take advantage of our optional
- The time we save you makes a huge difference in cost and efficiency
- So this time around, we are
- The most precious commodity these days is time
- It's only a matter of time before
- Not the first time that
- Time waits for no one
- Time spent with us is time well spent
- It's been a long time coming
- Finally, time to do what you want
- Regularly, good times and bad
- Timing is now perfect for

*See also:* **CLOCK**

## TIMELESS

- The over-all feeling is of timelessness and enchantment
- Timeless beauty at your fingertips
- Soak in the timeless feel of
- A place of timeless serenity and peace

*See also:* **CLASSIC**

## TIP

- Want a hot tip on
- Tip of the week
- Tips on everything from
- For interesting tips and information, tune in to
- Here you can find insider tips on latest
- Tips on how to improve and maintain
- Paved with golden tips

*See also:* **HELP, INFORMATION**

# TODAY

- Today is the big day
- Starts today
- Do it today
- Today is the day when you finally
- Today's products at yesterday's prices

*See also:* **NOW**

# TOE

- Starts your toes a-tingling
- Feel the thrill all the way down to your toes
- Keep on your toes
- Now you don't have to toe the line for anyone
- A top-to-toe makeover
- Feel terrific from top to toe

# TOGETHER

- Shows you how to put it all together
- Some things go together naturally
- Achieving more together
- Together, we can do it
- Bringing together some of the most famous
- The first time so many have come together to
- We pull it all together
- Together, we can see it through
- Bringing together some of the country's most respected experts

*See also:* **PARTNER, PARTNERSHIP, TEAM, TEAMWORK**

# TOMORROW

- The product of tomorrow is here today
- Ready to answer tomorrow's needs for
- Tomorrow's product and service today
- Striding boldly into tomorrow
- Don't wait until tomorrow
- Tomorrow may be too late
- Building a firm foundation for tomorrow
- Tomorrow's abilities today

*See also:* **FUTURE**

# TOOL

- A wonderful new tool for people who are searching for
- The best tool in you magic toolbox
- Don't forget the tools you'll need

- Creative tools for personal expression
- Are you getting the tools you really need
- The right tools for
- Giving you the tools you need to get the job done right
- All the tools you'll need to
- You need the right tools

*See also:* **INFORMATION, METHOD, WAY**

## TOP

- Climb to the top with our expert help
- Putting you at the very top of our list
- Has raced to the top
- Let them try to top this
- A product you can't top
- Takes you all the way to the top
- We're tops at
- Go to the top of the class

*See also:* **BEST, SUPERIOR**

## TOPIC

- The hot topic for today is
- A topic everyone is interested in
- We can't say enough about this topic
- Whatever topic you choose
- A topic for a very lively discussion

*See also:* **CONCEPT, IDEA**

## TOUCH

- Staying in touch with the people who matter most
- Other ways to get in touch with us
- We provide the human touch
- For that special touch
- Just the right touch
- The soft touch
- Touchably soft
- Next time you touch down, visit us
- Come in for a touch of
- We help you keep in touch with
- Gives it that sweet finishing touch
- And for the final finishing touch
- Add the perfect touch
- You can't afford to be out of touch
- Systems that keep you in touch

- Acquire the golden touch
- For the personal touch
- Keeping you in touch and up-to-date

*See also:* **COMMUNICATE, CONNECT, EFFECT, EXPERIENCE, FEELING, REACH, SKILL, TALK, TELL**

## TOUGH

- Tough on problems
- A tough act to follow
- When you're this tough, you don't bother with
- We built it tough and strong so that you can

*See also:* **STRENGTH, STRONG**

## TRACK

- On the right track for
- Now you can keep track of your entire
- Delightfully off the beaten track
- Get on track for big savings

*See also:* **PATH, ROAD, WAY**

## TRADE

- Buy, sell and trade
- Now running a special trade-in campaign
- Trade in your old items for new
- No trade offs
- Trade-in deals nobody can beat

*See also:* **BUY, CHANGE, PURCHASE, SELL, SWITCH**

## TRADITION

- A wonderful tradition since
- A great new tradition is born
- Committed to time-honored traditions of
- Steeped in tradition
- The meaning and tradition behind our product
- Start your own tradition today

*See also:* **HERITAGE, HISTORY, INHERITANCE, LEGACY**

## TRADITIONAL

- As traditional as they come
- There's nothing traditional in our approach to
- Not so traditional is the idea that you can
- Traditional savings are here again
- Isn't it time you stepped out of the traditional and into the modern

● The timeless beauty of traditional style
*See also:* **CLASSIC, HERITAGE**

## TRAFFIC
● Let us increase your traffic dramatically
● Stop traffic with
● Buy one of these traffic-stoppers and you'll be a hit
● And you don't have to fight traffic to get to our store
● Tie up traffic with

## TRAIN
● You're not just training bodies, you're shaping minds
● Our trained staff is waiting to help you
● We provide all the training necessary to
● You don't need special training to
*See also:* **LEARN**

## TRANSFORM
● Is instantly transformed into a bright and welcoming
● Transformed into something you'll be proud of
● You'll feel transformed
*See also:* **CHANGE**

## TRANSITION
● Thousands of people, just like you, have successfully made the transition
● You can make the transition too
● The transition is very easy
*See also:* **CHANGE. SWITCH, TRADE**

## TRAVEL
● You don't have to travel any farther than your local dealer
● Make us your travel destination
● Let's travel together down this exciting new road
● Experience the sheer comfort of travelling with
*See also:* **JOURNEY, MOVE**

## TREASURE
● Want something you'll treasure forever
● Will be treasured for years and years
● A real treasure waiting for you
● A store packed with treasures
● We treasure your good opinion of us

- A unique treasure to delight almost any age
*See also:* **SPECIAL, UNIQUE**

## TREAT

- Treat yourself or a special someone to
- Time to give yourself a treat
- A simple, effective way to treat
- The best treat of all is
- It's always a treat to
- Treat your family to health and happiness
- For this festive season a variety of delectable treats
*See also:* **EAT, PAMPER**

## TREND

- Designed to help you take advantage of the trend to
- A trend we're determined to dispel
- One of this year's key trends
- Trends come here first
- Starting a whole new trend to
- We create trends
- Trendy and smart
*See also:* **FASHION, STYLE, TASTE**

## TRIAL

- Three months free trial
- Do not wait for your free trial
- Give it a trial and see how well it works
- Try it on a trial basis
*See also:* **TRY**

## TRIBUTE

- Paying tribute to fifty years of
- As a tribute to our customers we're offering
- We want to pay tribute to you with this
- A tribute to honor your loyalty and
*See also:* **APPRECIATION, GIFT**

## TRIP

- A trip your family will never forget
- Easily worth the trip to
- One trip to our store and you'll realize
*See also:* **JOURNEY, MOVE, TRAVEL**

**TROUBLE**
- Double trouble for
- It's no trouble at all to help you
- Taking the trouble to make sure
- No amount of trouble is too much

*See also:* **CHALLENGE, EFFORT, HASSLE, PROBLEM**

**TRUE**
- What was true then remains true today
- Tried and true
- It's amazing but true that
- Is this chance too good to be true

*See also:* **REAL**

**TRUST**
- Complete trust in
- The store you trust
- Earning your trust every day
- People trust us
- Trust is what it's really all about
- More reasons to trust
- We give you a reason to trust
- Use it once and find out why it's trusted most
- There's no other product that's more trusted

*See also:* **CONFIDENCE, FAITH, GUARANTEE, RELY, WARRANTY**

**TRY**
- It's time you tried a
- You just can't wait to try
- If you haven't tried our product recently, you're missing out on something great
- A must-try product
- We are pleased to offer you one more reason to give us a try
- Beauty without even trying
- Isn't it time you tried it
- Give it a try for free
- Try it today
- Don't take our word, try it yourself
- You can try it before you buy it
- Just try it yourself
- You owe it to yourself to try

**Try:** attempt, endeavor, undertake, take a shot/crack at, strive, essay,

make an effort, venture, hazard, risk, check out, examine
*See also:* **EFFORT, TRIAL**

## TUMMY
- To satisfy a growling tummy
- A real tummy pleaser
- You'll feel good with this in your tummy
- Making tummies happy everywhere

## TUNE
- A first-time opportunity to tune in to what's happening
- Tune up for
- Tune in, turn on to
- Totally in tune with you
- Listen to a different tune
- We'll have you playing to a whole new tune
*See also:* **CONNECT**

## UNDERSOLD
- We refuse to be undersold
- We won't be undersold on
- We will not knowingly/willingly be undersold
- We will not be undersold by anyone
*See also:* **LESS, REDUCE**

## UNDERSTAND
- Customers come to us because we understand
- We understand very well that
- Come to someone who really understands
- It really helps that our people understand your needs
- Helping to understand what you're doing
- Specially trained to help you understand
- We understand your needs
- Taking the time to understand your goals
- And because we truly try to understand the needs of

**Understand:** comprehend, fathom, penetrate, figure out, grasp, recognize, see through, perceive, discern, make out
*See also:* **KNOW, INFORM, RECOGNIZE**

## UNDERSTANDING
- A greater understanding of
- For those who want a clearer understanding of
- Bringing deep experience and understanding to

- Working to increase your understanding of

**Understanding:** comprehension, consciousness, cognizance, knowledge, realization, awareness, conception

*See also:* **CONCEPT, IDEA, INFORMATION, KNOWLEDGE, WISDOM**

## UNEXPECTED
- Always the unexpected
- Such excellent results are not exactly unexpected
- Providing you with unexpected, built-in value

*See also:* **SURPRISE**

## UNIQUE
- Discover an incredibly unique
- Is what makes this fine product truly unique
- Embraces all that is unique and fascinating about
- You bet we're unique
- Because you're unique
- Unique and well-established

*See also:* **ORIGINAL, SPECIAL**

## UNIVERSAL
- Is ageless and universal
- Universally accepted standards
- The timeless and universal appeal of

*See also:* **CLASSIC, TIMELESS**

## UNLIMITED
- Just imagine the unlimited
- Tap into unlimited possibilities
- An unlimited offer for people just like you

## UNLOCK
- Unlock the secret of success
- Unlocks the door to a whole new universe
- Unlock your hidden beauty
- Unlock the inner you

*See also:* **FREE, RELEASE, SOLVE**

## UNTHINKABLE
- We just did the unthinkable
- What was unthinkable just last year is now possible
- Such advances used to be unthinkable

**UNWIND**
- Stretch out and unwind
- What better way to unwind than to
- Now you can unwind in style
- Relax and unwind with

*See also:* **PAMPER, RELAX**

**UPDATE**
- We are continually updating our
- Constantly revised and updated to keep you currant
- You'll receive updates on new products every week
- Call us for an update on
- The most exciting update yet

*See also:* **INFORMATION**

**UPGRADE**
- Upgrading fine minds since
- And it's so easy to upgrade when you're ready
- Buy something you can upgrade when you want
- Continually upgraded

*See also:* **IMPROVE**

**UPLIFT**
- A wonderful uplift of spirits
- Feel the uplift as soon you arrive
- A real mood uplift

**USE**
- Easy to use and even easier to
- Both for everyday and specialized uses
- However you intend to use it
- Unlike any you've ever used before
- Easy to use, easy to afford
- Makes exceptional use of
- Anyone can use it
- Designed for ease of use
- Another great use was born
- Handy products you'll use every day
- You won't find anything that's easier to use
- A hundred handy uses
- Simple to use and useful at the same time
- Another great use is born
- Yours to use whenever you want

- Ready to use
- Use them immediately to
- Ready for instant use
- Why would you use anything else
- Use it every day
- Easier to use than any other product
- You only pay for what you actually use

*See also:* **APPLICATION, FUNCTION, METHOD, SERVE**

**USEFUL**
- Widely useful in
- You'll find it very useful for
- A very useful addition to you
- Of almost unlimited usefulness

*See also:* **PRACTICAL, HELPFUL**

**UTILIZE**
- We utilize the best
- Helping you to utilize
- Now you can utilize all of your talents and options

*See also:* **FUNCTION, USE**

**VACATION**
- Go on a dream vacation this winter
- Like having a vacation every day
- Feel as though you're on vacation
- Have the vacation of a lifetime

*See also:* **HOLIDAY, TRAVEL**

**VALUABLE**
- Plus you can get valuable tips on
- Is immensely valuable
- Providing something unique and valuable
- Quite likely the most valuable available
- Giving you valuable experience with

*See also:* **TREASURE**

**VALUE**
- Your best value is
- If you value quality of life
- Continues to add value to
- Has the potential to increase in value
- Value really adds up

- Add up the value
- Long live value
- Hotline to value
- Rock solid value
- Value-packed
- Value-crammed
- Value-added
- Value power
- Economical value
- Value jammed
- Overflowing with value
- Double value
- Triple your value
- Creates new value
- Instant value
- Spot-on value
- Clean value
- Industrial strength value
- Open up to value
- Unbelievable value
- Exponential value
- Value blowout
- Explosion of value
- Grown-up value
- Space age value
- Old fashioned value
- Dawn of new value
- Out of this world value
- How do you unearth value
- Exceptional value in an ordinary world
- Fantastic values
- Experience incredible value
- Committed to quality, value, selection and service
- Add value to your home with
- Value-driven
- Our feature value
- An unprecedented value
- And perhaps nowhere else will you find such an exceptional value
- Strength, consistency and value
- With unbelievable value
- Spectacular values
- Enjoy values only a Mom and Dad could love
- More great values

- The values are outta sight
- Great values in-store

**Value:** worth, merit, utility, advantage, benefit, usefulness, gain, profit, avail, good, importance, prize, treasure
*See also:* **BENEFIT, BUY, MONEY, SALE, SAVINGS, USEFULNESS**

## VARIETY

- We bring a wide variety of
- Right now, our selection offers phenomenal variety
- A large variety of impressive
- A massive variety of styles and patterns
- A great variety of products to choose from
- A huge variety to suit your home
- Each form comes in a slight variation of

*See also:* **ASSORTMENT, CHOICE**

## VENTURE

- Consider a new venture
- Nothing ventured, nothing gained
- Venture boldly into this exciting world
- Join in this enthusiastic and far-sighted venture

*See also:* **ADVENTURE, INVESTMENT, RISK**

## VERSATILE

- It's all quite versatile
- More versatile than any other product
- Year-round versatility
- Renowned for serviceability and versatility

*See also:* **CHANGE, FLEXIBLE, USEFUL**

## VIABLE

- Makes them also commercially viable
- Always a viable choice
- Now giving you very viable options

*See also:* **POSSIBLE**

## VICTORY

- A victory over
- Chalk up another victory for our side
- Victorious, year after year

*See also:* **BEAT, CONQUER, WIN**

**VIEW**
- Offers breath-taking views
- We'd love to hear your point of view
- Giving you a whole new view of
- A view we enthusiastically endorse
- Suggesting a very different point of view

*See also:* **IDEA, INFORMATION, PICTURE**

**VINTAGE**
- Vintage-inspired
- A vintage idea whose time has come again
- Of a very superior vintage

*See also:* **HERITAGE, HISTORY, LEGACY**

**VISIBLE**
- A visible transition to excellence
- It's visibly better
- The difference is clearly visible

*See also:* **SEE**

**VISION**
- Our vision continues to grow
- And because your vision is boundless
- Searching for you vision
- Share our vision for a better future

*See also:* **CONCEPT, IDEA, MISSION**

**VISIT**
- Come and visit
- And exciting and educational place to visit
- We would like to invite to come visit us
- Please visit and enjoy
- We'd love to see you visit us
- To make sure you visit our store
- Our frequent visits and constant monitoring make sure

*See also:* **CALL, COME**

**VISITOR**
- Will be on hand to give visitors a rare opportunity to view
- A cordial invitation to all visitors
- Treat all our visitors wonderfully
- We love to pamper visitors

*See also:* **GUEST**

## VOICE
- A strong voice for change
- Another strong voice speaks up
- Your voice at
- Now you can really make your voice heard
- Really listen when you voice your concerns

*See also:* **EXPRESS, SAY, SPEAK, TALK, TELL**

## VOLUME
- Volume buying assures you of competitive prices
- How can you pump up the volume
- Bigger volume means bigger savings for you
- More volume in our stores

*See also:* **QUANTITY**

## WAIT
- You don't even have to wait while
- You aren't just going to wait around for success, you're going to go out and get it
- But wait, there's more
- No lag, no waiting
- Can't wait to tell you about
- Why wait any longer to
- Just wait until you see what's in store for you
- Alterations while you wait
- You've waited months or years for it
- Don't just wait for things to change
- Waiting on your every whim

## WAKE
- Something to wake up to
- Wake up to big value
- This can be a real wake up call to
- The world is waking up to the excitement of
- Wake up your senses with

## WALK
- Within easy walking distance of
- Walk away with a great deal
- Walk in anytime
- We warmly welcome walk-in traffic

*See also:* **MOVE, VISIT**

**WALLET**
- Without being hard on your wallet
- Now you can have a fat wallet too
- Saves your wallet
- Your wallet will love it too
- Big on value, easy on your wallet

*See also:* **BUDGET, POCKETBOOK**

**WANT**
- Whatever you want, whenever you want
- For people who want it all
- There's only one person who really knows what you want
- Goes just where you want it to
- You're going to get even more of what you want
- When the only thing you want is to
- We make sure you get exactly what you want
- Give them what they want
- Give it to them the way they want it
- We really know what you want

*See also:* **DESIRE, WISH**

**WAR**
- Waging war on problem
- We're declaring all-out war on
- The war on prices is heating up
- Be part of the war on overpricing

*See also:* **ATTACK**

**WAREHOUSE**
- We are your product warehouse
- Lots and lots of warehouse specials
- A huge warehouse crammed with values

*See also:* **SHOWROOM, STORE**

**WARM**
- All warm and fuzzy
- Warmed up instantly
- Just warm and serve
- A sensuously warm
- Makes you fell allwarm inside
- Warm up to great value

*See also:* **COMFORT**

## WARMTH
- Surround yourself with the warmth of
- A whole new dimension of warmth
- A place full of warmth and welcome

*See also:* **COMFORT, SOFT**

## WARRANTY
- Lifetime warranty on
- A thoroughly comprehensive warranty
- We'll honor the replacement warranty
- Full season warranty available
- Lifetime warranty available
- We will honor all warranties
- Extended warranty without charge
- Under complete warranty
- Hazard warranty guarantee
- Comprehensive warranty backed by an industry leader

*See also:* **CERTAINTY, GUARANTEE, PLEDGE**

## WATCH
- Just watch it get results
- The eyes that keep a close and constant watch on
- A steady watch on the well-being of
- Watch for our
- Always watching out for you

*See also:* **LOOK, MONITOR, SEE**

## WAY
- Coming your way soon
- One way to help maintain
- The best, fastest, most efficient, most technologically savvy way to
- We have to find the way
- Discover a better way
- The best way to make sure
- A convenient, economical way for you to enjoy
- It's the easy way to
- The way to go, the way to save
- Once you see how many ways you can
- Looking for a way to
- The surest way to get what you really want
- Is there a better way
- The most impressive way to
- So you can discover a new way to

- One easy, revolutionary way to
- Simply your cheapest, most convenient way to
- It's the best way to be sure you get what you want
- There's more than one way to get
- A surefire way to
- Discover quick and clever ways to
- Amazing new ways to
- Even more ways to save
- It's the best way to be sure you get exactly what you want
- There is no better way to
- Finding new ways to
- A couple of great ways to

*See also:* **METHOD, PATH, SYSTEM**

## WEALTH
- Achieve wealth in your spare time
- Working to preserve and enhance your wealth
- Get the look of wealth
- Giving you a wealth of choice

*See also:* **CASH, FORTUNE, LUXURY, MONEY, RICH**

## WEAR
- Since just about everything can wear out
- Refuses to wear out
- Coordinated wear collection
- Wears forever, almost
- Practically never wears out
- What you wear is just as important as how you wear it
- We make them very wearable

## WEATHER
- Weather permitting
- Weather-proof
- Handles any kind of weather
- Untouched by the roughest weather

*See also:* **ATMOSPHERE**

## WEEK
- This week's specials
- One week only
- Better get here before the end of the week
- This is the biggest week in
- In less than a week you can own it

## WEEKEND
- Big savings for the long weekend
- Spend the weekend of your life at
- Have yourself a lazy weekend
- This weekend only

## WEIGHT
- Boost energy, lose weight, take control
- Giving more weight to the idea of
- A very weighty matter
- Lifts a huge weight off your shoulders
- Watch the weight melt off

*See also:* **LOAD**

## WELCOME
- Welcome to our establishment
- We're welcoming even more of you to
- Always open to welcome you
- Welcome to drop in on a casual basis
- Transformed into a bright, welcoming
- You'll be welcomed with open arms
- Everyone is welcome
- Waiting to welcome you
- Our company welcomes you at any time
- Creates a comfortable and welcoming ambiance

*See also:* **HAPPY**

## WELL
- Did it and did it well
- No one else does it so well
- Making sure you're well and happy
- Transforms discomfort into a state of well being

*See also:* **GOOD**

## WEST
- The spirit of the wild west
- This is how the west was won
- Straight out of the old west

## WHAT
- We've got what it takes to be number one
- What to do if
- Just look at what we have to offer

- Doing whatever it takes

## WHERE
- Puts it exactly where you want it
- If you've been wondering where to go for
- Here's where you can get the best
- Where everyone is going these days

## WHO
- Revealing who you are
- Who says you can't
- We're the people who are famous for
- Let the world know who you really are

## WHOLESALE
- Below wholesale prices
- Get it wholesale at
- Now selling wholesale to the public

*See also:* **SALE, SAVE, SAVINGS, VALUE**

## WHY
- You'll see why right away
- This is why everyone is coming to us
- Here's why you should choose us
- Value, quality and service is why

## WILD
- Answer the call of the wild
- Try something wild
- Lets your wild side loose
- For the wild thing inside you
- Drive them wild with

*See also:* **EMOTION, FEELING, FREEDOM**

## WIN
- Get ready to win
- There's more to winning than just scoring points
- The difference between playing and winning
- If you want to win big
- Find yourself in a win win situation
- Winning big without losing big

*See also:* **BEAT, CONQUER, SUCCEED, VICTORY**

## WINNER

- Winner take all
- Go where the winners go
- You're a winner right from the start
- We want to congratulate all the winners of

*See also:* **LEADER**

## WINTER

- Say hello to winter
- Now actually enjoy winter
- Don't let winter get you down
- Now you can laugh at winter

*See also:* **SEASON**

## WIPE

- They simply wipe clean
- Wiping out your doubts about
- Now wipe out those pesty

*See also:* **CLEAN**

## WISDOM

- Ancient wisdom for a modern world
- Listen to the hard-won wisdom of
- We've accumulated a lot of wisdom over the years
- You need to find not only knowledge, but also wisdom
- The wisdom to make the right choices when they're most crucial

*See also:* **INFORMATION, KNOWLEDGE**

## WISH

- You'll wish you'd known about it years ago
- Whenever you wish
- Stop wishing and start doing
- Any time you wish, you can
- Bring us your wish list
- Ready to gratify your every wish
- Your wish is our command
- Send your heartfelt wishes with a
- Your fondest wishes realized
- Now you can realize your greatest wish
- We know what you're wishing for

**Wish:** desire, long for, want, yearn for, hope for, sigh for, care for, covet, have a yen for, hanker, fancy, bent upon, inclined to, prefer, aspire, set one's heart on, crave, relish, hunger for, fondness, liking, itch, appetite,

inclination, preference, leaning, have a mind for
*See also:* **DESIRE, WANT**

## WITHOUT
- Don't do without it
- No one should go without
- Without a doubt, it's the very best

## WONDER
- Wondering where you go from here
- No wonder we're number one
- It's one of the wonders of
- Why wonder when you can know for sure
- Small wonder it's the number one choice
- It's no wonder that
- The wonder of it is
- Is it any wonder that
- You might be wondering why we're doing this

*See also:* **MIRACLE**

## WONDERFUL
- Wide and wonderful
- Just so wonderful you can't resist
- The most wonderful product you'll ever come across

## WORD
- You have our word on it
- The word is out about
- We keep our word to you
- But don't take our word for it
- So amazing we can't quite express it in words
- Meaningful words, wise sayings
- The result is too good for words
- Words that truly inspire

*See also:* **GUARANTEE, INFORMATION, PROMISE**

## WORK
- To find out how we work, just call
- For heavy-duty work, try
- People who believe that hard work pays off
- We think hard work should pay off
- Working closely with you to achieve
- Works together with your

277

- Make light work of
- Making this product work harder for you
- They all work together for you
- You can do it while you work to
- Works the way you've always wanted it to work
- Put it to work for you right away
- If you think it's about time someone worked harder for
- Make it work for you, not against you
- We'll have you working with the best
- The hardest working part of your
- It works so well
- The work has just begun
- It really works
- All the benefits with none of the work
- It works for you
- Making quick work of
- Together, we can get down to work
- Designed to work together to
- It only works if we all do our part
- It works, period
- Begins to work immediately
- We look forward to getting to work for you
- It works well on
- It has worked for millions all over the world
- Works best when you need it most
- The harder you play, the harder it works
- And it works fast
- Here's how it works
- It's easy and it works fast
- No work, we do it all
- Helps you do a lot of work in less time
- You just know it's going to work
- It's about making your work easier and more productive
- Makes enjoyable work of even the most difficult
- So you too can put this amazing product to work for you

**Work:** effort, toil, labor, endeavor, sweat, performance, function, act, enterprise, undertaking, occupation, industry, business, trouble, pains, exertion, spare no effort, bring about, effect, attain, achieve, exercise
*See also:* **EARN, EFFORT, FUNCTION, JOB, PERFORMANCE**

**WORKOUT**
- Give yourself the ultimate workout
- Won't give your pocketbook a workout

- Give our brains a workout
- A lot more than just mental workout

## WORLD

- That's why the world's leading authorities recommend
- In today's fast-moving world you need
- Team up with world-renowned
- Explore new worlds
- Discover the exciting world of
- One of the largest in the world
- Where we go, the world tries to follow
- We select only the finest products from around the world
- Ushering you onto the world stage
- Just because you're on the other side of the world
- Some of the world's most interesting
- The world is wide
- It's a dog-eat-dog world out there
- From virtually anywhere in the world
- Making a world of difference
- Hold the world in your hand
- We'd like to hand you the world
- Enter a thrilling new world
- Thank you for inviting us into your world
- Already hard at work around the world
- Out of this world value
- Shut out the world
- Welcome to a brand new world of
- Someone who made a real difference to the world
- Your introduction to the world of
- Anywhere in the world
- Bring this exciting world right into your home
- Taste the world
- Travel the world as easily as going around the block
- Now you can enjoy one of the world's only
- It's the world's leading
- The brand new world of
- Flashing round the world
- The world's best is yet to come
- We've got the world covered
- Nobody in the world sells more
- Welcome to a whole new world of
- From the world to you
- From recognized world class

- Organized into easy-to-explore worlds
- Get the best of both worlds
- No longer worlds apart

*See also:* **EARTH**

**WORTH**

- It's time you got your money's worth
- For which you'll receive you money's worth
- We'd rather tell you what it's worth
- Undoubtedly worth the money
- Judged not by its price but by its worth
- Worth more than ever before
- Why it's worth holding onto

*See also:* **SAVINGS, VALUE**

**WRAP**

- Get wrapped up in
- Comes gift-wrapped and beautiful
- All wrapped up in savings
- We've been keeping it under wraps

*See also:* **SECRET**

**WRONG**

- All these people can't be wrong
- You're never wrong at our store
- You just can't go wrong with
- Stopping you from making the wrong choice
- Just might be wrong for you

**YEAR**

- Man/woman/idea/surprise of the year
- Every year for decades to come
- Enjoy more each year
- This is the year for you to
- Enjoy it for years to come
- Shaping up to be a very rewarding year

*See also:* **TIME**

**YES**

- Say yes to
- The answer is yes
- Yes, you can find it here
- We want you to say yes

# YOU

- It's all about you
- We do it all for you
- So we'll be there when you need us
- Then it's up to you
- Let us give you the best
- We did it, and you can too
- Time to be you
- Designed for people just like you
- It's all just for you
- Lets you do all this
- All you have to be is you
- Lets you be you
- Just be you
- And you are the reason for it all
- Made just for you
- Now you don't have to
- You can do it
- You got it
- Yes, this is the one for you
- You either have it or you don't
- You are who you are so be proud

# YOUNG

- No matter how old or young you may be
- For younger looking
- As young as you feel
- No longer the exclusive territory of the young
- Making you feel young again
- Younger looking than you ever thought possible

**Young:** adolescent, teenaged, minor, juvenile, unfledged, callow, childish, puerile, inexperienced, green, wet behind the ears, unsophisticated, naive, innocent

*See also:* **KIDS, TIMELESS**

# YOURS

- It's yours for just
- Yours for the asking
- Yours for a smile
- Get yours today
- Makeit truly yours by
- Irrevocably yours
- Something that's yours alone

281

## YOURSELF

- Doing it yourself will cost you more
- Treat yourself to the best
- Suit yourself
- Please yourself first
- Helping you take care of yourself
- Do it yourself for greater savings
- Always be yourself

*See also:* **YOU, YOURS**

## ZERO

- Zero in on who's right for you
- With zero disadvantages
- Like going from zero to a hundred in less than a second
- Zeroing in on featured values
- Start at ground zero

*See also:* **DISCOVER, FIND, SEARCH**

# NAME THAT SALE

1) Select anything from PART ONE, such as **"Blitz"**.

2) Use the name alone or match with anything from PART TWO, such as **"Holiday"**.

3) Combine to produce **"Holiday Blitz"**.

## PART ONE:

- BASH
- BLAST
- BLITZ
- BLOWOUT
- BONUS
- BUCK BUSTER
- CELEBRATION
- CLEAN OUT
- CLEAN SWEEP
- CLEAR OUT
- CLEARANCE
- CLOSE OUT
- DAYS
- DEAL
- DOORCRASHER
- EVENT
- EXPLOSION
- GIVEAWAY
- LIQUIDATION
- MADNESS
- MELTDOWN
- MONTH
- OFFER
- ROLLOUT
- SALE
- SALE-A-THON
- SPLASH
- SPECTACULAR
- SPECIAL
- SPIN OUT
- WEEK

## PART TWO:

- Adventure
- Anniversary
- Annual
- Annual Spring/Summer Fall/Winter
- Baby
- Back to School
- Bankruptcy
- Bi-annual
- Big and Tall
- Big Little
- Big Savings
- Big Value
- Birthday
- Blowout
- Boatload
- Buck Buster
- Cash and Carry
- Cash Only
- Celebration
- Centennial
- Children's
- Christmas
- Clean Out

285

- Clean Sweep
- Clear Out
- Clearance
- Clearing
- Close Out
- Closing
- Country-wide
- Doorcrasher
- Early Morning
- Easter
- Elephant
- End of Season
- Everyday
- Factory Outlet
- Factory
- Fall
- Father's Day
- Final
- Fire
- Founders Day
- Fresh Air
- Frosty Friday
- Giant Spring/ Summer/ Fall/Winter
- Going Out of Business
- Good Luck
- Goodbye
- Grand Opening
- Grand Reopening
- Half Price
- Halloween
- Happiness
- Hello Spring/ Summer/ Fall/Winter
- Holiday
- Hungry Man
- Infants
- Inside Outside
- In-store
- Inventory
- Inventory Blowout
- Kids Galore

- Kids First
- Larger Than Life
- Liquidation
- Lots-of-fun
- Lotsa Loot
- Lovers Only
- Lucky
- Lucky Saturday
- Lucky Day
- Madness
- Mail-in Rebate
- Manufacturer's Clearance
- Manufacturer's Overstock
- Marathon
- Mid-month
- Midsummer
- Mid-week
- Midwinter
- Mid-year
- Midnight Madness
- Month-end
- Mother's Day
- More for Less
- Neighborhood
- New Arrivals
- New Year
- No Worry
- Odd Size
- One Day
- One of a Kind
- Opening
- Oversize
- Overstock
- Penny
- Planeload
- Pre-season
- Price Basher
- Price Smasher
- Price Magic
- Public
- Purrrfect
- Rainy Day
- Red Tag

- Relocation
- Renovation
- Retirement
- Sale of the Month
- Saturday Sale Fever
- Save a Dollar
- Seasonal
- Semi-annual
- Shopfest
- Smash Hit
- Special Purchase
- Spin Out
- Spring Break
- Spring
- Store-wide
- Summer
- Super Duper
- Super Holiday Special
- Super Saver
- Super Special Madness
- Surprise
- Switched On

- Takeover
- Thank You
- Thanksgiving
- The Big One
- Time Out
- Tiny Tots
- Trainload
- Truckload
- Two For One
- Vacation Start-up
- Valentine's Day
- Value Added
- Vanload
- Warehouse Clearance
- Warehouse
- White
- White Elephant
- Winter
- Women's Day
- Worry Free
- Year End

# EXCLAMATIONS

- A dream come true!
- A name you can trust!
- A classic!
- Above the crowd!
- Add up the value!
- Admit it!
- All on sale!
- All new!
- Always in stock!
- An incredible secret!
- An absolute must!
- And that's not all!
- Apply today!
- Ask the experts!
- Attention pet lovers!
- Attention!
- Back by popular demand!
- Back page deals!
- Bang on savings!
- Bank on us!
- Bargain alert!
- Bargains galore!
- Be your own boss!
- Be first in line!
- Believe it!
- Best grade!
- Best in its class!
- Best buy!
- Best buy anywhere!
- Best of all!
- Better than ever!
- Better hurry!
- Brand names, low prices!
- Break out now!
- Buck buster!
- Buy one, get one free!
- Buy now, pay later!
- Buy, sell and trade!
- Call our toll-free number
- Call us today!
- Call today!
- Can you dig it!
- Cash savers!

- Cash in!
- Charge it!
- Check these deals!
- Check us out today!
- Come see what we are doing!
- Coming soon!
- Coming soon to an outlet near you!
- Command performance!
- Company's coming!
- Congratulations!
- Cool!
- Crazy days!
- Dial that phone!
- Day or night!
- Deal of the month!
- Dealers wanted!
- Do it right!
- Dollar days are here again!
- Don't miss this special offer!
- Don't miss it!
- Done!
- Don't guess!
- Don't miss out!
- Don't hesitate!
- Don't be left out!
- Don't pay for six months!
- Doorcrasher offer!
- Dreams can come true!
- Embrace temptation!
- Ends Saturday!
- Enroll now!
- Enter now!
- Environmentally sound!
- Environmentally friendly!
- Everything included!
- Factory direct!
- Factory outlet!
- Factory to you!
- Fast forward!
- Fast track value!
- Fast, friendly service!

- Final week!
- Final 3 days!
- Find out what's cooking!
- Finest quality!
- Free preview!
- Free delivery!
- Free with any purchase!
- Free with every purchase!
- Free sneak peek!
- Free trial!
- Free estimate!
- Free trial offer!
- Free!
- Fresh!
- Full steam ahead!
- Fun! Fun! Fun!
- Get the whole series!
- Get dialing!
- Get it fast!
- Get it done fast!
- Gets things moving!
- Give us a call today!
- Give yourself a head start!
- Go for broke!
- Go for it!
- Go team!
- Good news!
- Grand opening!
- Great buy!
- Heed the call!
- Help yourself today!
- Help yourself!
- Here they come!
- Here's how it works!
- Here's what you get!
- Hot deals!
- Hot buys!
- Hotline to value!
- Hottest thing going!
- Huge market demand!
- Huge price drops this week!
- Hurry in!
- Hurry in now!
- Hurry!
- Hurry! Hurry! Hurry!
- In the spotlight!
- Incredible profits!
- It works!
- It's back!
- It's that easy!
- It's a buy!
- It's time for a change!
- It's basic!
- It's your lucky day!
- It's remarkable!
- It's hot!
- Join the party!
- Just think of it!
- Just for the fun of it!
- Just rarin' to go!
- Just released!
- Kid stuff!
- Kids participate free!
- Know it all!
- Less is more!
- Lets you be you!
- Limited quantities!
- Limited time offer!
- Limited time only!
- Liquidation sale!
- Listen up!
- Long live value!
- Look for this symbol!
- Look no further!
- Look what's new!
- Look no further!
- Look here!
- Look!
- Make it happen!
- Make your dollar go further!
- Make the break!
- Make history!
- Making good things happen!
- Money-back guarantee!

- More famous brands!
- More great buys inside!
- More please!
- Need help?
- New this year!
- New and improved!
- New and improved!
- New lower prices!
- New on the market!
- New!
- News flash!
- No compromise!
- No kidding!
- No end in sight!
- No catch!
- No gimmicks!
- No way!
- No fee!
- No money down!
- No wonder!
- No problem!
- No extra cost!
- No problem!
- No mixing required!
- Nobody beats our prices!
- Nothing else to buy!
- Now on!
- Now you're talking!
- Now discounted!
- Now open!
- Now reduced!
- One week only!
- One of a kind!
- Only at this location!
- Open 7 days a week!
- Order immediately!
- Order today!
- Party time!
- Picture this!
- Picture perfect!
- Please call us!
- Please order today!
- Prices slashed!

- Quality guaranteed!
- Reach for the stars!
- Read all about it!
- Ready to install!
- Ready to use!
- Reduced again!
- Reduced!
- Reply now!
- Right on!
- Rise and shine!
- Round the clock!
- Satisfaction a must!
- Saturday only!
- Save dollars today!
- Save more!
- Save, save, save!
- Save!
- Savings alert!
- See you soon!
- Seeing is believing!
- Send no money now!
- Shop by phone!
- Show off!
- So call today!
- Something for everyone!
- Special offer!
- Special extended!
- Special purchase!
- Specially priced!
- Spectacular values!
- Start smart!
- Starting today!
- Stay cool!
- Stock up now!
- Stock up while you can!
- Stop traffic!
- Super special madness!
- Super buys!
- Super savers!
- Surprise!
- Switch and save!
- Talk about service!
- Talk about a full plate!

- That's all there is to it!
- That's impossible!
- That's right!
- The big one!
- The word is out!
- The pleasure is yours!
- The call of the wild!
- The end is near!
- The king is back!
- Think big!
- Think again!
- This week's events!
- This month's specials!
- This weekend only!
- This Saturday only!
- Three years to pay!
- Thumbs up!
- Time is running out fast!
- Today's super seller!
- Tried and true!
- Try it free!
- Try something wild!
- Unbeatable buy!
- Updated daily!
- Wake up!
- Warehouse clearance!
- Warning!
- We guarantee it!

- We do it all!
- We deliver!
- We're back!
- Week-long savings!
- Welcome y'all!
- What next!
- What a pleasure!
- What a find!
- What a natural!
- What a catch!
- When they're gone, they'gone!
- While quantities last!
- While supplies last!
- Why buy new!
- Wow, look at the sales!
- Wow!
- You win!
- You ain't seen nothin' yet!
- You can too!
- You can say that again!
- You can do it!
- You got it!
- You'll be glad you did!
- Your best buy!
- Your complete shoppingguide!
- Your choice!
- You've got it made!

# REPLY COUPONS

- As seen on TV
- As a valued customer, I will also be entitled to receive, for free examination
- Bill me in three months
- Bill me in full
- Choose a payment method
- Clip and mail right away before this great offer ends
- Clip and save
- Complete and mail this postage-paid reply card
- Complete all information
- Enroll me under the terms outlined here
- Enter me to win one of these incredible products
- Four easy payments of
- I understand there is no sign-up or monthly fee
- I would like to get more information sent to me free of charge on the advertised product or service
- I may cancel at any time
- I need send no payment now
- I understand the mailing of this card places me under no obligation
- I understand this information is free, and I am under no obligation to purchase
- I understand I need send no money now
- I understand I qualify for the seniors and pensioners discount
- I will enjoy three added bonuses
- I may return any product within thirty days for replacement or refund
- I am under no obligation
- I am interested in knowing more about
- I can't wait to receive my new
- I may purchase only those products I wish to own
- If you decide to purchase more than one product, please take note of the following volume rates
- If I continue as a member, I will receive
- Just complete and main the Request Form below
- Mail this card today
- Mail check or money order payable to
- My satisfaction is guaranteed
- My main interest is
- My signature authorizes
- No purchase necessary
- Not available in any retail store
- Offer expires on this date
- Payment enclosed
- Phone or fax for faster response

- Photocopy this form for a friend
- Please, tell me more about the following programs
- Please check off the service offer(s) you would like
- Please send the following titles
- Please read this important information and sign below
- Please print clearly
- Please makes cheques payable to
- Please check off which product you wish to purchase
- Please accept my enrollment and send me
- Please enter me into the contest to win a complete set
- Please send your cheque or money order to
- Please have a specialist phone me about
- Please send me my free
- Please take a minute to answer the following questions, so we can better provide the solutions you need
- Please register me for the
- Please help us keep our records up to date by telling us if you have recently moved, or of any other change in information
- Please fill out the information below so we can direct our communications to
- Pre-register before this date
- Reply now for a full color catalogue
- Reserve your place today by filling in your name and address
- Return order form to
- Risk-free guarantee
- Rush me these products now
- Send no money now
- Send me the product and bill me only
- Send my free bonus as soon as you receive my order
- Send me more information now
- Send my friend a
- Send me the next issue of
- service you need for your
- These offers are valid at all participating
- This information is strictly confidential and will be used for the sole purpose of
- Three easy ways to sign up
- Use the attached coupon and save
- Yes, I would like to order
- Yes, enter my subscription to
- Yes, I want to save on
- Yes, I want to participate
- Yes, please reserve for me

- Yes, I want to know more about
- Yes, please send me
- Yes! Please enter my order for
- Yes! I'd like to find out more about
- Yes! I request access to
- Yes! I want access to
- Yes! My career needs a boost
- Yes! Please rush me more details about
- Yes! Please give me all the facts about
- Yes! Please send me the product
- Yes! I want to give a one-year gift subscription for only
- Yes! Please give me all the facts about
- Yes! I want to switch to
- Your comments would be appreciated

# BEGINNINGS
# AND
# TRANSITIONS

- A dramatic shift in
- A clear indication that
- As further analysis shows
- According to the myth
- Add to that
- Additionally
- Advocating a dramatic departure from
- Again and again
- Also
- An apt description of
- And in preparation for
- And you know what
- And you must remember
- And best of all
- Anyway
- Apparently
- Apropos to
- Arguably
- As a matter of fact
- As an added bonus
- As a result
- As you read this crucial message
- As an example
- As you can see
- As you know
- As well
- Assuming that
- Assuredly
- At this time
- At one point
- At first glance
- At the end of the day
- Because ultimately
- Behind the scenes
- Believe me
- Best of all
- Better still
- Beyond that, however, is
- But there it is

- But as usual
- But on the other hand
- But thanks to
- But you know what
- Candidly speaking
- Categorically
- Certainly
- Contributing to the shift away from
- Cost-effectively
- Covered exclusively by
- Did you know that
- Diplomatically
- Don't ever forget that
- Either way
- Elsewhere
- Equally important is
- Especially when
- Even now
- Even better yet
- Even as you read this ad
- Ever faithful
- Every minute, every day
- Examples include
- First and foremost
- Firstly
- For openers
- For the first time ever
- For emphasis
- For starters
- For example
- Fortunately
- Frankly
- From time to time
- Happily
- Has always been our calling card
- Here is a perfect example
- Honestly
- How otherwise could we
- However

- We want you to know
- You may wonder if
- You understand that
- In many instances
- In case you're wondering why
- In conclusion
- In so many instances
- In anticipation of
- In the meantime
- In any case
- In the beginning
- In the first place
- In addition
- In brief
- In the tradition of
- In accordance with
- In particular
- In addition
- In essence
- In a nutshell
- In recent years
- In keeping with
- In this regard
- Inasmuch as
- Indisputably
- Initially
- Invite you to
- Inviting as it seems
- It is impossible to even estimate
- It is estimated that
- It also explains why
- It really comes down to this
- It also explains a lot about
- It all adds up to
- It's interesting to note
- It's not just a plan to
- It's even more unthinkable that
- It's obvious by now
- It's imperative that

- It's quite obvious that
- It's no coincidence that
- It's essential that
- It's a foregone conclusion
- Be certain that
- You can be sure that
- Just in case
- Just between us
- Just one example is
- Last year alone
- Lastly
- Lessons can be drawn from
- Let us assure you that
- Make no mistake about it
- May we introduce ourselves
- Meanwhile, back on the farm
- More certain than ever
- More efficient than ever
- More recently
- Moreover
- Most of all
- Most sincerely
- Naturally
- Needless to say
- Nevertheless
- No one likes to
- No doubt about it
- Not if you want to
- Of course
- Of course, on the other hand
- Often, all it takes is
- On behalf of
- On a scale of one to ten
- On the other hand
- On a positive note
- On second thought
- On an absolute scale
- On the home front
- Once and for all

- Once again
- One way or the other
- One good example is
- One of the strongest pieces of evidence is
- Only natural that
- Overly optimistic projections can
- Please read on
- Please be sure to
- Primarily
- Provide access to
- Quite simply
- Rationally speaking
- Realistically
- Regardless
- Rest assured, however, that
- Revealed by further analysis is
- Right now
- Secondarily
- Secondly
- Shortly
- Simply put
- Since our founding back in
- Sometimes
- Speaking of which
- Starting from the top
- Surely, however
- That distinction is reserved for
- The most intriguing thing about this is
- The list goes on
- The prognosis is
- The other day
- The data are quite clear on
- The irony is that
- The important thing is
- The way we see it is
- The thing is
- The truth is
- The crowning touch
- There's no such thing as

- There's no denying that
- Thirdly
- Thousands, to be exact
- To begin with
- To be honest
- To say the least
- To improve matters
- To put it mildly
- To commemorate
- To start with
- Today
- Truth to tell
- Truthfully
- Ultimately
- Undeniably
- Understandably
- We pride ourselves on
- We watched in admiration as
- What's more
- When it comes to
- Whether you're concerned about
- With this in view
- Without quibbling too much
- You can call it what you like
- You have the option to
- You might want to consider
- You might conclude that
- You should also know that
- You may not know this, but
- You even have the choice of
- You see

# POWER WORDS

**A blast**
- Blast-off
- Boom
- Booming
- Bursting
- Dynamite
- Explosion
- Explosive
- Fireworks
- Pow
- Pyrotechnic
- Rocket
- Thunder
- Thundrous

**Ablaze**
- Afire
- Blazing
- Blistering
- Conflagration
- Fiery
- Fire
- Flame
- Furnace
- Heated
- Hot
- Hotter
- Hottest
- Ignite
- Incandescent
- Kindle
- Red hot
- Scalding
- Scorching
- Searing
- Sizzle
- Sizzling
- Smouldering
- Spitfire
- Torchy

**Able**
- Affect

- Capable
- Capacity
- Practical
- Pragmatic
- Resourceful
- Self-starting

**Abound**
- Abundance
- Abundant
- Bonanza
- Crammed
- Double
- Enriched
- Enriching
- Extensive
- Free-flowing
- Full-blown
- Fully-loaded
- High-yield
- Lavish
- Liberal
- Loaded
- Lots
- Luxuriant
- Numerous
- Packed with
- Plentiful
- Triple
- Unconditional

**Absolute**
- Ageless
- Eternal
- Everlasting
- Forever
- Perpetual
- Universal

**Absorbent**
- All-weather
- Flesh
- Geometric

- Material
- Molded
- Pre-owned
- Prefinished
- Retouch
- Woody

**Accelerated**
- Fast forward
- Fast
- Fast-paced
- Faster
- Fastest
- Gallop
- High-speed
- Hurry
- Overdrive
- Presto
- Prompt
- Quick
- Quick 'n
- Quicken
- Quickest
- Race
- Racing
- Racy
- Rush
- Speeded-up
- Speedy
- Stampede
- Swift

**Accent**
- Acknowledge
- Attention
- Highlights
- Juxtapose
- Limelight
- Notice
- Notice-me
- Privilege
- Selected
- Target

## Accentuate
- Beef-up
- Boost
- Booster
- Deepen
- Enhance
- Enhancing
- Enrich
- Enriching

## Access
- Accessible
- Accommodate
- Automatic
- Available
- Built-in
- Convenient
- Frequent
- Handle
- Handy
- Handy for
- In-store
- One stop
- Portability
- Portable
- Suitable for

## Accessory
- Accompanied by
- Blend
- Companion
- Compatible
- Complimentary
- Cross-reference
- Juxtapose
- Matching
- Paired
- Shared
- Simultaneous
- Supporting
- Together

## Acclaimed
- Acknowledged
- Celebrated
- Established
- Recommended

## Accolade
- Adoration
- Applause
- Praise
- Kudos

## Achieve
- Achievement
- Achiever
- Create
- Feat
- Performance

## Acknowledged
- Blockbuster
- Blowout
- Champion
- Hero
- Outstanding
- Overwhelming
- Towering
- Winner
- Winning

## Action
- Action-packed
- Activate
- Adventure
- Aggressive
- Bounce
- Bouncy
- Bounding
- Contagious
- High performance
- Made-for-adventure

## Actual
- Genuine
- Honest-to-goodness
- Palpable
- Real
- Real-world
- Reality
- Template
- Undeniable
- Valid
- Verified
- Virtually
- Visibly

## Adapt
- Adaptable
- Compliant
- Comply
- Compromise
- Options
- Pliable
- Programmable

## Add
- Add-on
- Additional
- Adopt
- Alternate
- Bonus
- Plus
- Topped with
- Upgrade
- Upload

## Adjustable
- Agile
- All-purpose
- Diverse
- Ever-evolving
- Flexible
- Interchangeable
- Multi-

- Multi-function
- Multi-media
- Multi-purpose
- Multi-use
- Reversible
- Supple
- Transitional

**Adore**
- Adored
- Bask
- Beloved
- Care
- Caring
- Compassionate
- Heart
- Heartfelt
- Indulgent
- Love
- Worship

**Advance**
- Advanced
- Advancement
- Ahead
- All-new
- Au currant
- Avant-garde
- Breakaway
- Breakthrough
- Cutting-edge
- Early
- Early bird
- Educated
- Enhancement
- Forward-looking
- Fusion
- Future
- Futuristic
- Initiate
- Initiative
- Innovation
- Innovative

- Latest
- Leading-edge
- New dawn
- New
- New-age
- Newborn
- Newest
- Nouveau
- Novel
- Novelty
- Pioneer
- Revolutionary
- Space age
- Trial run

**Advertise**
- Conjure
- Develop
- Download
- Promote
- Represent
- Upload

**Advocate**
- Help
- Helpful
- Helping
- Welcome
- Welcoming

**Afford**
- Affordable
- Available
- Buyable
- Low cost
- Save
- Savings
- Thrifty
- Value

**Age**
- Century
- Eon

- Era
- Millenium

**Age-defying**
- Ageless
- Taut
- Younger-looking
- Youthful

**Aged**
- Ancient
- Old
- Oldest
- Retro
- Timeless
- Vintage
- Vintage-inspired

**Aim**
- Destination
- Goal
- Intention
- Target

**Alchemy**
- Enchanting
- Enchantment
- Enchantress
- Magic
- Magical
- Mysterious
- Mystery
- Mystical
- Secret
- Sorcerer
- Sorceress
- Sorcery
- Spell
- Spellbinding
- Spellbound
- Wizard
- Wizardry

## Alert
- Alive
- Avid
- Go-ahead
- Lifelike
- Magnetizing
- Never dull

## All-inclusive
- All-time
- Every
- Everything
- Everywhere
- Panacea

## All-star
- Compelling
- Five star
- Highest
- Must
- Must-have

## Allow
- Let
- Release
- Treat

## Allure
- Attractive
- Beautiful
- Draw
- Entice
- Enticing
- Handsome
- Lovely
- Sharp-looking

## Alone
- Idiosyncratic
- Independence
- Independent
- Individual
- Individualist
- Individually

- One of a
- One-of-a-kind
- One-touch
- Only
- Original
- Originality
- Particular
- Particularly
- Private
- Single
- Singular
- Singular
- Solitary
- Solo
- Unique

## Alp
- Apex
- Beyond
- Conqueror
- Hero
- Jackpot

## Amazing
- Astonishing
- Awe-inspiring
- Dazzling
- Dizzying
- Drop-dead
- Extraordinary
- Eye-popping
- Incredible
- Knock down
- Knockout
- Mind-boggling
- Outrageous
- Shattering
- Smashing
- Spectacular
- Staggering
- Startling
- Stunning
- Stupendous

- Traffic stopper
- Unbelievable
- Uncanny

## Ambiance
- Ambient
- Atmosphere
- Bathed in
- Limpid
- Misty

## Amok
- Boffo
- Giddy
- Hilarious
- Howling
- Out-there
- Outrageous
- Pandemonium
- Socko
- Uproarious
- Whoop-up

## Angle
- Ball
- Bat
- Flag
- Page
- Shoot
- Texture
- Track
- Wall

## Anticipate
- Discover
- Explore
- Find
- Found
- Intrigued
- Look for
- Rediscover
- Reinvent
- Search

314

- Seek
- Unravel

**Appeal**
- Appealing
- Beguile
- Clear
- Colorful
- Crisp
- Dandy
- Delight
- Desire
- Effortless
- Elegy
- Evocative
- Eye-catching
- Fashionable
- Favorite
- Gold
- Golden
- Good
- Picturesque
- Precious
- Preferred
- Quaint
- Yearn

**Appetite**
- Eagerness
- Hunger
- Ravenous
- Yearning

**Appointed**
- Esteem
- Motherhood
- Respect
- Respectful
- Revere
- Reverence

**Aristocratic**
- Arrogant

- Blue chip
- Diva
- Imperious
- Privileged
- Swish

**Aroma**
- Aromatic
- Breathable
- Musky
- Perfume
- Scented
- Unscented

**Arouse**
- Catapult
- Jazz
- Juicy
- Jump
- Lightning
- Revved up
- Rocket
- Surrender
- Swath
- Synergistic

**Art**
- Artful
- Artfully
- Artistry
- Creative
- Creativity
- Picture
- Portrait
- Sculpture

**Ask**
- Aspire
- Challenge
- Compare
- Estimate
- Inquire
- Reckon

**Assemble**
- Deliver
- Furnish
- Install
- Provide
- Serve
- Service

**Assorted**
- Assortment
- Blend
- Eclectic
- Ensemble
- Medley
- Random
- Scattershot
- Variety

**Assure**
- Certainty
- Certified
- Cinch
- Complete
- Ensure
- Guarantee
- Ingrained
- Patented
- Proof
- Surefire
- Truth
- Warranty

**Astronomical**
- Celestial
- Comet
- Cosmic
- Divine
- Extraterrestrial
- Heavenly
- Stellar

**Astute**
- Canny

315

- Clever
- Discerning
- Genius
- Intelligent
- Learn
- Savvy
- Sharp
- Sharpest
- Skillful
- Smart
- Sophisticated
- Talented
- Tricky

**Attribute**
- Condition
- Conditioning
- Tone

**Audacious**
- Audacity
- Bold
- Brash
- Daring
- Dash
- Dashing
- Derring-do
- Sass
- Sassy
- Spirited

**Avail**
- Effective
- Equipped
- Functional
- Functionality
- Serviceability
- Use
- Useful
- Usefulness
- Utilize
- Work

**Award-winning**
- Deserve
- Deserving
- Esteemed
- Highly-regarded
- Reputed
- Respectable

**Awe**
- Impress
- Interest
- Interesting

**Baby**
- Childish
- Childlike
- Germinate
- Infant
- Young
- Youth

**Background**
- Heritage
- Historical
- History
- Legacy
- Story

**Balance**
- Harmony
- Join
- Link
- Range
- Setting

**Ballad**
- Cavalier
- Celebrate
- Celebration
- Gala
- Ode
- Poem
- Poetry

**Banish**
- Discontinued
- Elimination
- Fewer
- Impossible
- Less
- Minimize
- Nadir
- Never
- No
- Notorious
- Overstatement
- Preventable
- Prevents
- Reduce
- Unacceptable
- Zero

**Basted**
- Buttery
- Chewy
- Confection
- Creamy
- Delicious
- Flavor
- Fruity
- Gourmet
- Mouth-watering
- Recipe
- Savoury
- Scrumptious
- Slice
- Smack
- Smothered
- Succulent
- Tasteful
- Tastefully
- Tasty
- Yummy

**Battle-tested**
- Durable
- Endurance

- Endure
- Indelible
- Indestructible
- Indispensable
- Lasting
- Lastingly
- Stamina

**Bedazzle**
- Bright
- Brightest
- Brilliance
- Brilliant
- Burnished
- Gilded
- Glistening
- Glitter
- Glittering
- Glitzy
- Phosphorescent
- Scintillating
- Shimmer
- Shimmering
- Shine
- Shiny
- Sparkling

**Bedecked**
- Decorative
- Decorator-inspired
- Embellished
- Ornament
- Ornamental

**Bedew**
- Dew
- Dewy
- Greased
- Moisture-rich
- Sheen
- Slick
- Wet-look

**Begin**
- Beginning
- Dawn of
- Debut
- Initiate
- Introduce
- Introducing
- Introductory
- Self-starting
- Springboard
- Start
- Start-up
- Unfold
- Unleash

**Believe**
- Believer
- Optimist
- Optimistic

**Benchmark**
- Example
- Hallmark
- Measure
- Metaphor
- Model
- Namesake
- Reference
- Standard

**Best**
- Best-ever
- Finest
- Master
- Masterpiece
- Masterwork
- Maximum
- Olympian
- Olympic
- Optimum
- Optimal
- Optimize
- Peak

- Premium
- Prime
- Purest
- Smartest
- Supreme
- Tiptop
- Unbeatable
- Unrivalled
- Unsurpassed
- Zenith

**Best-loved**
- Bestseller
- Conquer
- Conquering
- Notable
- Notch above
- Noteworthy
- Remarkably

**Better**
- Improve
- Improvement
- Refine
- Refinements

**Better**
- Finer
- Mainstream
- More

**Big**
- Biggest-selling
- Bigtime
- Colossal
- Enormous
- Epic
- Epoch
- Extra-big
- Extra-long
- Extravaganza
- Extreme
- Gargantuan

317

- Giant
- Gigantic
- Ginormous
- Grand
- Grandeur
- Great
- Heroic
- High-capacity
- Huge
- Humungous
- Imposing
- Jumbo
- Large
- Legion
- Lofty
- Major
- Mind-boggling
- Monster
- Monstrous
- Mountain
- Outsize
- Sky-high
- Ultra strong
- Ultra
- Vast
- Whopper
- Whopping

**Bioforce**
- Chemical-free
- Earth bound
- Earth
- Earth-friendly
- Earth-safe
- Earthy
- Eco-friendly
- Environment
- Habitat
- Lake
- Life
- Live
- Mother
- Motherly

- Natural
- Naturally
- Nature
- Ocean
- Rooted
- Sea
- Solar
- Summer
- Sun
- Sunshine

**Bloom-crazy**
- Blooming
- Bouquet
- Floral
- Flowery

**Bolt**
- Chug
- Click
- Quiver
- Rack up
- Rap
- Smack

**Bond**
- Destiny
- Fate
- Guarantee
- Pledge
- Vow
- Warranty

**Boundless**
- Countless
- Limitless
- Unlimited

**Branch**
- Branching
- Multiply
- Propagate

**Bravo**
- Hit
- Home-run
- Win

**Break**
- Contrast
- Controversial
- Drift away
- Drifts
- Open
- Out of this
- Out

**Breathless**
- Breathtaking
- Rapture
- Rapturous
- Thrill
- Thriller
- Thrilling
- Tingle
- Viva
- Vive
- Vivid
- Volatile

**Breeze**
- Breezy
- Brio
- Festive
- Fizz
- Fizzy
- Jazzy
- Perk
- Perky
- Pizzazz
- Snazzy
- Zip
- Zippy

**Bridge**
- Byway

- Country
- Distance
- Highway
- Hub
- Journey
- Map
- Odyssey
- Vacation

**Broad**
- Empire
- Global
- International
- Internationally
- World
- Worldwide

**Broad-based**
- Inclusive
- Rangy
- Wide

**Buccaneer**
- Catch
- Capture
- Cavalry
- Control
- Force
- Kingmaker
- Militant
- Military
- Outperform
- Overcome
- Piratical
- Prevail

**Buckbuster**
- Bucks
- Budget
- Cash
- Cash in
- Cash
- Commercial
- Cost

- Dollars
- Earn
- Financial
- Invaluable
- Invest
- Investor-owned
- Millions
- Money tree
- Money
- Moolah
- Nonrefundable
- Payoff
- Pocketbook
- Precious
- Pricey
- Profit
- Profitable
- Recession-proof
- Refundable
- Spendable
- Valuable
- Value
- Value-driven
- Value-packed

**Busy**
- Countdown
- Enthusiastically
- Hardest-working
- Industry
- Nurse
- Push
- Shopfest
- Strategy
- Street smart

**Calm**
- Calming
- Candle light
- Cradled
- Nestle
- Relax
- Relaxing
- Serenity

- Soft
- Soften
- Soothing
- Tempered

**Carefree**
- Cheers
- Enjoy
- Glad
- Hallelujah
- Happiness
- Happy
- Joy
- Joyful
- Joyous
- Light-hearted
- Merriment
- Merry
- Rejoice
- Rejoicing

**Careful**
- Risk-free
- Safe
- Safety
- Sanctuary
- Shield
- Worry-free

**Carnival**
- Escapade
- Festival
- Festivity
- Jubilee
- Party

**Cataclysmic**
- Delirious
- Extremist
- Madly
- Madness
- Manic
- Obsess
- Obsessed

- Obsession

**Center**
- Genre
- Headquarters
- Showroom
- System

**Ceremony**
- Courtesy
- Development
- Event
- Holiday
- Scenario

**Chameleon-like**
- Change
- Metamorphosis
- Restructure
- Revised
- Transform
- Transforming
- Versatile
- Versatility

**Champagne**
- Decadent
- Fancy
- Luxurious
- Luxury
- Magnificent
- Opulence
- Opulent
- Rich
- Splendor
- Sumptuous
- Wealthy

**Chance**
- Factor
- Opportune
- Opportunity
- Potential

- Preview
- Test

**Charged up**
- Crackle
- Dynamic
- Electrifying
- Energize
- Energy
- Supercharged
- Voltage
- Zap

**Chase**
- Headlong
- Pursue
- Pursuit

**Cheeky**
- Contagious
- Impish
- Infectious
- Kicky
- Saucy
- Whimsical

**Chi-chi**
- Chic
- Elegant
- Elegantly
- Fashion
- Sporty
- Style
- Stylish

**Chivalrous**
- Chivalry
- Fervor
- Inspiration
- Inspire
- Inspiring
- Intense
- Intoxicating

- Passion
- Possessed
- Romantic
- Sentimental

**Choice**
- Choose
- Choosey
- Decide
- Decidedly
- Decision
- Determine
- Pick
- Picky
- Select
- Selection

**Chuckle**
- Giggle
- Laughs
- Laughter
- Smile
- Smiling

**Circle**
- Spin
- Rotate
- Turn
- Whirl

**Civic**
- Correct
- Obey
- Right

**Civil**
- Civilized
- Kind
- Polish
- Polished
- Sophisticated
- Suave
- Urbane

**Clarifying**
- Contemplate
- Rational
- Reasoned
- Reflect
- Reflection
- Sense
- Sensibility

**Class**
- Group
- Kind
- Sort
- Species

**Classic**
- Classy
- Dress
- Dressy
- Eloquent
- Exquisite
- Grace
- Graceful
- Gracious
- Hauteur
- Refinement
- Signature

**Clean**
- Clean-cut
- Flawless
- Immaculate
- Pristine
- Pure
- Purer
- Purest
- Sanitary
- Virgin

**Close-up**
- Confidential
- First-hand
- Intimacy

- Intimate
- Intricate
- Lock-in
- Nuances
- Personal
- Personalize

**Cloud-light**
- Delicate
- Downy
- Fluffy
- Gentle
- Gentleness
- Soft
- Velvety

**Cloud-soft**
- Featherweight
- Light
- Lightweight
- Ultra light

**Comeback**
- Refund
- Restorative
- Restores
- Revive

**Comfort**
- Cool
- Friendly
- Refreshing
- Forgiving
- Friendship
- Serendipitous
- Serendipity
- Simple

**Comic**
- Frivolity
- Froth
- Fun
- Fun-loving

- Funhouse
- Funky
- Funny
- Hopscotch
- Joke
- Kidding
- Quip

**Commitment**
- Devoted
- Devotional
- Faith
- Faithful
- Loyalty
- Patriotic
- Trust

**Communication**
- Flyer
- Message
- Offer

**Competition**
- Contest
- Provocation
- Rival
- Rivalry
- Victory

**Competitive**
- Entrepreneurial
- Enterprise
- Venture

**Completely**
- Comprehensive
- Filled
- Extensive
- Extra
- General
- Stranglehold
- Thoroughly
- Ubiquitous

- Unfiltered
- Utterly

**Computer-friendly**
- Computerized
- Cyber
- Cyberpal
- Wired

**Concept**
- Idea
- Instinct
- Thought

**Conservative**
- Consistency
- Consistent
- Dependability
- Dependable
- Fail-proof
- Goofproof
- Guaranteed
- Proven
- Reliable
- Rely
- Stable
- Steady
- Time-tested
- True
- Warranted

**Content**
- Peace
- Peaceful
- Peacemaker

**Contour**
- Proportions
- Shape
- Shaped

**Convenience**
- Ease

- Easier
- Easiest
- Easy
- Easy-to-use
- Elementary
- Immediate
- Instant
- Instantly
- Low-maintenance
- Low-tech

**Copy**
- Imitate
- Mimic

**Craft**
- Crafted
- Fashioned
- Hand-formed
- Hand-picked

**Craze**
- Crazy
- Fad
- Insane
- Loony
- Nuts
- Nutty
- Wacky

**Creditable**
- Credit
- Respected
- Tested
- Trustworthy
- Truthful

**Crescendo**
- Suspense
- Tension

**Critical**
- Critically

- Crucial
- Crunch
- Urgency
- Urgent
- Urgently

**Crowd-pleasing**
- Promotable
- Popular

**Crucial**
- Important
- Limelight
- Mission-critical
- Vital

**Cultivate**
- Develop
- Exponential
- Grown up
- Growth
- Plow

**Cut above**
- Exceptional
- First
- First class
- Grade A
- Superb
- Superior
- Top form
- Top drawer
- Top quality
- Top-rated
- Topnotch
- Tops
- Unprecedented
- World class
- World-beater
- World-beating

**Dance**
- Danceable

- Dancing
- Flowing

**Danger**
- Hazard
- Peril
- Risk
- Warning

**Darling**
- Dear
- Huggable
- Lovable
- Love-struck
- Loved
- Lover
- Sweet
- Tender

**Dedicated**
- Determined
- Diligent
- Disciplined
- Dogged
- Effort
- Highly-motivated
- Insistence
- Perseverance
- Persistence
- Relentless
- Remorseless
- Uncompromised
- Undaunted

**Deep**
- Discreet
- Sensible
- Serious

**Defining**
- Especially
- Exclusive to
- Exclusive

- Special
- Specialize
- Specially
- Specialty
- Specific

**Demonstrate**
- Display
- Present
- Show

**Deserving**
- Excellence
- Excellent
- Quality
- Quality-crafted

**Design**
- Order
- Organize
- Plan

**Desirable**
- Erotic
- Hunk
- Hunky
- Kissable
- Lusty
- Seduce
- Seductive
- See-through
- Sensuous
- Sexiest
- Sexy
- Slinky
- Sultry
- Sybaritic

**Diaphanous**
- Sheen
- Sheer
- Transparent

**Different**
- Distinct
- Divide
- Division
- Spin-off

**Distinctive**
- Impressive
- Remarkable
- Significant

**Domestic**
- Domestically
- Home
- Home-style
- Homebody
- Homecoming
- Hearth
- Lair
- Refuge
- Sojourn

**Door**
- Doorway
- Enter
- Gate
- Gateway
- Key

**Drama**
- Dramatic
- Dramatically
- Theatrical

**Drench**
- Flood
- Flooded
- Free-flowing
- Overflows
- Poured

**Ecstacy**
- Ecstatic

- Gripping
- Rhapsodic
- Rhapsody

**Efficient**
- Efficiency
- Energy-saving
- Practiced
- Well-oiled

**Element**
- Essence
- Fundamental
- Lasting
- Substance
- Root

**Elevate**
- Profound
- Radical
- Speechless
- Transfix
- Transported

**Emotion**
- Emotional
- Evoke
- Excite
- Excitement
- Experience
- Feeling
- Haunting
- Moving
- Touch
- Touching

**Emperor**
- Imperial
- King
- Kingpin
- Prince
- Princely
- Princess

- Queen
- Queenly
- Royal

**End**
- Final
- Finale
- Finish

**Enlighten**
- Illuminating
- Inspirational
- Vision
- Visionary
- Vista
- Wisdom
- Wise
- Wiser
- Wisest

**Essence**
- Nirvana
- Quintessential
- Seminal
- Ultimate

**Example**
- Model
- Paradigm
- Replica

**Exotic**
- Rare
- Rarified
- Uncommon
- Unusual
- Weird

**Expanded**
- Extended
- Extra
- Plus

**Expert**
- Expertly
- Master
- Mistress
- Virtuosity
- Virtuoso

**Fabled**
- Fabulous
- Fantastic
- Marvel
- Marvelous
- Wonder
- Wonderful
- Wondrous

**Famous**
- Newsworthy
- Reputation

**Fearless**
- Fierce
- Fight
- Feisty
- Ferocious
- Roar

**Flair**
- Impact
- Punch

**Florid**
- Flourish
- Plump
- Plush

**Flow**
- Pool
- Splash
- Spurt
- Wave
- Well

**Fly**
- Flight
- Leap
- Leapfrog
- Soar
- Wind
- Wings

**Fortunate**
- Fortune
- Positively
- Productive

**Free**
- Free trial
- Freebie
- Gift
- Unload

**Fresh**
- Fresh-picked
- Freshen
- Fresher
- Freshest
- Freshly

**Generous**
- Gratifying
- Gratitude
- Thank you
- Thanks

**Glamorous**
- Glorious
- Gorgeous
- Lush

**Gleam**
- Glimmer
- Gloss
- Glossy
- Lambent
- Lustre
- Lustrous

- Moon
- Moonlight
- Moonshine
- Translucent

**Groove**
- Groovy
- Hip
- Hipper
- Hippest
- Yuppie

**Habit**
- Method
- Methodical
- Step-by-step
- Way

**Hammer**
- Physical
- Practical
- Tool

**Handful**
- Heap
- Load
- Trove

**Healthy**
- Healthy-looking
- Hearty
- Rosy
- Shapely
- Tonic
- Vital
- Wholesome

**Heavy**
- Heavy duty
- Heavyweight
- Hefty

**Height**
- Heights

- High
- Higher

**Honest**
- Honesty
- Integrity
- Truly

**Horsepower**
- Potency
- Potent
- Power
- Power-packed
- Powered
- Powerful
- Pressure
- Prowess
- Rigor
- Rigorous
- Steam
- Strength

**Humanity**
- Kindness
- Soul
- Soul mate

**Humble**
- Modest
- Neat
- Nice
- Nicely
- Nifty

**Husky**
- Industrial
- Reinforced
- Resistant
- Rock
- Rugged
- Shock-absorbing
- Strenuous
- Strong

- Stronger
- Strongest
- Tough

**Hybrid**
- Integrated
- Interface
- Merge
- Merger
- Synthesis

**Hypnotic**
- Hypnotize
- Magnetizing
- Mesmerize
- Rivetting

**Ideal**
- Ideal for
- Perfect
- Perfecting
- Perfection

**Indefinable**
- Mysterious
- Secret

**Invigorate**
- Regenerate
- Regeneration
- Rejuvenate
- Rejuvenating
- Rejuvenation
- Revitalize
- Revitalizing
- Stimulate
- Stimulating

**Invincible**
- Irresistible
- Unbeatable
- Undefeated

**Leader**
- Leadership
- Leading
- Pacesetter
- Premier
- Premiere
- Star
- Top of the Top
- Topdog
- Uncontested
- Undisputed

**Legendary**
- Renowned
- Storied

**Lifetime**
- Long-range
- Preserve

**Long**
- Lanky
- Tall
- Tiptoe

**Lyrical**
- Melodic
- Musical
- Operatic
- Song
- Tinkling

**Magnificent**
- Out-there
- Rewarding
- Smash
- Smash hit
- Splendid
- State-of-the-art
- Stunner
- Super duper
- Super
- Treasure

**Meaningful**
- Memorable
- Persuasive
- Remember
- Resonance
- Resonant
- Unforgetable

**Move**
- Relocate
- Shift

**Outlaw**
- Iconoclast
- Maverick
- Rebel
- Rebellion
- Rebellious

**Own**
- Possess
- Possession

**Participate**
- Partnership
- Share

**Pleasure**
- Satisfy
- Satisfaction

**Position**
- Profile
- Presence
- Stand

**Precise**
- Precision
- Spot on

**Problem-solving**
- Troubleshoot
- Troubleshooter

**Progress**
- Progressive
- Spearhead
- Tomorrow
- Uncharted

**Project**
- Series
- Scientific
- Statistically

**Purveyor**
- Salesperson
- Seller
- Staff
- Vendor

**Quiet**
- Silent
- Whisper-quiet
- Whisper-smooth

**Radiant**
- Star-studded
- Starry
- Starstruck
- Sun-loving
- Sunny
- Twinkling

**Raging**
- Rambunctious
- Rampage
- Reckless
- Riot
- Riotous
- Rip snorting
- Rip roaring
- Untamable
- Untamed
- Widest
- Wild
- Wilder

- Wildest

**Ready**
- Ready-made
- Ready-mixed
- Ready-to-use
- Ready-to-wear

**Recycled**
- Refillable
- Removable
- Renewable
- Replacement
- Reusable

**Reliable**
- Steady
- Unshakable
- Unsinkable
- Unswerving
- Unwavering

**Remedy**
- Results
- Reward
- Solution
- Success
- Successful
- Yields

**Resilience**
- Resiliency
- Resilient
- Responsive
- Responsiveness

**Ripe**
- Mature
- Maturity

**Roomy**
- Spacious
- Capacious

**Satiny**
- Seamless
- Silkier
- Silky
- Sleek
- Sleeker
- Smooth

**Seal**
- Stamp
- Wrap

**Sponsor**
- Sponsored
- Support

**Storm**
- Stormy
- Tempest
- Tempestuous

**Subtle**
- Subtlety
- Understated
- Undertones

**Swell**
- Swing
- Swirl
- Swoop

**Thumbs up**
- Vocal
- Wow
- Wowed

**Total**
- Complete
- Whole

**Unexpected**
- Spontaneous

- Surprise

**Wash 'n wear**
- Washable
- Waterproof
- Wear-resistant
- Wearable
- Weatherproof

**Well-balanced**
- Well-established
- Well-prepared
- Well-validated

# *Marketing Phrase Book*

## Professional Edition

Do you have more complex, demanding promotional needs? Give yourself the added advantage of the *Marketing Phrase Book, Professional Edition.*

The Professional Edition is a major resource, greatly expanded all round and offering large additional sections on:

### Computers and the Internet

Today, as technology increases more and more of the market is moving onto the Web. Get a head start with the language that sells in cyberspace.

### Contests and Sweepstakes

Boost the excitement of contests and sweepstakes that add extra drawing power to so many of your promotions.

### Telemarketing

The telephone is one of your most crucial sales tools. Improve the effectiveness of your telephone selling techniques and make every call yield great marketing results.

### Colors

You never dreamed there were so many different words for color. Choose from a vast and dazzling array of tints, shades, hues and nuances to find that very special description you've been looking for.

Spiral bound to lie flat for easy reference.

Two volumes
667 Pages
$64.95
ISBN 0-9680853-3-4

# Fundraiser's Phrase Book

The *Fundraiser's Phrase Book* provides you with thousands of winning phrases designed for the nonprofit professional.

## INSIDE YOU'LL FIND:

- Hundreds of ways to ask for help, support, donations, gifts, assistance, aid, sponsorship, MONEY, members, volunteers, etc.

- All the "trigger words" that set donors reaching for their check books.

- Columns of creative, donor-friendly salutations as well as clever envelope teasers and urgings your lapsed donors and members can't resist.

- Dozens of ways to persuasively word that vitally important reply device.

- Help to communicate in a warm, one-to-one manner so essential in getting your message across with powerful emotional impact.

## INVALUABLE WHEN:

- You know what you want to say but you just can't put your finger on the right words.

- You want to revitalize and update your work.

- You need new ideas to jump-start your imagination.

## TERRIFIC FOR:

- Letters
- Newsletters
- Speeches
- Grant applications
- Proposals
- Web pages

**and**

**Fundraising Packages that really work!**

*Fundraiser's Phrase Book*
Standard Edition:
301 pages, spiral bound
$44.95
ISBN 0-9680853-0-X


*Fundraiser's Phrase Book*
Deluxe Edition
526 pages, spiral bound
$74.95
ISBN 0-9680853-1-8
Expanded edition, featuring large bonus sections on today's
hottest topics – the **Internet, Contests and Sweepstakes** and
**Telephone Campaigns**.

\* \* \*

*"What a great idea! Old hands like me often need some starter
phrases. Entry level fundraisers can quickly find a phrase without
trying to invent the wheel."*
**Jerry Huntsinger**
**Fundraising Expert**


*"Building blocks you can actually use in your letters, proposals or
presentations...an easy escape hatch when you just can't find the
right words yourself."*
**Canadian Fundraiser**


*"I have been using the book since I purchased it... It sits on my
desk for easy reference."*
**Kathleen Bradshaw**
**Women's College Hospital, Toronto**

# ORDER FORM

Please send me _____ copies of the *Fundraiser's Phrase Book*
**Standard Edition,** 301 pages, at $44.95 ea.

Please send me _____ copies of the *Fundraiser's Phrase Book*
**Deluxe Edition,** 524 pages, at $74.95 ea.

Please send me _____ copies of the *Marketing Phrase Book*
**Professional Edition,** 667 pages, 2 volumes, at $64.95 ea.

**Shipping and handling:** Add $4.00 for first book and $2.00 for each
additional book.

All international orders in U.S. funds.  Ask about quantity discounts.

| | |
|---|---|
| **Price of copies:** | $_____ |
| **Shipping and handling:** | $_____ |
| **Subtotal:** | $_____ |
| **GST:** 7% (Canada only) | $_____ |
| **TOTAL** | $_____ |

☐   My check or money order payable to **Hamilton House** is enclosed.

**Name:** _____

**Address:** _____

_____

**City:** _____   **Prov./State:** _____

**Code:** _____   **Country:** _____

**Telephone:** _____   **Fax:** _____

**E-mail:** _____

Mail to:     **Hamilton House,  27 Leuty Ave.,
Toronto, ON, Canada M4E 2R2
Phone (416) 694-8394     Fax (416) 694-6138
E-mail: hamil@interlog.com**